D0330581

THE
GIRL

THE
GIRL

MARILYN MONROE,
THE SEVEN YEAR ITCH,
AND THE BIRTH OF AN
UNLIKELY FEMINIST

MICHELLE MORGAN

RUNNING PRESS

PHILADELPHIA

Running Press
Hachette Book Group
1290 Avenue of the Americas, New York, NY 10104
www.runningpress.com
@Running_Press

Printed in the United States of America

First Edition: May 2018

Published by Running Press, an imprint of Perseus Books, LLC, a subsidiary
of Hachette Book Group, Inc. The Running Press name and logo is a trademark of
the Hachette Book Group.

The Hachette Speakers Bureau provides a wide range of authors for speaking events.
To find out more, go to www.hachettespeakersbureau.com or call (866) 376-6591.

The publisher is not responsible for websites (or their content) that are not owned
by the publisher.

Print book cover and interior design by Ashley Todd.

Library of Congress Control Number: 2017961025

ISBNs: 978-0-7624-9059-2 (hardcover), 978-0-7624-9060-8 (ebook)

LSC-C

10   9   8   7   6   5   4   3   2   1

This book is dedicated to:

Jim and Zena Parson. I will never forget your kindness.
Thank you so much for all you've done for me.

And

My beautiful and immensely talented friend, Gabriella Apicella.
I'm sure Marilyn would have loved you, just as much as I do.

Contents

Introduction

WHEN I FIRST DISCOVERED Marilyn Monroe, it was 1985 and I was a teenager. I was at first attracted to her beautiful, glamorous image, but the moment I began reading about her, my feelings went far deeper. I soon realized that Marilyn had become a highly successful woman despite having many odds stacked against her. While her ultimate story was one of tragedy, the woman herself was a fighter, someone who began life as Norma Jeane—a little girl who lived in a series of foster homes—and yet fought her way to become not only an actress, but one of the most famous women in the entire world.

Yet while I could quite clearly see that Marilyn was an intelligent person, I found myself forever bombarded with comments such as "Oh, she was just a dumb blonde" or "You can tell she's just playing herself on-screen." These statements baffled me and always came from people who knew nothing at all about her (nor wanted to learn). More than thirty years later, I have covered aspects of Marilyn Monroe's life in five books and find myself still dispelling myths, correcting untruths, and trying to educate people on one of the most universally intriguing stars of the cinematic pantheon. Happily, now many want to learn what Marilyn was really like. But it cannot be denied that history has been rewritten in the decades since her death, and the woman who achieved so much in the 1950s is often lost in a haze of modern-day Internet memes and rumors. I regard this book, therefore, as a means of redeeming her reputation.

The Girl, titled after her character in the 1955 comedy *The Seven Year Itch*, tells the story of how that film transformed Marilyn Monroe from another Hollywood star into "The Girl" of modern times—a true icon—and sent her on an unparalleled adventure of self-discovery and reflection. The years 1954 to 1956 were Marilyn's most powerful and inspirational, and it was during this time that her most substantial decisions were made. Before *Itch*, she had been known for her mostly fluffy, dumb-blonde roles, and she was unhappily married to baseball legend Joe DiMaggio. But by the time the film opened, Marilyn was the president of her own film company, a student at New York's Actors Studio, and embroiled in a battle with Twentieth Century Fox that would eventually gain independence not only for herself, but others working under the constraints of the studio system too. Shortly after the release, she legally changed her name to Marilyn Monroe, thereby divorcing herself from the troubled past of Norma Jeane once and for all. Her rebellion was remarkable and exceptionally rare during a time when women were expected to strive to be fantastic homemakers and actresses had to accept every kind of behavior imposed upon them by their male bosses.

While *The Seven Year Itch* played a pivotal part in Marilyn's life, so it did in mine too. I can remember the exact date when I first watched the movie: it was December 24, 1986, and I was sixteen years old. I had been a fan for just over a year and had seen only a few of Marilyn's movies at that point. I desperately wanted to see *The Seven Year Itch* because of the famous skirt-blowing scene, but what I remember most of all is just how luminous Marilyn Monroe looked in the film. Her hair, her skin, her costumes—everything glowed, and the magic of her personality shone straight out of the screen.

At some point during the evening, my grandparents came to visit. They sat down and watched the film with me, laughing when Marilyn made quips about keeping her undies in the icebox, and making comments about her strange habit of dunking potato chips in champagne. My grandparents were born just three years before Marilyn, which made her a star of their generation, not mine. However, I don't ever remember them querying why their granddaughter was suddenly so obsessed with her. It was merely accepted that Marilyn—and *The Seven Year Itch*—could transcend generations and entertain in the same way they had during the 1950s.

Thirty years later, my thirteen-year-old daughter sat down to watch the same film and declared Marilyn to be "so pure." This made me smile. The magic of The Girl, *The Seven Year Itch*, and, of course, the actress captured the imagination of a teenager once again. And so it is that Marilyn's influence continues to inspire each new generation.

Marilyn always searched for ways to make her life more meaningful and profound. She was an exceptionally modern woman and fought the studio and her male bosses as if it were the most natural process in the world. She was glamorous but not scared to be seen without makeup. She could be flirtatious but demanded respect. She posed nude and totally owned the fact that she had done so. In an era of female restraint, Marilyn was an unlikely feminist and a person of such determination that she never ceased to amaze anyone lucky enough to meet her. In turn, her life, work, and rebellion have impacted the lives of people around the world.

This book presents Marilyn Monroe in a fresh light: strong, independent, brave, and authentically unique; a woman of Yeats, Shakespeare, Chekhov, and Tolstoy; a real-life human being who strived to better herself through education and action. Marilyn Monroe continues to inspire women well over half a century since her death. *The Girl* explores the many different ways this has come to pass.

—Michelle Morgan, October 2017

Rebellious Starlet

NORMA JEANE BAKER ALWAYS had a rebellious streak. As a child in the 1930s, she had sneaked out of her strict foster parents' home to see a movie. Being told she'd go to hell for it did little to curb her desire to go again. Then, while living in an orphanage, she and a group of friends were dared to scale the hedge and run away. Norma Jeane was only too happy to get involved, but was soon caught and severely reprimanded for her trouble.

In 1942, the sixteen-year-old was actively encouraged to marry the boy next door, James Dougherty, which would allow her foster parents to make a guilt-free move out of state. She went through with the marriage, though never became a contented housewife. When her husband was sent abroad during the war, the teenager moved in with the Doughertys and started work in a local factory. However, this soon turned into a period of rebellion after she was spotted by a photographer who recommended she start a modeling career. Norma Jeane grabbed the opportunity with both hands and signed with the Blue Book Modeling Agency in Hollywood. There, she was coached by agency boss Emmeline Snively and told that she would go far if she dyed and straightened her brunette hair. When her in-laws started complaining about her interest in this newfound career, Norma Jeane moved out of their house, and in 1946, she traveled to Las Vegas to obtain a divorce from her husband. Shortly afterward, the model landed a contract with one of the top movie studios, Twentieth Century Fox, and assumed the identity of Marilyn Monroe.

After a few false starts, Marilyn's star began to rise, but for the most part, she found herself playing the role of dumb blonde in film after film at Fox. For a while she was content to work this way because she was simply happy to have a job. When asked if she felt so-called cheesecake/glamour roles would interfere with any dramatic plans she might have, Marilyn was steadfast in her opinion. "Oh, I don't think so," she said. "I think cheesecake helps call attention to you. Then you can follow through and prove yourself."

In March 1952, Marilyn's burgeoning career threatened to implode when it was discovered that she had posed for nude photographs during her modeling days. Three years earlier, the unemployed starlet had been living at the Hollywood Studio Club and was behind on her rent and car payments. Faced with being homeless and remembering that a photographer by the name of Tom Kelley had once asked her to pose nude, she phoned him in the hope that he could help. A short while later she reclined on a red velvet sheet while Kelley took a handful of photographs of her au naturel. Today the snaps are considered artistic, but in the late 1940s they were scandalous, so to protect herself, the actress signed the model release form as Mona Monroe. Since Marilyn had already posed seminude for artist Earl Moran earlier and never been recognized, she convinced herself that the Kelley pictures would never be seen, picked up her $50 check, and paid her bills.

Eventually Tom Kelley sold the photographs to a calendar company and they caused a sensation. Because of the calendar's popularity, it did not take long for word to reach the offices of Twentieth Century Fox. Vice president of production Darryl F. Zanuck was outraged and instructed the actress to categorically deny that she was the model in the photographs. Once again, however, Marilyn's defiant nature shone through. She absolutely refused to say the girl was not her, and instead admitted the story was true and released a statement with her version of events: "I was broke and needed the money. Oh, the calendar's hanging in garages all over town. Why deny it? You can get one any place. Besides I'm not ashamed of it. I've done nothing wrong."

While Twentieth Century Fox thought the starlet had completely sabotaged her own career, Marilyn contacted several columnists to tell them how worried and nervous she was to hear the reaction of press and public. This was a genius move on her part, because it encouraged the reporters to write sympathetic articles about her predicament. "If anything, the busty, blond bombshell probably has just struck a gold mine," wrote Gerry Fitz-Gerald. "She is the favorite movie actress of practically every garage mechanic and barber in Hollywood."

Fitz-Gerald was correct. The honesty with which Marilyn owned the drama, coupled with the story of her penniless situation, touched the hearts of the public. Instead of vilifying her, fans sympathized with her plight and admired the fact that she had finally been able to achieve success. When it was discovered that she was dating baseball legend Joe DiMaggio, it became the ultimate Cinderella story: the girl who once had no pennies to rub together had now met her Prince Charming. Newspaper columnists and the public were ecstatic, and Marilyn had won her first battle as a star.

At the same time Marilyn was admitting to the nude calendar, German actress Hildegarde Neff was causing outrage after performing a nude scene in the film *The Sinner*. When she arrived in New York City to promote the US release, columnist Earl Wilson asked if she condemned Marilyn for posing for the nude calendar. "No!" Neff snapped. "I'm for her. She won. The public accepted her. She needed a job. Nobody's attacked her for it." Wilson asked if the actress thought it paid to go nude. "No, it doesn't pay to go nude," Neff replied. "It pays to be honest."

Marilyn survived the scandal with dignity intact, but someone not so lucky was Phil Max, a fifty-year-old camera shop owner in Hollywood. He had watched the story carefully and in 1953 bought a supply of the calendar for his store on Wilshire Boulevard. Displaying one of the items in the window, Max enjoyed brisk sales for the next two weeks. Unfortunately for him, this success ended when passersby noticed a group of junior high school students giggling and pointing outside the shop. The police were called and Max found himself arrested for violating an ordinance forbidding the display of nude photos that could be seen from the street. Several days later, the man appeared in court, where he pleaded guilty and was fined $50. Just like Marilyn, he was not apologetic. "I didn't think there was anything wrong with putting the calendar in the window," he said. "And I still don't. I've seen pictures like that displayed in lots of places." Someone else who didn't see anything wrong was entrepreneur Hugh Hefner. In late 1953, he licensed the calendar photograph for the first issue of his magazine, *Playboy*. The resulting sales helped create a multimillion-dollar enterprise and made Hefner into a legendary—if controversial—figure.

Another upheaval surfaced a short time after the initial calendar scandal when it was discovered that Marilyn had been withholding information about her estranged mother, Gladys Baker. Baker had been in and out of mental hospitals for much of her adult life, and Marilyn had never enjoyed a positive relationship with her. In fact, as a child she'd only lived in her care on one occasion, and that ended when Gladys was taken away after suffering a complete mental breakdown. Since then, Marilyn had only seen her for short periods of time, and as soon as fame beckoned, the actress claimed that Gladys Baker had passed away. However, enterprising reporters went searching for the truth and discovered that the woman was actually alive. The story broke and once again Zanuck despaired.

While Marilyn was sickened that her ill mother was now subject to rabid media scrutiny, she owned up to her lie about being an orphan and explained that she had never wanted the public to find out about Gladys, due to her illness. The honesty worked yet again, and the public sympathized and understood.

AFTER SEVERAL YEARS OF working in films that required little more than smiles and wiggles, Marilyn grew bored and anxious to take on more significant parts. Thankfully, her spirits were buoyed when she was asked to work in dramatic films, including *Don't Bother to Knock* (1952) and *Niagara* (1953). Henry Hathaway, director of the latter, thought the actress magnificent, bright, and easy to work with, but the public preferred their Marilyn funny.

The actress had become a major star in lightweight comedy roles and musicals, as well as sultry publicity photographs angled to emphasize the blonde-bombshell look. Recognizing that these films and photos were a winning formula for Marilyn, Zanuck was happy to cast the actress in cheesecake roles forevermore. What he and others didn't count on, however, was that Marilyn was not. In fact, she was growing more frustrated with every script that came her way.

Jane Russell, Marilyn's costar in *Gentlemen Prefer Blondes* (1953), predicted in March 1953 that the actress would not remain quiet about her discontentment for long. Speaking to Erskine Johnson, she said, "[Marilyn's] going through the same thing I went through. She doesn't like what the studio is doing to her and she doesn't know how to say no. One of these days she will learn as I did. She'll start swinging axes."

Unfortunately, in an era and industry filled with male dominance, this was easier said than done. The cheesecake image was stifling, as was the fact that Fox insisted on putting Marilyn into film after film with scarcely any break in between. This gave her no time to really engage with the character, and it was literally a case of taking off one costume and putting on another, while still trying to remember all the dialogue and cues. Eventually, the twenty-seven-year-old actress came to realize that she would have to do something to rectify this situation. And as Jane Russell predicted, she did indeed.

In late 1953, Fox announced that Marilyn's next picture would be the frothy musical *The Girl in Pink Tights*. Described by the publicity department as "a spectacular musical romance of little old New York," the film was to be set in 1900 and feature Marilyn as a small-town schoolteacher who wants to sing opera. She moves to the city, only to find that her dreams aren't so easy to fulfill, and ends up working as a saloon singer and dancer. Along with Marilyn, the cast was to include Frank Sinatra, Dan Dailey, Mitzi Gaynor, and Van Johnson.

Marilyn contractually had no right to question any role the studio wanted her to do, nor did she even have to read the script. Instead, the studio would merely give her a date to show up on set and expect her to get straight to work. However, Marilyn had just finished the role of Kay in the western *River of No Return* (1954) and had no interest in playing another showgirl. She would be happy to read the script, she told casting director Billy Gordon, but without access to it, there was no way she would appear on set.

Darryl F. Zanuck always saw Marilyn as something of a hindrance to production—a woman who had the nerve to ask for a dressing room when she was making *Gentlemen Prefer Blondes* and who wondered aloud why Jane Russell was being paid more than she was on the same film. He decided to ignore her demands, but could only do that for so long. When no amount of coaxing got her to the studio, it was decided that Marilyn would be sent the script, if only to shut her up. As soon as the actress received the document, she read it, disliked it immensely, and sent it straight back.

Zanuck was absolutely furious. He instructed Marilyn's drama teacher, Natasha Lytess, and a member of the Fox publicity department to tell her to get back to work. They were both prohibited from seeing Marilyn by her boyfriend, Joe DiMaggio. Her agent, Charles Feldman, then got involved, but with no clause for script approval in her contract, there was really nothing he could do to help. He told the rebellious star that she must be on set for *Pink Tights* on January 4, 1954, and hoped for the best.

Marilyn traveled to San Francisco to spend the holidays with DiMaggio and his family. The New Year came and went, and the studio got everything in place to begin the new picture. Everything, that is, except the star. Marilyn stood her ground; she stayed in San Francisco and gave the studio the silent treatment. The executives responded by suspending her immediately, and announced that they would groom starlet Sheree North to take over all of Marilyn's future parts. Marilyn retaliated by releasing her own statement, this time explaining that if she continued to play the same kind of roles over and over, the public would soon grow tired of her. She would not play in *Pink Tights*, she insisted. Instead, she decided to marry Joe DiMaggio.

The marriage may have come as a surprise, but actually Marilyn and Joe had been dating since 1952, and rumors of a wedding had long since filled newspaper columns. As the couple kissed outside San Francisco City Hall on January 14, 1954, dozens of reporters were ecstatic. It was a match made in media heaven: the retired baseball player and the beautiful actress, who had met on a blind date set up by friends. "I liked his seriousness," Marilyn said in January 1954. "I can spot a phony, and this man was real. We came separately to the date but we left together—ahead of everybody else."

Zanuck was left with a predicament. He still believed that Marilyn was being unnecessarily disruptive and did not wish to pander to her whims. However, at the same time he knew that the marriage to Joe DiMaggio had captured the public's imagination, and any further prodding by the studio could be seen as bullying. After meetings with lawyer Frank Ferguson and general manager Lew Schreiber, Zanuck decided to lift the suspension and told Marilyn to report to Fox by January 25.

The studio bosses may have thought they were doing her a favor, but they did not consider Marilyn's strong backbone. If she did not want *Pink Tights* before her marriage, she most certainly did not want it now. She refused to show up on set, and the humiliated studio told her that the suspension was well and truly back on. Marilyn retorted by asking her lawyer, Lloyd Wright, to speak on her behalf. "Miss Monroe has authorized me to make this statement," he said. "She has read the script and does not care to do the picture."

When reporters pounced on the actress at the San Francisco airport, she had little to say except to repeat that she had no interest in the *Pink Tights* script. "My only interest is Joe," she said. "My only desire—to continue our honeymoon."

Instead of fretting that her rebellion might signal the possible end of her career, Marilyn and Joe traveled to Japan, where he attended baseball training and she went to Korea to entertain the troops. This not only kept her name firmly in the public eye, but also gave her a chance to give back to those soldiers who had continually supported her since the early pinup days. Marilyn adored doing the shows, and if anything, the sight of thousands of marines chanting her name only reinforced her idea that she now had the clout to take charge of her career.

Back home, the DiMaggios moved from San Francisco and eventually settled into a house at 508 North Palm Drive in Beverly Hills. The home was just yards away from actress Jean Harlow's last residence at 512, and just down the road from number 718, the house Marilyn had once shared with Hollywood agent and former lover Johnny Hyde. Returning to the street where she had lived during the early days of her career must surely have affected Marilyn. It would not be far-fetched to imagine that she thought about her former mentor when passing number 718. Neighbors revealed that they often observed the actress walking up and down the street at dusk. Was she remembering those heady days when her dreams for her career seemed so bright and within her grasp?

Whatever Marilyn's thoughts about North Palm, Joe DiMaggio disliked the location intensely. "Too many kids know where we live, because the picture of the house we're renting was published in a magazine," he said. "They ride up and down the street and even ring the front door bell." He vowed to find another property as soon as the lease expired.

While Marilyn stuck fast to her aversion to *Pink Tights*, Twentieth Century Fox finally realized she was actually needed on the lot. Not being a fan himself, Zanuck could not understand the public's fascination with the blonde star, but the fan mail continued to roll in to the studio regardless. By April 1954, it was clear that something had to be done. Agent Charles Feldman had meetings with Fox president Spyros Skouras to try to sort the problems out. Luckily, the mogul seemed sympathetic to Marilyn and advised Feldman on the best way to handle the stubborn Zanuck.

Many urgent meetings were held because Zanuck, Schreiber, and lawyer Frank Ferguson were all painfully aware that after the release of *River of No Return*, they would have no more Monroe vehicles to present. Marilyn was demanding more creative control over her projects, and while a new contract negotiation began, no one could come to any kind of agreement as to what clauses should be included. Even Feldman told Marilyn to scale down her list of demands, which only resulted in the actress becoming angrier and more determined.

Eventually, after Marilyn threatened to strike until her contract ran out, it finally occurred to the studio chiefs that she had won this particular battle. Zanuck reluctantly took her off suspension, told her that she would not be required to make *Pink Tights* after all, and instead offered her a part in *There's No Business Like Show Business*, with Ethel Merman and Donald O'Connor. In the meantime, the new contract negotiation was conveniently forgotten.

In addition to being an agent, Feldman produced movies, his most notable being *A Streetcar Named Desire* (1951), which won four Academy Awards, including Best Actress for Vivien Leigh. His latest plan was to make the Broadway smash hit *The Seven Year Itch* into a movie, and he was convinced that Billy Wilder would direct the film for release by Twentieth Century Fox. Feldman believed that the role of The Girl was perfect for Marilyn and could totally change her career. After immersing herself in the story and sitting through a successful meeting with Wilder, the actress felt the same way. Feldman told Monroe that Zanuck was sure to give her the part in *The Seven Year Itch* as a reward if she accepted *There's No Business Like Show Business*, so she decided to take Feldman's advice. *Show Business* was once again a lightweight musical, but if taking it meant there was a chance of claiming her coveted role in *The Seven Year Itch*, she was willing to stay quiet about her concerns.

It was a gamble that almost didn't pay off, however. Soon after Marilyn agreed to do *Show Business*, Feldman told her he had been unable to strike a deal with Fox's Skouras to have *Itch* released by the studio. He would have to forget about Marilyn playing the role and instead take the film to another studio. The actress was justifiably furious and reminded her agent that the only reason she had agreed to return to work was because of his promises regarding *Itch*. Her strong reaction sent Feldman running back to Skouras once again, and eventually it was settled that *Itch* would be a Fox movie after all.

Marilyn was then cast as The Girl. She was pleased with the outcome, but her relationship with Feldman eventually soured. No longer did she trust that he was completely on her side, and it was only a matter of time before she would move on.

For anyone who believes that Marilyn was a dumb blonde or victim, the *Pink Tights* episode confirms that she was, in fact, the complete opposite. Bob Cornthwaite, who acted with her in *Monkey Business* (1952), saw firsthand just how brave she could be: "Marilyn was very likeable and also stubborn, which is what saw her through. She was persistent and that stood her in good stead. Marilyn was ambitious and didn't want to spoil her chances of success but knew if she stuck to her guns and made demands, she might get away with it."

Marilyn had won an important battle, not only for herself, but for other actresses coming up behind her. Refusing a role she was contracted to play was an astonishingly brave position for an actress of the studio era to take. However, the media downplayed the move in spectacular fashion, and some were downright patronizing, such as reporter Mike Connolly: "Marilyn Monroe told me, in all seriousness, that she's sick of playing empty-headed blonde chorus girls and musical comedy dolls. That's why she turned down the first script of *Pink Tights* and walked out of Twentieth Century Fox. 'My ambition,' said Marilyn, 'is to play Juliet in *Romeo and Juliet.*' Very serious. Hey, how about that gal!"

Whether they liked it or not, that "gal" was indeed extremely serious. However, that still didn't stop some from claiming that Marilyn's strength came from the knowledge that she now had a husband behind her. "This was her first triumph in studio negotiations," wrote reporter Jack Wade, "and Marilyn realizes that she won largely because she had a husband to back her up."

It is true that, in private, Joe tried to help Marilyn by reading through terms for a new contract. However, the fight itself was definitely made via the actress's own thoughts and representation. The notion that a woman must surely need a husband to make strong decisions would be proven wrong just eight months later. For now, though, Marilyn got on with making *There's No Business Like Show Business* so that she could then prepare for the most iconic film of her life.

CHAPTER ONE

The Girl

THE SEVEN YEAR ITCH was a George Axelrod–penned play, exploring the idea of how, after seven years of marriage, partners can develop an "itch" to experience sex with a person other than their betrothed. It told the story of Richard Sherman—a middle-aged, married man who is left alone for the summer while his wife and son go to the country. He works in publishing by day, and by night wiles away the hours in the company of his own far-fetched but relatively innocent imagination. However, all this comes to a climax when one evening he is almost killed on his terrace by a falling plant pot, innocently knocked off the balcony above by the beautiful single woman living upstairs.

She is The Girl—a woman with no name, not for reasons of mysteriousness but simply because George Axelrod could never decide on a perfect name for her. For the purposes of the story, the character is never referred to by name, though Axelrod later mused that in retrospect, perhaps he should have called her Marilyn. As soon as Richard sees The Girl, he becomes obsessed with imagining who she is and what kind of personality she may have. He invites her downstairs for a cocktail, and before she arrives, he goes through all manner of adventures in his head, including an exploration of his own masterful (but vastly overstated) prowess. When The Girl actually enters his apartment, Richard is shocked to discover that although young and seemingly naïve, she is actually quite experienced in the ways of the world and has posed nude in *U.S. Camera* magazine.

Suddenly, Richard's imaginative thoughts turn to reality when events move on and the two spend the night together. By morning, however, he is almost paralyzed by the fear that his wife is going to find out and murder him in cold blood. He decides that the dalliance must never happen again, and heads out of New York to see his wife and deliver a yellow skirt she has forgotten to take on her trip.

When the play opened at New York's Fulton Theatre on November 20, 1952, it did so to tremendous applause. Stars Tom Ewell and Vanessa Brown delighted critics and audiences alike, and the Axelrod script was shown to be a mix of lively entertainment and clever dialogue. J. Fletcher Smith, writing for *The Stage*, described it as a "riotously funny comedy" and made mention that despite the fact that the play was in three acts, Tom Ewell was onstage the entire time. "[He] has vaulted to the front rack of contemporary light comedians," he wrote, before announcing that the play was clearly the smash hit of the season.

Writing for the *New York Times*, critic Brooks Atkinson concurred, recognizing that every part of Ewell's performance was polished and fresh. The same amount of success came when *The Seven Year Itch* opened at London's Aldwych Theatre on May 14, 1953. Starring Brian Reece as Richard and Rosemary Harris as The Girl, the *Tatler* declared it to be an "ingeniously amusing comedy."

The original play even managed to name-check one of Marilyn's friends in a scene where Richard shows an author the cover of the writer's book. The picture depicts a man chasing a beautiful woman, which the writer—a humorless doctor—dislikes immensely, mentioning that the cover was supposed to depict a would-be attacker chasing a middle-aged woman. Instead, he complains, the victim looks more like actress Jane Russell, Marilyn's costar in *Gentlemen Prefer Blondes*.

With the runaway success of the play, it wasn't long before Axelrod's script was touted as a film. Director Billy Wilder and producer Charles Feldman took up the challenge of turning it into a movie, but from the beginning it was going to be problematic. At its core, *The Seven Year Itch* is a sex comedy that pushes boundaries and shows that even a plain, middle-aged man can get into intimate scrapes if he puts his mind to it. This theme was fine for the liberal theater crowd, but the ferociousness of the movie censors was something else entirely. Wilder and Axelrod tried to push the dialogue as much as they could, but the censors decided that the story would need to be watered down considerably. So it was that by the time it went into production in the summer of 1954, the story no longer involved actual infidelity. Instead, Richard Sherman merely let The Girl stay in his apartment because she had no air-conditioning to beat the blistering summer heat. He then worried what would happen if his wife found out and thought they had slept together.

Of course, with the changing of this vital point in the story, the explanation of the *Seven Year Itch* theory changed too, and some wondered if the film could work at all. One of these was George Axelrod, who complained that his original story was supposed to show the hilarious reactions of Sherman when he felt guilty for cheating. Now that the actual cheating had gone, he was concerned that the entire story would make absolutely no sense.

Fortunately for all involved, the reworked script was actually hilarious, and showed the paranoid Sherman still feeling guilt, but mainly because of his active imagination. Added to the mix is a janitor who spots The Girl lounging in the apartment one evening and makes his own mind up as to what is going on there. His ability to arrive at the most inappropriate moments creates a real reason for Sherman to feel despair.

Even the character of The Girl was watered down for the movie. Whereas in the play, critics described her as being a potential schemer who didn't worry about sleeping with married men, in the film that couldn't be further from the truth. The Girl is shown as a sensitive, funny young woman, who only kisses Sherman in an attempt to show him how attractive he is to other women. She then sends him off to his wife, and innocently waves good-bye from the window.

A running theme throughout is Sherman's preoccupation with a boat paddle that his wife has left behind by mistake. He knows his young son will need the item to have fun on his holiday so goes through numerous ways of trying to wrap it, including bandages and a brown paper bag. This prop proved to be far funnier than the yellow skirt mentioned in the play, and is a centerpiece of several humorous scenes.

While Marilyn was safely cast as The Girl, there were still numerous roles to fill. One of them came as quite a surprise when actress Roxanne (aka Dolores Rosedale) was given the part of Elaine, a friend of Mr. and Mrs. Sherman. Some months before, the outspoken woman apparently talked to columnist Earl Wilson about Marilyn. "She should take about fifteen pounds off her fanny," she was quoted as saying, before adding that a girdle and bra were essential accessories too. When Wilson asked Marilyn if she had anything to say, she replied, "No comment," but the statement had upset Joe DiMaggio quite considerably. While the two women would never be seen on-screen together, they did run into each other at a *Seven Year Itch* party in Manhattan. Marilyn remained calm and dignified, but when the opportunity arose, she evidently asked Roxanne about the statements. The actress was shocked that Marilyn was brave enough to bring the charges up and denied ever saying them.

The casting of the male lead in *The Seven Year Itch* caused a stir when executives could not decide who would be best to play Richard Sherman. The man should not be too good-looking, as the emphasis was always on the fact that he could pass for the man next door, not a movie star. At first, Billy Wilder was keen on actor Walter Matthau, whose lived-in looks made him a perfect choice. He was screen-tested and looked ideal for the part, but Fox was unwilling to invest in the actor due to his being a relative newcomer. Years later, he was asked about his feelings toward Marilyn. "I never worked with her, but if she'd lived, I think she would have been all right. She would have been President of the United States."

It was suggested that Bill Holden be cast in the part, but Wilder balked at the idea, saying that the stunningly handsome actor just wasn't right for the role and until he found someone who was, the picture would be stalled. At long last, Tom Ewell—the actor who played the role on Broadway a staggering 730 times—was asked to test. Having been in the play for so long, he knew Richard Sherman better than anyone else, and his performance in the test proved to be superb. Added to that, the actor most certainly did not have generic, film-star features, which made him even more ideal for the story. After some discussion between Wilder and Fox, Ewell was cast.

For Tom Ewell, the success of the play and now the opportunity to reprise the role on film was a dream come true. He had worked hard for many years but found it difficult to make a real name for himself in either theater or film. For a time, he had moved to Hollywood, but without much luck, so he moved back to New York City, where he went from theater to theater looking for a lead—any lead—that would end in a job. Between gigs he studied with various coaches and attended the Actors Studio on a regular basis. He took odd jobs, including washing dishes and selling cigarettes, but although he appeared in many plays over the course of his career, it wasn't until *The Seven Year Itch* that Ewell truly felt successful.

While Marilyn was already a well-known and established star by the time *The Seven Year Itch* crossed her radar, the status of being given the part of The Girl was just as important to her. Ultimately, the experience would inspire her so much that her life would change beyond all recognition, and it is interesting that she was not the only one influenced that way. Once his time on the film was over, George Axelrod decided to move to Los Angeles so that he could have closer control over the adaptations of his plays. Even Tom Ewell's wife was inspired by the movie, and told journalists that while her husband had always been a worrier like the character of Richard Sherman, she now hoped he could lighten up and cease the anxiety once and for all.

WHILE IN THE PLAY the mention of Jane Russell was dropped into a scene, in the film a mention of Marilyn was even more cleverly managed, thanks to the fact that The Girl has no name. In one scene, it is clear that Richard has no idea what she is called and stumbles over a botched-up introduction between her and the apartment janitor. Later, however, when his love rival enters the picture and asks who the blonde in the kitchen is, Richard replies, "Wouldn't you like to know?! Maybe it's Marilyn Monroe!"

Oddly enough, there were several parallels in the lives of Marilyn and The Girl. For starters, The Girl is a model/actress who has also posed seminude. We know this to be so when she shows Richard Sherman a saucy picture of herself in a copy of *U.S. Camera*. As we have seen, Marilyn herself was a successful model for several years and posed nude for Earl Moran and Tom Kelley. The subsequent calendar pictures ignited a scandal for Marilyn, which The Girl also says she experienced.

During a conversation with Sherman, The Girl complains about once living in a club, where she had to be in early and was restricted in what she could and could not do. As a starlet, Marilyn lived at the Hollywood Studio Club for a few years and shared the same feelings toward the strict rules and regulations. The Girl expresses her opinion that being married would be just as bad as living back at the club. Since Marilyn was struggling with the restrictions of married life to Joe DiMaggio, one can't help but wonder if she felt the same way.

By the time shooting began, Marilyn's relationship was coming undone at a furious rate. During the making of her previous film, *There's No Business Like Show Business,* Joe had become jealous over her friendship with voice coach Hal Schaefer. He also disliked some of the scenes in the movie, particularly the "Heat Wave" number, which depicted Marilyn dancing with a group of men while wearing a skimpy costume. He detested living in Los Angeles and wanted desperately for the couple to return to San Francisco, settle down, and have children. The more time went on, however, the less this looked like a possibility.

While Marilyn was going through one of the most stressful times of her life as a result of her fractured marriage, her character of The Girl seemed to be having a ball: acting, modeling, dating, going to the cinema and out to dinner, and making her own decisions. Indeed, her biggest worry in the entire movie seems to be the lack of air-conditioning in her apartment—a problem that requires her to keep her undies in the icebox. In short, The Girl was living a fairly carefree life in Manhattan. She made it all look so wonderful.

When Marilyn flew into New York on September 9, 1954, for location filming on *Itch*, Joe did not arrive with her. Reporters eagerly pressed her to answer why, but all the actress would say was, "Isn't that a shame." There then followed a press party at the St. Regis Hotel, some time spent with friends, and DiMaggio arrived on September 12.

Any signs of trouble between the pair were kept well hidden. On walking into Sardi's restaurant, the couple literally caused everyone to stop what they were doing and gape at them. Costar Tom Ewell was in attendance that evening and said he had never seen anything like it before. "Everybody worships this girl," he told columnist Hedda Hopper. He then disclosed that before the end of the night, Joe DiMaggio had sought him out to reveal that he had seen *The Seven Year Itch* on Broadway and loved Ewell's performance. The actor was thrilled.

The next few days were a flurry of activity. There were theater visits and photo sessions and even the opportunity to meet Italy's biggest glamour star, Gina Lollobrigida. However, Marilyn was not in New York City to mingle; she was there to work. In that regard, the actress was filmed at an apartment window, where she waved and spoke to Tom Ewell, who was down on the sidewalk. Of course, word that Marilyn was in the vicinity soon spread to fans, and the street became packed with curious bystanders all trying to catch her attention. She did not fail to impress them and posed for amateur and professional cameras alike. These public shots were exciting, but they were nothing compared to what was to come on a dark New York street just days later.

"MARILYN MONROE IS HERE, shooting scenes for Twentieth's *Seven Year Itch*. . . . May be seen at the 52nd and Lexington Trans-lux at 6 am Saturday." It was a seemingly innocuous mention toward the end of the September 10, 1954, Walter Winchell column, and yet this would turn into legendary reporting from the famed gossip columnist. The time originally noted was wrong, but when it was corrected to the even earlier 2 a.m. of Saturday the fifteenth, 1,500 fans, photographers, and curious folk got out of bed, rushed to the normally nondescript corner, and craned their necks to see Marilyn Monroe in the flesh.

As the crowd watched the film crew set up, whispers quickly gathered pace. What was about to happen? Was Marilyn Monroe really going to make an appearance? The fans were curious, excited even, but not one person on that New York City street knew that they were watching history being made—the birth of an icon.

When Marilyn finally walked out into the night, it was like a thunderbolt had struck. She looked absolutely luminous. Fans cheered and clapped while the actress posed for anyone with a camera, though the snappers soon got on the nerves of Billy Wilder, who just wanted to get on with the scene. When he had first chosen the Trans-Lux Theater as a location, he apparently did so because he'd seen it at 2 a.m. and the whole street was somewhat quiet. Now that word had leaked, it was packed to the point of bursting. Still, he tried to ignore the chants and instead concentrated on the matter at hand—yelling "Action."

Wearing a Travilla-designed, white pleated dress with a halter-neck top, Marilyn stepped onto a subway air vent, and *whoosh*! Her skirt flew up into the air, revealing long legs and white panties. The crowd was not expecting such a spectacle and went crazy. So much so, in fact, that Wilder had to strike a deal with them: if they could be quiet while the scene was shot, the camera would then be withdrawn and their photographs could be taken.

It didn't quite work that way, however. Reporter Saul Pett was there to witness the event and noted that the scene required at least twenty takes, and every time the skirt blew up, fans "howled, whistled, and applauded." When he got close enough to Marilyn to ask if she minded all the attention, she exclaimed, "Oh, I love it! I love it!"

One person who did not love it, however, was Joe DiMaggio. He took one look at the scene and turned on his heel. "Tell my wife I'll see her back at the hotel," he told friends as a film crew captured him stalking away in disgust. When Marilyn returned to her room later that evening, she did so knowing that her husband had greatly disapproved of the night's spectacle. Over the years, many rumors have sprung up about what really happened that evening, with stories of Joe becoming violent and Marilyn deciding there and then to divorce him. Interestingly, drama coach Natasha Lytess quite contrarily stated that the room was firmly locked and the actress did not get inside at all. We can only speculate as to the private moments they shared in (or out of) that room, but it is worth pointing out that several friends reported a degree of violence during the entire marriage, not just on that particular evening.

The DiMaggios flew back to Los Angeles and Marilyn called in sick at the studio, claiming a cold. When reporters phoned the house, they were eager to know if the draft caused by the fans during the skirt scene was the reason for the illness. This, however, was laughed off by her doctor, who explained that Marilyn was suffering from a case of nervous exhaustion, brought on by the busy schedule of *The Seven Year Itch.*

In reality, the reporters weren't far off the mark to think that the skirt scene was the cause of Marilyn's absence, but at that point in time, no one knew just what kind of fallout it had created. When journalist Pete Martin later asked Marilyn if Joe had been furious or calm with the scene, she quietly replied, "One of those two is correct. Maybe you can figure it out for yourself, if you'll give it a little thought."

Ironically, the noise and fuss caused during the location shot in New York led to a retake on a Fox soundstage. The resulting scene was far more innocent than the one filmed on the street, and editing cut it down even more. In the end, anyone hoping to see Marilyn's skirt fly high above her ears in the finished movie would be left disappointed.

Some fans asked if the scene had been shot more discreetly in the first place (or even left out altogether), would her marriage have imploded the way it did? The reality is that even if the scene had never gone ahead in front of an audience of thousands, the chances of the DiMaggio relationship surviving were pretty low. Marilyn was at the height of her career; she had enjoyed great success and was hungry for more. Joe, on the other hand, was a retired baseball player who was somewhat floundering between his past success and future career plans.

On the evening they met in 1952, Joe was the one who garnered attention from fans in the restaurant. Marilyn later remembered that they slapped him on the back and greeted him in such a way that she realized she was obviously in the company of a legendary man. Until that point, the actress had no interest in baseball and had barely heard of Joe DiMaggio. By 1954, however, it was Marilyn the fans wanted to see, and Joe did not appreciate that one bit. The two were headed in different directions, and there could be no possible outcome at that point in their lives except to divorce.

Earlier in 1954, columnist Earl Wilson had asked Marilyn if her career would intrude on her marriage. "Why should it?" she demanded. "I had my career when Joe and I met. He understands all that. I want him to have one now, a whole new one. He's wonderful on radio and television. We'll help each other. . . . A happy marriage comes before everything." With that in mind, at the beginning of production on *Itch*, Marilyn had kept a copy of *How to Cook Italian Foods* in her dressing room and read it between takes. Just weeks later, it seemed like everything had changed.

Recovered from her illness and back on the set, Marilyn's behavior was sometimes difficult to deal with. Tom Ewell said that during the marital problems, "she would slink off by herself, plainly miserable. I don't think I ever felt more pity for anyone in my life." Billy Wilder told Pete Martin that Marilyn seemed so upset and unconfident that he sometimes wished he was her psychoanalyst. He did note, however, that at no time during the entire shoot was she ever malicious to anyone on set.

It would be unfair to suggest that the marital problems were the sole reason there were various issues during filming. Historically speaking, making a movie with Marilyn was often fraught with difficulties, among them her lateness, anxiety, and stumbling over lines. Even worse was a reliance on acting coach Natasha Lytess, who would often take on the role of unofficial director, overriding production decisions whenever she saw fit. The teacher had driven numerous directors to distraction over the years, but she had never worked with Billy Wilder before, and he had an idea that she was completely oblivious to. Knowing that Natasha would take over the whole show if allowed to run free, Wilder devised a plan that would help everyone. Instead of allowing her to give Marilyn directions once the scene was shot, he would take Lytess to one side beforehand and explain what he would like the actress to do. The coach then took the instructions to Marilyn, and Wilder ultimately received his version of the scene and not Natasha's.

Now that Marilyn's marriage was in the midst of breaking down, a childhood stammer returned and she would often seem distant and in a world of her own. The fact that Marilyn had been able to make it onto the set at all was a miracle, considering what she was going through in her personal life, but with money firmly in their eyes, the studio bosses were not about to praise her bravery. Instead, they seethed over the actress's holdups, and production executive Sid Rogell kept Zanuck up-to-date with every development. Everyone at the studio prayed that despite everything, the film would be finished successfully.

On September 27, just before Joe DiMaggio returned to the East Coast to cover the World Series, the couple decided to separate for good. They managed to keep it quiet for several days, but then word inevitably leaked out. On DiMaggio's return to Los Angeles, he went back to the North Palm residence, but by this time the couple was on such bad terms that the house was divided. He took up residence downstairs while Marilyn remained in her upstairs bedroom.

On October 4, 1954, Marilyn's lawyer, Jerry Giesler, served papers to the baseball star and then left the house to face a barrage of reporters waiting outside. These so-called "gentlemen of the press" acted disgracefully during days camped on the lawn of the DiMaggio home. Later, the *Los Angeles Times* complained that the scene played out like a rowdy film premiere, and one unnamed columnist actually kicked a powerful news anchor on the backside.

Giesler reassured reporters that Marilyn would not leave the house that day, but he'd try to arrange a press conference as soon as possible. According to the lawyer, his client was sick and not up to talking publicly at that time. He also added that Joe did not have any kind of legal counsel and that the charges would be mental cruelty, incompatibility, and a conflict of careers. No alimony would be sought, Marilyn was not pregnant, and the two remained friends. When asked if the skirt scene had anything to do with the decision to separate, Giesler steadfastly denied it. Instead, he said, the estranged couple had discussed their situation and come to an understanding.

When the couple did eventually leave the house separately, photographers recorded every moment. Joe DiMaggio went straight to his car, while Marilyn hung on to Giesler's arm, tried to speak, and then began to cry. She was distraught, but being free from the stifling, pent-up atmosphere that had haunted her for months was ultimately liberating. Marilyn returned to the studio several days later, and was overheard telling her makeup man that she had finally had a good night's sleep and felt "alive for the first time in days." Meanwhile, Joe went to San Francisco for a short time, where he was greeted by reporters camped outside his front door. Unusually for him, DiMaggio actually invited the media into his home, where he explained that while he understood they had to ask such questions, he had absolutely no intention of speaking.

Some friends refused to believe that the marriage was actually over. Mark Scott, radio and television broadcaster and associate of DiMaggio, reported that the couple still appeared to be in love with each other. He described the situation as not irreconcilable and gave fans hope that there could be a halting of divorce proceedings. Joe's brother Tom explained that he had been with him before the World Series. "There was no suggestion that anything was wrong," he said. This was backed up by DiMaggio's friend Reno Barsocchini, who claimed that everything was absolutely fine just a week before. According to him, Joe had been in San Francisco and had traveled back to Los Angeles to see Marilyn before planning a return to New York for work.

One reporter for the *Bridgeport Telegram* said that the separation had come like an "A-bomb. . . . There had been no hint of anything but harmony in the DiMaggio home." This was wishful thinking at best, because Rex Barley, staff writer for the *L.A. Mirror*, was in the press box with DiMaggio for the World Series and described him as being exceptionally tense and quiet. "If you mentioned marriage, he was even more clam-like," he said.

One person who was not shocked was Natasha Lytess. She had long hated Joe DiMaggio, and recalled an evening when the actress turned up at her door, disheveled and face puffy from crying. The couple had quarreled once again, and this time Marilyn begged Natasha to allow her to stay the night so that she did not have to return to North Palm. Shortly afterward, the couple separated and the drama coach breathed a sigh of relief. Calling him an "often morose baseball-star-with-muscles," Lytess said that the couple had absolutely nothing in common and claimed to have once heard Marilyn shout at her husband in an effort to discover anything they might be able to do together. DiMaggio apparently replied that perhaps they could grow a little garden. Lytess said it was the most pathetic speech she had ever heard.

Nowadays, Joe DiMaggio's desire to have a wife who did not work, stayed at home, cooked, and looked after him seems sexist and restrictive. However, it is important to remember that he was not living in the twenty-first century. In the 1950s, women were not expected to be ambitious. Instead, society predicted that they would leave school; seek employment somewhere like an office, factory, or shop; meet a nice young man; and get married and have babies. Many new wives gave up their jobs to take care of the home, and those who did not would likely stop working as soon as they started a family.

For an idea of the kinds of duties expected of a 1950s housewife, one does not have to look further than newspapers of the time. In one article by an unnamed "doctor," a list of responsibilities included: bringing the husband his pipe, slippers, and newspaper; answering the front door; turning on the radio; making dinner; and of course, looking after the children. The "doctor" then gave a few tips for husbands to make their wife's life easier. These included not allowing her to do housework in the evening, not keeping her waiting when food was on the table, occasionally making breakfast on the weekend, and always dealing with argumentative neighbors or tradesmen. This was necessary, according to the author, because men were better equipped for such matters. Women, it seemed, were just too sensitive to handle it.

In a 1955 issue of the *Australian Women's Weekly*, there was a competition to win a new car. However, instead of the kind of trivia questions one would expect to answer today, the competition centered on "the qualities of an ideal wife and mother." Each week, the magazine gave a list of elements that contributed toward "making a woman ideal for marriage." These included cleanliness in the home, patience, sewing skills, personal attractiveness, and housework competence. The women contestants then had to choose twelve points they deemed most appropriate to their life in the home, and the winner would be decided by a panel of men.

This extraordinary article was by no means rare; in fact, it was the rule more than the exception to show women safely at home, cooking and cleaning. Advertisements during the 1950s confirm this ideal, often depicting women holding feather dusters and dressed in an apron while their husbands are chasing promotion in smart offices. Even presents were directed toward the household. What woman wouldn't want a vacuum cleaner from her husband? "Christmas morning she'll be happier with a Hoover," claimed one seasonal ad.

Educational films aimed at newly married couples had an emphasis on what a wife's role should entail. One such production, released by Coronet Instructional Films in 1951, presented a young couple going through various stresses over the course of one year of marriage. The wife was shown as having given up her job after the wedding to maintain a happy house for her husband. She spends her days cooking, cleaning, organizing bridge parties, and seething that her husband visits his mother too often. Ironically, the overriding theme was to demonstrate that a marriage is a partnership, but the subtext relied heavily on the idea that it could only ever be that way if a woman was willing to compromise herself.

It was not often that these ideals were questioned. This was confirmed in November 1954 when United Press sent out a questionnaire to the editors of 143 newspapers and magazines. They wanted to know what kinds of subjects their female readers were interested in reading about and then the answers were compiled into a survey. The results showed that while some women were keen to know about Marilyn's views on marriage, others were apparently tired of hearing about her. The average woman was happy to learn about politics and education, but what she really wanted to know was how to be better at housekeeping, dressing well, and being attractive.

Occasionally a woman would buck the trend and decide that her life goal was not to wait for a man to come home from work. Although she later claimed to have offered to give up her career to save her marriage, in October 1954 Marilyn Monroe was the person wishing to get more out of her life. Joe DiMaggio could not give the support she needed, inflicted tight rules on how she should dress and behave, and wanted no part in her film career. In fairness, he was a fairly typical 1950s spouse; Marilyn Monroe, however, was not.

There were many issues that forced her hand in the breakup with DiMaggio, and during the divorce hearing on October 27, Marilyn mentioned some of them. There were weeks when her husband refused to speak, she said, and he would accuse her of nagging when she asked what was wrong. He had also caused her grievous mental suffering and anguish, and had refused to allow friends into their home. Her lawyer called it a "conflict of careers," and neither party spoke about the rumors of domestic assault. DiMaggio was not in court and did not contest the separation, so the judge granted Marilyn a temporary divorce to be made final around a year later.

As she walked out of the courtroom and into her new life, another marriage was about to end in a far more tragic way. Santa Monica court reporter Mack Silbert was covering the Monroe/DiMaggio divorce, and his twenty-eight-year-old wife, Selma, asked if she could go along with him. The man agreed, and as Mack worked in the thick of the action, his wife sat at the back of the courtroom and observed Marilyn giving her testimony. No one will ever know what went through her mind as she watched the proceedings unfold, but at the end of the case, Selma Silbert calmly picked up her purse and walked to the nearby Bay Cities building. There, she was to meet her husband for lunch.

Instead of going to the restaurant, the woman walked up to the tenth-floor restroom. Once there, she opened the window as far as it would go, balanced herself on the windowsill, and threw herself out. She landed on top of an adjoining building, where she died instantly. When Mack Silbert arrived on the scene, he was so overcome with grief that he collapsed. Selma was his first wife and the mother of his two young children.

In newspapers the next day, it was stated that the woman had "been upset" and had tried to take her life on several occasions in the past. In reality, however, Selma was suffering from postpartum depression after giving birth to her last child just the year before. Her death was so traumatic to the family that it was rarely spoken about, and the fact that she had been watching Marilyn just moments before was never mentioned.

The diagnosis and treatment for postpartum depression during the 1950s was almost nonexistent. For women showing signs of it, the term "neurotic" was often bandied around, and in some cases, electric shock treatment was recommended. Tragically, because of the severe lack of understanding of women's mental health, there was no hope for the young mother. While Marilyn obtained her freedom through divorce, Selma Lenore Silbert found hers in quite another way. There was just a two-month age difference between the women.

This was not the only time Marilyn's name was used in the context of a tragic or depressing story. Another came almost three years later, when a young wife appeared in court to divorce her emotionally abusive husband. According to Mary Parks, her spouse continually humiliated her in private and in the company of friends because she did not look like Marilyn Monroe. With dark hair and a slim build, Mary was actually the complete opposite in appearance, and her husband allegedly reminded her of this on a constant basis. The stress and anxiety took its toll, and the woman lost even more weight before finally filing for divorce.

ON NOVEMBER 2, 1954, Marilyn was back on the set of *The Seven Year Itch*. There, she filmed a scene where the plumber (played by Victor Moore) is called to rescue The Girl from a dilemma: that of having her toe stuck up the bath faucet. The scene was a fantasy, imagined by Richard Sherman when he worries that The Girl will tell everyone about his unsuccessful attempt to seduce her on a piano bench. On hearing her story, the plumber was to drop his wrench into the tub and then go rifling around for it under the water. The scene was a funny one, but by the time the censors got hold of it, it was cut so that at no time was Victor Moore seen to drop the wrench, never mind grope around for it.

Just two days later, the film was finished, much to the relief of everyone involved. As director Billy Wilder recovered from the ups and downs of the shoot, he had the following to say to reporter Steve Cronin: "Working with Marilyn is not the easiest thing in the world, but it was one of the great experiences of my life. I have a feeling that this picture helped her in formulating an idea of what she herself is all about."

He was correct. During the filming, twenty-eight-year-old Marilyn had been thinking earnestly about her future, the kind of roles she wanted to play, and how she was going to achieve her ambition. Shortly before the movie wrapped, she was asked by a reporter what she hoped 1955 would bring. "I wish to grow as an actress and a person," she said. "That means this must be a year of hard work and study for me."

Around the same time as the film wrapped, British photographer Baron arrived in Hollywood to take photos of fifteen different actresses. Marilyn was one of his choices, though when he took the first photograph, he wasn't sure how it would turn out. He explained what happened to reporter Elizabeth Toomey: "Marilyn has a brassy smile she turns on for the cameras. But if you tell her to stop that you will find a truly amazing girl with great expression; great warmth." He also described her and actress Pier Angeli as being the most exciting subjects he had ever photographed.

On November 6, 1954, Charles Feldman hosted a party in Marilyn's honor at Romanoff's restaurant, which had been a favorite hangout since her starlet days. When Feldman told her about the event, the actress's first reaction was to worry about who to invite. Tom Ewell later recalled her saying that perhaps she could invite her costars from *How to Marry a Millionaire* (1953). She then borrowed a gown from the studio and drove herself to the party. According to the actor, the car broke down and she was late. Nevertheless, when she did eventually arrive, Marilyn made a huge impression on everyone she met. "Although she is personally shy and reserved," explained Ewell, "she can turn on her personality so that you forget anyone else is present."

Meanwhile, Marilyn's favorite childhood actor, Clark Gable, made her day when he asked her to dance, though she would later regret not being brave enough to tell him how much she adored him. It didn't take the newspapers long to declare (falsely) that the two were in love, a rumor that grew legs thanks in part to the release of a photograph of them dancing together. Just for good measure, it was also said that the actor had been sending Marilyn three dozen red roses every day. The fact that Gable was actually in a relationship with future wife Kay Spreckels (and that she was at the Romanoff's party with him) was totally ignored by the press.

Everyone appeared to have a great evening, and even Darryl F. Zanuck managed to say a civil word and raise a smile or two. Meanwhile, actor Clifton Webb watched Marilyn intently as she moved from one table to another. "She was an absolutely perfect hostess," he recalled. "Here was a girl who behaved so much more like a lady than many ladies." Groucho Marx—who had given her a break in *Love Happy* (1949)—was one of the guests, and told reporter Hedda Hopper that Marilyn looked like the front page of a good magazine. "I looked like the back," he quipped.

Marilyn swept around the room like a member of royalty, greeting everyone she met and accepting dances from several of her male friends. If there was ever a moment when she felt like the Queen of Hollywood, this must surely have been it. However, underneath the red velvet gown and platinum hairstyle, everything was not as it seemed. Marilyn had reached her peak on the West Coast and felt that it had no more to offer. While everyone admired the star as she danced, no one had any idea that she was about to give it all up. Marilyn, the Queen of Hollywood, was an illusion, and a new woman was about to be born.

CHAPTER TWO

No Dumb Blonde

IT SHOULD NEVER HAVE come as a shock that inside the ditzy blonde characters she played on-screen, Marilyn Monroe was a determined woman with intellectual ambitions. No one in the industry ever wondered if Bette Davis was really Margo Channing, or James Stewart was really George Bailey; it was merely accepted that they were actors playing a part. Yet when it came to Marilyn, the sight of her as Lorelei Lee in *Gentlemen Prefer Blondes*, and Pola in *How to Marry a Millionaire*, seemed to greatly confuse not just cinemagoers but industry workers too.

While Marilyn's characters were often larger than life—almost dreamlike in a way—there was no reason to assume that they were a reflection of who the woman really was, and yet that is exactly what happened. Unbelievably, this is still the case today, some fifty-five years after her death. Marilyn spoke about the problem herself in 1957: "People identify me personally with the parts I play. It isn't so much that I mind, but it just isn't so. But I've played so many different parts by now they must be confused."

Nominated for three Academy Awards during the 1940s, including for *Laura* (1944) and *The Razor's Edge* (1946), heavyweight actor Clifton Webb had no problem seeing through the persona. He shared his memories with reporter Ernie Player in 1955: "Marilyn is very sweet, very serious. She likes to talk about the theater and the kind of thing that makes people tick. She is intense and completely straightforward. She reads all the time. She is in complete earnest towards her career. Ambitious and anxious to know her job. This girl, when she was making very little money, spent practically every cent she made on various coaches. Now she will work all day, go to her little flat for a bit of dinner on a tray, and then work with her coach on the next day's scenes. And often they will work until early morning."

Webb was not the first person to see how earnest Marilyn was about her craft. Early boyfriend Bill Pursel remembers: "Back when we were close in 1946–1950, we wrote lots of notes to one another on napkins in restaurants; often scribbling a little poetry. . . . We both liked to dabble with simple poetry and I still do. Norma Jeane liked to read and seemed to always have a book with her. She mentioned that Carl Sandburg was her favorite, and I know she met him when she was in New York. I remember reading about it in the papers."

In the early days of her career, Marilyn had attended the Actor's Lab in Los Angeles, where she took part in many scenes and encouraged Pursel to do the same. He resisted her pleas, however, as he was already studying at Woodbury College, and to enroll at the Actor's Lab would have meant leaving in his final year.

Marilyn had gone to other classes too, such as private ones with teachers Helena Sorell and Lotte Goslar, as well as those offered to starlets at the Fox studio. There, she met Jean Peters, Arlen

Stuart, and Vanessa Brown. Brown went on to play The Girl in the Broadway version of *The Seven Year Itch*. Peters, meanwhile, acted with Marilyn in 1953's *Niagara*. The women took the young actress under their wing and were surprised at how sweet, innocent, and childlike she was. Marilyn would arrive in class wearing a gray skirt, pink angora sweater, and high heels, and was continuously sincere about her training.

No matter what her employment status was, Marilyn would always—without exception—study. Friends expressed that she had few clothes of her own, because she would spend her money on books and records instead. In fact, her first charge account was not at a famous or fancy store; instead, it was at Marian Hunter's bookshop.

Another popular hangout was Martindale's bookstore. Marilyn would spend hours browsing the shelves, and she would almost always leave with an armful of new additions to her library. In 1954, shop manager Rachel Brand spoke to columnist Earl Wilson about her famous customer: "Marilyn's a great reader," she said. "Marilyn has been a great reader since way back, long before she was Marilyn Monroe. She reads Kafka, Thomas Mann, and authors like that—no cheap stuff."

Just to show how thoughtful Marilyn was about her education, she enrolled in an arts and literature class at UCLA, during the early days of her stardom. Recognition by fellow students forced the actress to retire from her studies there, but this did not stop her learning. At various times, Marilyn could be seen walking around a film set with works of great literature in her hands, and she would read ferociously about acting teachers such as Konstantin Stanislavski.

Cofounder of the Moscow Art Theatre, Stanislavski devised what he described as the System: a way of acting that encouraged actors to draw on emotional experiences to get the best out of their own performance. The goal was for the actor to feel "himself in the role, and the role in himself." Marilyn admired Stanislavski greatly, though by the time she had discovered him, he was long passed. It is perhaps just as well she met him through his literature and not actual classes, because the man was known to be extremely brutal in his approach. Actor Mikhail Yanshin studied with Stanislavski and wrote about him in an article for *Theatre World*. According to Yanshin, he and his fellow students "feared the rehearsals under [Stanislavski's] direction as they would fear to touch a fire." After watching a scene, the teacher would go over each aspect of the performance in minute detail and criticize anything he felt was wrong in the approach. However, despite the anxiety, Yanshin still felt that every student in the room had benefited from Stanislavski's methods.

While Marilyn never met the teacher herself, she did have a chance to study with one of his students—Michael Chekhov. Chekhov had been friendly with Stanislavski for some years, but eventually questioned his system and branched off to create his own—less abrasive—version of it. Marilyn began classes with him in July 1952, and despite also studying with Natasha Lytess, continued until the end of 1954. "First of all, he's a rare human being, and a great artist," Marilyn explained. "I don't know which to put first. He's Anton Chekhov's nephew, but on his own he is one of the greatest artists of our time. . . . There's a very noble thing about him. Recently he wrote a book, and put in everything he's learned about himself as an artist, a writer, a director."

The relationship with Chekhov was intense. Marilyn held him in such high regard that she once gave him an engraving of Abraham

Lincoln with a note that explained that until she met Chekhov, Lincoln had been the man she had admired most in her life. In his classes, she learned about history, psychology, art, and, of course, acting. Talking to author Ben Hecht in 1954, Marilyn described how Chekhov's style of teaching had completely opened her eyes to the fact that acting was an art form, not just something one did on a movie set. Together they studied texts such as *The Cherry Orchard*, by Chekhov's uncle Anton, and Shakespeare's *King Lear*.

Chekhov introduced Marilyn to the writings of philosopher Rudolf Steiner and believed in her as a thoughtful, worthwhile actress. Not only that, his wife, Xenia, loved her too, often buying her nightclothes as she was worried by rumors that Marilyn slept in the nude. However, the relationship was also often troublesome, since the actress found it difficult to get to class on time. To keep their student/teacher relationship on track, she sent him a note, pleading with him not to give up on her. "I know (painfully so) that I try your patience," she wrote.

Far from abandoning his student, Chekhov wanted her to go deeper into her studies. He was honest—a little too honest, perhaps—about why the studio thought of her in less than complimentary terms. According to the teacher, Marilyn gave off too many sexual vibrations, making it impossible for Fox to see her as anything but a sex symbol. He told her that if she just stood in front of a camera and did nothing at all, she could still make a fortune. It was this conversation, according to Marilyn, that gave her the confidence to begin her fight with the studio. Being a sex symbol had been fine at the beginning of her career, but now she wanted to be known as an actress of great standing, as well as a worthwhile human being.

Marilyn had expressed a wish to go in another direction when she'd reconnected with ex-boyfriend Bill Pursel just a few years before. "Marilyn said she was thinking about shedding the cheesecake, as I called it, and taking up more serious acting lessons. I had encouraged her to do this earlier; I thought she could become a great actress, especially in feminine comedy. Now she wanted drama. Had she lived, she would have turned acting heads."

After the deep learning curve of 1954, Marilyn was finally ready to take the leap into her fight with the studio. While it all came very naturally to the actress, her decision on a larger scale was earthshattering. It was brave enough to fight for roles she wanted, but it was something else entirely to drop her existing career to search for a new one. Throwing off any worries about the loss of her stardom, Marilyn launched into a new era. To do this, she enlisted the help of a young photographer named Milton Greene.

Greene had first met Marilyn in 1953, when he was sent to Los Angeles on an assignment for *Look* magazine. The actress saw some of his photos and insisted they work together—even through the night if they needed to. At the time, Milton was actually in the room but she did not realize it; she thought that he was just "this young fellow, standing around all the time." When the two were introduced, Marilyn was amazed. "He's thirty-two," she later explained, "but I think he looks nineteen years old."

They hit it off immediately, and Milton took photos of Marilyn that were completely different from the standard Hollywood portrait, showing her dressed down, relaxed, and with little makeup. Most remarkable about the pictures is that while Marilyn was now a Hollywood star, the essence of her real-life personality came shining through. She later wrote that while she'd met many top photographers during her life, Greene was so unique that she wished he could always be her photographer: "He's not just a photographer, he's an artist really. . . . One of the things that make him such an artist is he's so sensitive and introspective. It was the first time I didn't have to pose for pictures. He just let me think, but he always kept the camera going."

When the two first met, Marilyn was at the beginning of what would become her first major rebellion against the studio. Greene, meanwhile, was making changes of his own. Firstly, he was about to get married to a beautiful, confident woman by the name of Amy, and second of all, he was looking to create a new career for himself. The photographer had long been known for his outstanding pictures in *Life*, *Look*, and *Vogue*, but now in his thirties, he wanted to branch into books and films. It was fate that the two should meet at such crossroads in their lives, and it wasn't long before they began talking about how they could eventually work together.

Over the course of the next year, Marilyn became a close confidante to Milton and Amy Greene, sent dozens of roses on the day of their wedding, and spoke to Amy on the telephone two or three times a week. The women eventually met when Milton again traveled to Los Angeles, and they became firm friends. From then on, the idea of actress and photographer working together bubbled away in the background, and when Marilyn complained about her ongoing studio troubles, Milton suggested she walk out and start her own company. Marilyn was surprised but delighted. Nobody had ever proposed such a solution before, and she promised to give it some serious thought. Indeed, during the New York location shoot for *Itch*, Marilyn met with Greene and his lawyer,

Frank Delaney, to secretly discuss the real possibility of reaching out for independence.

IN EARLY NOVEMBER 1954, Marilyn checked into Cedars of Lebanon hospital for minor gynecological surgery. Joe DiMaggio was at her side, and the media wondered if the two were about to reconcile. The reality, however, could not have been further from the truth. Shortly after their separation, Joe had hired a team of private detectives to find out if Marilyn was in a relationship with her voice coach, Hal Schaefer. This incident led to various scuffles and climaxed when DiMaggio and his friend Frank Sinatra kicked down the front door of an apartment, believing they would find Marilyn inside. Instead, the men discovered that they were in the wrong apartment, and while a middle-aged woman inside screamed at the sight of them, Marilyn and her voice coach made a run for it from next door.

The episode had been traumatic to everybody involved, but unbelievably, it did not stop Marilyn from remaining on amicable terms with her ex. Perhaps she felt it was easier at that time to be conversational, but if friends and reporters took her good nature to be one of reconciliation, they were very much mistaken.

One day while she was still in her hospital bed, Marilyn received a phone call from Amy Greene, asking if she would like to stay with her and Milton at their Connecticut home. With *The Seven Year Itch* finished, her divorce waiting to be finalized, and nothing on the horizon, the time was finally right to free the shackles of the Hollywood studio system and branch off on her own. She accepted Greene's invitation. Milton flew to Los Angeles and the two decided that on their return to the East Coast, they would create their own film company—Marilyn Monroe Productions.

The philosophy for the film company was simple: to create films and other projects that were worthy of the public's attention. Marilyn would provide the talent but was unable to put money into the venture, since she knew that walking out of her Fox contract would leave her without an income. Greene truly believed that the company would eventually be a resounding success and agreed to invest his own money into it, so that Marilyn could forget about cash problems and concentrate on the creative work.

During the next few weeks, there was a rush of activity. Despite having much to do, Marilyn was eager to watch Ella Fitzgerald perform at the Tiffany Club on November 18 and 19. Two days later, Marilyn was stopped and charged with driving without a license. Putting that behind her, she got on with the plans to move east, which included instructing her agent, Charles Feldman, of her intentions. Since he had been one of the producers of *The Seven Year Itch*, it put him in an unfortunate position. Because he was so closely associated with Fox, Marilyn believed him to be more inclined toward their interests than her own, and she still hadn't forgotten that he had previously told her to tone down her demands. While she did not tell him at that point, Feldman's days as her agent were numbered, and it wasn't long before she quietly fired him in favor of MCA agent Jay Kanter.

From November until mid-December 1954, Marilyn and Greene set about making their plans reality. Her contract with Fox was carefully studied, and the actress wrote a stern letter to Fox, disclosing that she felt her old contract was no longer relevant because new negotiations had never been finalized or signed. As far as she was concerned, her last two films were made under a separate agreement and no formal written contract existed between herself and the studio. On that note, Milton booked flights to New York for them both.

In the middle of it all, *There's No Business Like Show Business* was premiered to great fanfare. Darryl F. Zanuck announced that it would be released to 275 theaters over the Christmas season, making it one of the biggest Fox Cinemascope releases. The premiere would aid the Actors Fund of America, and it was reported that the publicity campaign would top one million dollars. In addition to the usual television, radio, and print media, the promotion would also include fashion shows and contests. The Natlynn Junior Originals dress company announced that they would be releasing women's outfits inspired by the film, while Westbrooke Clothes took on the male element. The former featured day dresses with full skirts, petticoats, and a small V-neck complete with bow, while the latter was based on suits worn by Donald O'Connor in the film. The entire campaign was due to run for six months, with the main hope being that the film *There's No Business Like Show Business* would become universally known overnight.

Motion Picture Daily described the movie as "most assuredly and unreservedly, worthy of its title and living proof of it." It praised all the performances, including Marilyn's, and declared that "it has so much to offer, so much to sell and be talked about, that this excellent show is certain to attract a huge crowd which can but go their way as salesman for it, after seeing it."

The *Motion Picture Herald*, however, showed a different side. They printed a regular feature that asked theater managers to report on business and the opinions of their customers. One manager, Mr. F. P.

Gloriod from Rodgers Theater, Poplar Bluff, Missouri, was steadfast in his opinion of *Show Business*: "Leave Monroe out of this and give it to someone else and this would have been an excellent show. Most comments were 'Monroe sure was terrible.' Business was good first day, off other three."

The opinion that Marilyn gave a "terrible" performance was harsh, to say the least. However, when she was later asked what her worst role was, she replied, "The one in *There's No Business Like Show Business*. I was miscast. I had to be continually taking off my shoes because of the difference in statures between Donald O'Connor and me. I admired Donald very much. He can be serious and I can be serious but we can't be serious together."

Joe DiMaggio had hated the "Heat Wave" dance number and he was not the only one. Columnist Ed Sullivan shocked readers by complaining that the film would have been far better if two of Monroe's songs had been cut out. "'Heat Wave' frankly is dirty," he griped.

Things were not helped when O'Connor did his best to disassociate himself with Marilyn's involvement in the film. He told acidic columnist Hedda Hopper that Marilyn might as well act on another soundstage, as far as interacting with her costars went. He observed that it was hard to have any kind of rapport with her, and then swiped that she had, after all, been up against incredibly experienced people.

MARILYN FLEW TO NEW York with Milton Greene. To avoid publicity, she used a false name: Zelda Zonk. Amy met them at the airport, and the three drove to the Greenes' Connecticut farmhouse, which was to be Marilyn's base for the foreseeable future. There, she met Milton and Amy's baby son, Joshua, and their maid, Kitty, both of whom would become firm friends with Marilyn in the weeks and months ahead.

In December 1954, Clifton Webb hosted a New York party for playwright Noël Coward. The actor had invited Coward's favorite stars, including Barbara Stanwyck, Rosemary Clooney, and Judy Garland. He then asked who else the writer would like to meet, and was somewhat surprised by the answer. "I would adore to meet Marilyn Monroe," Coward said. On the night of the party, Webb noticed that the playwright and actress sat together and talked intensely about their life and work. "She talks very seriously," he remembered.

After babysitting Joshua on Christmas Eve, Marilyn awoke in Connecticut to find presents under the tree. Milton photographed her unwrapping gifts while chaos ensued all around her. It was a happy day spent as part of her new family. Just minutes away from the Greenes' house, there was another stranger to the East Coast. Bertha Spafford Vester was an American philanthropist who had lived and worked in Jerusalem for most of her life. In 1925, she created a children's center and from then on ceaselessly helped that and other causes she felt passionate about. By December 1954, Bertha was almost seventy-six years old, but still spent much of her time fund-raising and sharing awareness of her charitable enterprises related to the American Colony in Jerusalem. In that regard, she traveled to New York City to give talks and hopefully persuade fellow philanthropists to come on board with her mission.

Journalist and editor Fleur Cowles—married to Gardner "Mike" Cowles, founder of *Look* magazine—knew a great many wealthy people who could be called upon to give their support. So it was that

Bertha found herself spending Christmas 1954 with the Cowles family at their home in Weston, Connecticut. Although the couple was "cordial and pleasant," she still felt out of place. "I am in Connecticut and alone," she wrote on the evening of December 25. "The first time I remember spending Christmas without one of my family being present. A stranger in a strange place."

On December 26, Bertha woke to breakfast in bed, but her room was so cold she spent the rest of the morning in the library and sun parlor. During this period of relaxation, Fleur caught up with her and disclosed some startling news. Bertha wrote in her diary about what followed next: "Fleur cautioned us all not to disclose it, but Marilyn Monroe was coming to lunch. She had run away from Hollywood (where she had spent her whole life) I suppose from a husband or a lover and was living with a neighbor, a Mr. and Mrs. Green [sic], a photographer. Fleur made me promise that I would ask Marilyn to help me collect money for my work. So I did, after, I am sure, Fleur made the introduction, and got her all excited about me being a wonderful woman. Marilyn is a pretty girl without any background—is a coming movie star—bleached hair, limpid blue eyes—straight, small nose, lovely mouth. The day passed listening to modern crooners and jazz and watching [a] football game. About 5 o'clock all guests and children departed. At 6 Fleur and Mr. Cowles and I had tea and sandwiches, and the Cowles left for New York by car to take a plane tomorrow for California to meet the Shah and Empress."

Many years after the event, Fleur Cowles wrote about her friendship with Marilyn, as well as the meeting with Bertha Spafford Vester. With the passage of time, her story became disfigured somewhat: she wrote that Bertha was over ninety years old (a good fourteen years older than she actually was) and implied that Marilyn was actually staying at her house during the meeting. Nevertheless, it is a joyous little story, with Bertha being delighted but terrified of spending time with such a glamorous woman, and Marilyn winning her over immediately with her dressed-down clothes and casual manner. Photographs show the two women deep in conversation and at ease in each other's company. According to Cowles, Marilyn listened intently to Bertha's fund-raising stories and told the older woman that she was determined to do good for the world and would not waste her life away.

MARILYN ADORED HER TIME in Connecticut, and for the first time in many years, she was able to just be herself, as well as recover from a recent bout of anemia and exhaustion. Not used to experiencing real seasons, she loved the winter trees and thought it was a miracle that they'd soon wake up and sprout leaves. Nobody bothered her during her long walks alone, and the peace gave the actress a chance to think about her future and plan the next step.

When she wasn't walking, Marilyn passed the time quietly in the Greenes' farmhouse and made sure nobody had to fuss over her. She read many books, enjoyed scented bubble baths (her favorite was jasmine and gardenia), and entertained the Greenes' toddler, Joshua. His earliest memories would be of Marilyn playing games and reading stories. The home became her safe place—an environment where she and Milton could build their business together. She also spent a lot of time chatting with Amy Greene: "We'd discuss everything from clothes to housekeeping to babies to headlines," recalled the photographer's wife. "Sometimes we'd giggle like a couple of school kids. Others, we'd come up with some sure-fire formula for saving the world. You know, the way women do."

Milton and Marilyn's conversations centered on organizing the running of their film company. Marilyn would be the president, as well as the majority shareholder with 51 percent of the stock. Milton was the vice president and owned 49 percent. Directors were appointed, lawyers hired, and paperwork completed. At the end of it all, the two partners had what looked—on paper, at least—to be the basis for a productive, creative, and worthwhile organization.

Milton was ecstatic. Starting the company had been a huge risk both financially and creatively, but he was confident that everything would work out, especially since Marilyn proved herself to have a fantastic business head. Reporter Earl Wilson thought the same way: "I think Marilyn knows exactly where she's going—and that it's forward. It's just possible that she'll turn out to be not only the sexiest but the smartest blonde of our time."

On January 7, 1955, it was time to present the "New Marilyn" to the world. This was done by way of a press conference held at the home of attorney Frank Delaney. Unbelievably, while Marilyn was readying herself for her first public appearance in months, Fox put out a statement to say that as far as the executives were concerned, the actress was still living in Hollywood and nowhere near the East Coast. Marilyn's arrival at the conference would, of course, prove Fox wrong, but as reporters waited for that moment, rumors swirled as to what exactly this new Marilyn would look like. Would she still be blonde? Still be glamorous? They didn't have to wait long to find that the answer to both questions was yes. As the actress waltzed into the room, several journalists noted that the fresh Monroe looked rather like the old one. "Tell us about your new look," demanded one reporter. The actress blinked, pretended to be confused, and declared that this was the first time she'd heard of it.

Marilyn looked particularly beautiful, dressed in a white ermine coat, satin cocktail dress, and heels. She was keen to show that the move to New York had little to do with dress style and everything to do with control. Announcing that she had just formed her own production company with Greene, Marilyn explained that the purpose was to expand her career into producing films, as well as television and other projects. When Marilyn added that she now believed herself to be a free agent, lawyer Frank Delaney nodded and confirmed that she no longer had a contract with Fox. As far as he was concerned, the agreement negotiated in 1951 had been abandoned by both parties, and *The Seven Year Itch* was filmed under a single-picture contract.

This answer seemed to buoy Marilyn's confidence to no end, and when asked why she had walked out of the studio, the actress replied that her two most recent movies—*River of No Return* and *There's No Business Like Show Business*—were not to her taste. She did not like herself in them, she explained, and in the future she wanted nothing more than to be able to choose her own roles. The actress then cited *The Brothers Karamazov* by Fyodor Dostoyevsky (aka Dostoevsky) as an example of the kind of part she'd like to be considered for in the years ahead.

The press reaction to the conference was mixed. Hedda Hopper wondered if Marilyn had ambitions above her limits and told readers that she seemed to be carried along by her new advisors. She reported that some attendees at the press conference were heard to query what they were even doing there. "There has been a change in her public relations," said another journalist, "and even the most charitable of her admirers can't think this change is for the better."

Reporter Jim Henaghan had a long friendship with Marilyn, but even he was worried. "Milton Greene has been a disturbing influence on Marilyn's life," he said. "He has brought about changes that might very well end her career." He described the press conference as "one of the most bizarre in entertainment history."

Even Marilyn's friends and colleagues wondered if she had made the right decision by fleeing Hollywood. Natasha Lytess—who was fretting about the possible loss of her job—declared that nobody was indispensable and Marilyn may be forgotten if she didn't return. Director Jean Negulesco said, "She is one of the most talented actresses I've ever worked with, but I don't think the public would accept her in different roles. She's stubborn." He made clear his belief that she should have stayed working for Fox instead of branching out with Milton Greene.

The truth was, Marilyn wanted to show the world that a woman could be glamorous and blonde but still be an intelligent human being. In her mind, it did not have to be one or the other, but because this was such a revolutionary idea for a woman in her position, she was ridiculed for it. "I realized that just as I had once fought to get into the movies and become an actress, I would now have to fight to become myself and to be able to use my talents. If I didn't fight I would become a piece of merchandise to be sold off the movie pushcart."

Struggling to be treated as a serious human being was not a new experience. Marilyn had been laughed at in the past and just carried on striving toward her goal. It was all she could do. "I was born under the sign of Gemini," she said in 1952. "That stands for intellect. I don't care if people think I'm dumb. Just as long as I'm not!"

One person who did enjoy the press conference was reporter and high-society hostess Elsa Maxwell. While she was as perplexed as everyone else about the true nature of the event, it had given her the opportunity to meet Marilyn, which she had wanted to do for quite some time. Afterward, she wrote that an unnamed Fox employee had reprimanded her for being sympathetic toward the actress in her articles. "You don't seem to get the idea that she's on her way out," he said. "A year off the screen and she'll be washed up! We can find a dozen like her!" Maxwell laughed the incident off and insisted that if executives thought they could find another Marilyn, they were wrong.

After the press conference, the two women met again many times. Describing her as the most exciting girl in the world, Maxwell told Marilyn that it must have taken a great deal of courage to walk away from Hollywood. "No Elsa," she replied. "It didn't take any courage at all. To have stayed took more courage than I had. . . . All any of us have is what we carry with us; the satisfaction we get from what we're doing and the way we're doing it. I had no sense of satisfaction at all. And I was scared."

Several days after the MMP press conference, Marilyn quietly flew back to Hollywood with Milton Greene to reshoot the skirt-blowing scene for *The Seven Year Itch*. When friends caught up with her in the studio commissary, she told them that she was still intent on running her own company and had no intention of speaking to studio lawyer Frank Ferguson or any other Fox executive. When she returned to the studio on January 13, it became clear that they wanted her there to do publicity photos and tests for a film called *How to Be Very, Very*

Popular. Instead, Marilyn locked herself in her dressing room and refused all communication. The studio was incensed and demanded that she report to Lew Schreiber's offices on January 15 to discuss the new film. Instead, Marilyn hopped onto the next available plane and was back in Manhattan before many realized she was gone.

Dented by the realization that Marilyn was still determined to live on the East Coast, Twentieth Century Fox announced that no matter what the actress might say, she was still signed with the corporation until August 1958. They added that everyone was incredibly happy with the dividends earned from her latest movies and there was no intention of ever putting her into *The Brothers Karamazov*. The spokesperson then took a pointed swipe toward her acting talents. As far as he was concerned, while Marilyn had tried her luck at other studios as a starlet, no one but Fox had chosen to sign her to a long-term deal. "That, brother, was criticism," wrote columnist Thomas M. Pryor.

Still sure that Marilyn would run back when she came to her senses, Fox continued preproduction on *How to Be Very, Very Popular*. They then made the unprecedented decision to release full details of Marilyn's salary, and said that her current financial grievances were of her own making. According to the studio, she had actually been offered a supplemental contract in 1954, which would have seen her earn no less than $100,000 per picture. Since she hadn't signed it, however, her previous contract was still in force. Ironically, it was this same issue that convinced Marilyn and her representatives that she no longer had any ties to the studio, since the introduction of a new contract must surely mean that the old one had been dropped.

Zanuck was not convinced and a statement was prepared by the legal department. "The studio will use every legal means to see that she lives up to every provision of [the contract]," it said. It was then added that during her time at Fox, every effort had been made to give Marilyn the greatest worldwide publicity possible, and to surround her with the best artistic talents available. As far as the Fox top brass were concerned, nothing was wrong at their end, and all blame was to be placed at Marilyn's door.

Back in New York, the undeterred actress waved their comments off. She still did not consider herself under contract, and would most certainly not appear in the next inferior picture they had planned for her. In the end, Fox had to admit defeat in this particular battle. On January 18, the studio announced that Marilyn was suspended, and that Sheree North would star in *How to Be Very, Very Popular.* The studio went all out in trying to frighten Marilyn with the thought that North could replace her not only in movies, but in the public's heart too. To that end, they enrolled the help of *Life* magazine, which gave North a full-color cover and five pages depicting how she was being groomed for stardom.

Full-page ads also appeared in other magazines, telling fans to look out for the new face, and similar press continued to be printed during 1955. When *How to Be Very, Very Popular* was eventually released, the studio pulled out all the stops in their Marilyn/Sheree comparisons. A photo of North and her costar, Betty Grable (who had also acted with Marilyn), appeared in many ads for the film, accompanied by the following Marilyn-themed declaration: "Remember *Gentlemen Prefer Blondes?* Want another one like *How to Marry a Millionaire?* Wasn't it great with *There's No Business Like Show Business?*" An arrow then pointed to Sheree, with the words "Sheree North! All the fireworks you'll need in July!"

The ads continued in the same fashion in 1956 when another North film—*The Lieutenant Wore Skirts*—was released. Alongside a photo of Marilyn standing over the subway grate, one such poster asked, "Remember the skirts that blew up all over America? Now there's something new in skirts," with an arrow pointing toward Sheree North, who just happened to be starring with Marilyn's *Seven Year Itch* costar, Tom Ewell.

But in early 1955, Marilyn remained unworried. They had tried to threaten her with Sheree North in 1954 when she rejected *The Girl in Pink Tights*. On that occasion, columnist Dorothy Kilgallen even announced that North would soon be working on a biopic of Jean Harlow, knowing full well that Marilyn was an enormous fan of the 1930s star. Nothing came of the movie at that point, however, and shortly afterward Marilyn was actually offered the role herself. She did not like or accept the script, but it surely must have felt good to know that despite the veiled threats, no actress could ever replace her and the studio knew it.

At the end of January 1955, Zanuck sent a memo to Fox president Spyros Skouras to inform him that the studio had shown a rough cut of *The Seven Year Itch* at the Fox Theater in Oakland, California. There had been great excitement from the audience, and at the end of the show, 253 people said it was excellent and 153 described it as good. Only one person out of the more than 400 who watched thought it was terrible. Zanuck was extremely pleased by the results of the test screening.

Shortly afterward, an anonymous but disgruntled Fox stockholder complained about Marilyn to none other than columnist Hedda Hopper. He insisted that Marilyn brought nothing good to the organization and should be fired permanently. This statement infuriated the manager of the Oakland theater where the recent preview had taken place. He wrote to Hopper himself and said that while the stockholders might not want Marilyn, the exhibitors most certainly did. "I thought the audience would tear the house down," he said about the preview.

CRITICS WONDERED ALOUD IF Marilyn's rebellious streak was just for show. *Modern Screen* even printed an article entitled "Don't Call Me a Dumb Blonde," which argued that "there is a small shrewd group that insists that the curvaceous blonde is mixed up . . . is suffering from delusions of grandeur . . . will never make any man a happy wife . . . has been following poor advice and has more luck than talent."

Not so, said an unnamed but charitable friend. "More than anything else, Marilyn craves recognition as an artist, as an actress—not as a lucky, fatuous personality. She would like to cremate the dumb blonde reputation she never deserved."

Journalists were intrigued by the whole situation, especially when it was revealed that she had been reading classical literature and visiting theatrical actors backstage. Marilyn herself showed no patience with their curiosity. When asked if her attitude toward life had changed, she merely replied, "I don't think so." She was speaking the truth. For many years, Marilyn had harbored a great love of classical literature and took part in various acting classes and courses. When asked in 1951 what she was currently reading, the starlet revealed she was engrossed in a biography of German philosopher Albert Schweitzer and the entire works of French novelist Antoine de Saint-Exupéry.

Nineteen fifty-one had been a pivotal time for Marilyn, in terms of putting down roots in serious acting, books, and music. Notes made by early biographer Maurice Zolotow reveal that her favorite authors that year included Thomas Wolfe and Arthur Miller, while the role she most wanted to play was Gretchen in *Faust*. An interview that also appeared in 1951 disclosed that Marilyn loved to discuss author Walt Whitman and composers Mozart and Beethoven.

Actor Jack Paar witnessed Marilyn's literary tastes during the making of the 1951 movie *Love Nest*. When asked about the experience in 1958, he had the following to say: "Please get this straight. Some published quotes attributed to me have given the impression that I disliked Marilyn while I was working with her in *Love Nest*. This is not true. She was a nice, big, little girl, one who was constantly carrying books of poetry with the title visible, so you could see what she was reading. It seemed to me she always wanted to be an intellectual, but she thought it was something you had to join. This naturally bored me, and I was also annoyed because she was always late."

People might have seen Marilyn purely as a young, sexy starlet, but in 1951—at just twenty-five years old—the actress made every effort to further her education. "A girl can get along for quite a while just because her contours are in the right pattern," she said. "It isn't enough, though, for a long-term program, especially if you want to pick up a thing or two about emoting." While making *Let's Make It Legal* (1951), Marilyn spoke to journalist Michael Ruddy: "I'd like to be smart and chic and sorta—sorta assured like Miss [Claudette] Colbert. But I guess first I want to be an actress—a good actress."

In 1953, reporter Logan Gourlay met up with Marilyn in her small apartment. There, he spotted books by Shakespeare, Somerset

Maugham, and Ibsen. "I'm beginning to understand Shakespeare," she said. "Michael Chekhov has helped me a lot. I don't like Somerset Maugham. He's too cynical, but I like Oscar Wilde." During the interview, she told the journalist that she was learning lines from *The Ballad of Reading Gaol* by Wilde. When they met up again, she recited the last verse perfectly and told him not to be so surprised that she enjoyed poetry. To another reporter she declared, "I've just discovered Tolstoy. He's wonderful. I'm blonde but neither dumb nor dizzy."

Marilyn disclosed to reporter Aline Mosby that she read the classics because she felt comfort from learning that like her, the characters often felt alone inside. "I'm trying to find myself now," she said, "to be a good actress and a good person. Sometimes I feel strong inside but I have to reach in and pull it up. You have to be strong inside of you. It isn't easy. Nothing's easy, as long as you go on living." Marilyn surprised photographer Philippe Halsman when he took a glance at her bookshelves and spotted works by Russian authors and other highbrow volumes. He recognized straightaway that despite her public image, she was trying desperately to improve herself.

Someone else who saw Marilyn walking around with great works of literature was David Wayne, her male costar in *How to Marry a Millionaire* (1953). He later told columnist Earl Wilson that she carried books by Kafka. "I don't know whether she knew what she was reading," he said, "but she was making a hell of a try. She was out to get somewhere."

Photographer Earl Leaf confirmed how smart she was in December 1954. Talking of her early days in Hollywood, he stressed, "Marilyn thought of herself as a serious-minded, sober-sided dramatic actress. True, producer Lester Cowan's praise department tried to pin the

'Mmmm Girl' label on her for the benefit of those wolves who can't whistle, but sex had not raised its pretty head very high in her own dreams of the future."

For anyone who thought they were original by laughing at Marilyn's ambitions during 1955, they were mistaken. Four years earlier, she had spoken about the mentality she had come up against from a young age. "I was afraid to talk about what I wanted," she said, "because I'd been laughed at and scorned when I'd seemed ambitious. You can't develop necessary self-confidence unless you express yourself, and even after I got to Hollywood, I was afraid that if I did, I'd be conspicuous."

By 1955, she didn't care about being conspicuous, but this was met with a hostile reaction in certain quarters. Stories began to leak to the press from generally unnamed men who saw Marilyn's strength as a threat to their manhood. An old friend of agent Johnny Hyde contacted columnist Steve Cronin to complain about the newfound independence. "I once thought that this girl had a good head on her shoulders; the kind of steady head success would never turn. Now I'm not so sure. I can't understand why Marilyn fought with her studio. What made her turn down a new contract at $100,000 a picture? A few years ago the girl was starving. That's why she had to pose for those calendar pictures. Now, she's ready to start her own company. What does she know about producing pictures? I can't help feeling that she has been the victim of bad advice."

Another anonymous individual was said to have worked as a crew member with her on many movies, including *There's No Business Like Show Business* and most recently *The Seven Year Itch*. His opinion was not positive: "I've been on a lot of pictures with her, and I must say

I was surprised when she ordered a closed set [on *Itch*]. Didn't want any visitors, didn't want any reporters. That was the tip-off, at least to me. She was getting a little big in the head. I've seen a lot of players in my time. Tell 'em they're getting conceited, and they call you a liar. But gradually success has a way of swelling the head. It certainly has swelled Marilyn's, or she wouldn't have gone off half-cocked."

The way some reporters spoke about Marilyn made it look as though she had been coerced into taking her career in another direction by her new colleagues: chiefly Milton Greene and his lawyer and agent. While she did value the advice of Greene and respected his position in her company, she never forgot that she was the majority shareholder. "I would listen to his advice about a film script," she said, "but I wouldn't necessarily take it. I make up my own mind about everything."

Reporter Milton Schulman could see clearly who was in charge. To him, Greene admitted that he was not a trained businessman and was willing to ask for advice. "I have no doubt as to who is the real Svengali of this relationship," wrote Schulman, "and it is not Greene. Undoubtedly the partnership has already achieved considerable success. But the big decisions come from Marilyn."

CHAPTER THREE

Behind the Tinsel

REPORTERS, STUDIO EXECUTIVES, AND the downright curious seemed to concentrate on finding that one issue that made Marilyn give up her Hollywood career. The truth, however, was that it really wasn't just one particular event or person. Yes, Marilyn wanted to be able to choose her own projects and work with respected directors, but there were other problems that had made living in Hollywood quite unbearable.

First of all, the tide of fame that had come to Marilyn from 1952 onward gave rise to a host of people anxious to sell their stories to the press. Her ex-sister-in-law, Elyda Nelson, released her story in 1952; Marilyn's first husband (Elyda's brother), Jim Dougherty, went to the press in 1953; and then a former roommate at the Hollywood Studio Club sold her tale just as the DiMaggio marriage broke up.

All these issues played a part in Marilyn's anger with Hollywood. However, while trying to understand the full reason for her decision to move east, it is imperative that we take into account the atmosphere of the entire industry not only at the point of her rebellion, but at its history. For all the glamour and sparkle that moviegoers believed there to be in the film capital, there were also wolves, gossip queens, and catty has-beens, all waiting to rip apart anyone they felt was beneath them in talent or stature. Some of the situations actresses were subjected to and witnessed were staggering. Knowing about them puts into perspective just how very tough it was to even attempt a career in show business during Hollywood's so-called golden age.

During the early days of cinema there were various sex scandals to soil the snow-white image of Tinseltown. Clara Bow, Lottie Pickford, and a variety of other "naughty" actresses all gave their studio heads anxiety over what they would do next to sully Hollywood's reputation. By the time the mid-1930s rolled around, however, the Motion Picture Production Code had been enforced, movie storylines were cleaned up, and studios were desperately trying to keep their actors and actresses on the straight and narrow. Even major stars such as Carole Lombard had behavior clauses added to their contracts, and rewards were often given to those who could keep their reputations unsullied. If a star or industry professional did misbehave, any mention of inappropriate behavior was strongly and absolutely denied. A perfect example of this is in an article published in the February 1941 issue of fan magazine *Modern Screen*, which sought to dispel the sordid rumors once and for all: "The day of the 'Casting Couch'—when a girl had to exercise her libido instead of her talent for a job—is almost dead. The much-publicized and traditional Hollywood orgy died that evening when Fatty Arbuckle became involved in the community's most colossal scandal which meant the end of Virginia Rapp[e]. Today Hollywood parties are pretty dull and business-like affairs."

Whether or not Hollywood liked to admit it, there is absolutely no doubt that the industry Marilyn knew was a brutal and hostile place. Everything was geared toward the satisfaction of men, and the words "sexual harassment" were never muttered or even considered. Tragically, any form of abuse that actresses went through was merely accepted as an occupational hazard. Marilyn spoke of her own experience with harassment early on in her career. Her decision to speak out was not commonplace, and credit must be given for the guts it took to actively criticize men still working in the industry.

Marilyn's first experience of assault was actually while she was just a child and living in foster care. Her foster mother took in boarders, and one was an older gentleman who called Norma Jeane into his room and proceeded to molest her. Afterward, her guardian refused to believe that he had done such a terrible deed, and the child was told never to speak of it again. But speak she did and in 1954—through interviews she gave to writer Ben Hecht—the world knew exactly what had happened and how much it had affected her life. Marilyn told Hecht that she had developed a stutter directly after the assault, and named the perpetrator as a Mr. Kimmel. It is now widely believed that the attacker could have been Murray Kinnell, an actor who had a prolific career during the 1930s and was professionally associated with Marilyn's foster father.

Her next encounter with sexual harassment was during the mid- to late 1940s, when a "producer" told her she should be in the movies and invited her to his office for an audition. However, after he asked Marilyn to act out all manner of bizarre situations, she soon realized that the interview was not leading anywhere professionally, and she left the room. Later the actress discovered that the man was not a producer at all; instead, he was merely a predator who had rented a production office for his own inappropriate fantasies.

This kind of behavior wasn't just reserved for would-be producers; there were also a great deal of genuine filmmakers who behaved in a similar fashion. Head of Columbia Pictures Harry Cohn was a notorious womanizer and disliked by a great many people in the industry. During Marilyn's starlet years, she had been contracted to Columbia for just six months, but during that time Cohn saw an opportunity. Knowing that she was a friend of Twentieth Century Fox cofounder Joseph Schenck, the mogul presumed (wrongly) that Marilyn was sleeping with him. Cohn believed that he too should be allowed this privilege and called the young actress into his office. There, he invited her to spend the weekend with him on his yacht, but he hadn't counted on Marilyn's quick thinking and steely personality. She told him that she would come, but only because she looked forward to spending time with Cohn's wife. This statement sent the lecherous man into a tailspin, and as Marilyn headed for the door, he shouted that she'd had her last chance in Hollywood. When it came time to renew her option, the actress found herself booted out.

In an era when it was uncommon to speak out against sexual harassment, Marilyn was one of a kind. She told the Harry Cohn story to writer Ben Hecht, though she sensibly changed his name to Mr. A. She also frequently spoke to other journalists about the wolves of Hollywood. "I didn't have much trouble brushing them off," she said. "I found out in those days if I looked sort of stupid and pretended I didn't know what they were talking about, they soon gave up in disgust."

Marilyn always insisted that she never slept with anyone for a part, and from 1952 onward she was far too big a star to have to fight off the advances of lecherous executives. However, even then she still encountered various opportunists who didn't recognize who she was. One such wolf was actually a taxi driver, and when Marilyn got into his cab with no makeup on and wearing old clothes, he looked her up and down. Explaining that he was an amateur photographer in his spare time, he asked if she would pose nude. "I beg your pardon?" she asked, to which he replied that she shouldn't be so quick to say no. "Look what it did for Marilyn Monroe," he said.

This encounter was just one example of the kinds of occurrences that were still going on throughout the entertainment industry. The truth was that many of the men working (or pretending to work) in films showed little respect for women, no matter who they were. One actress interviewed for this book shared her experience of the sexual harassment that was rife in the acting industry during the 1950s and 1960s:

> *I never did sleep with anyone for a job, but it was often suggested and several times I was offered the role anyway. One notable situation arose just as I was to be flown to Hollywood for makeup, design, etc., for a big movie I had been cast in, and I discovered I was pregnant. My agent and I had a meeting with the producer (who had initially propositioned me at the Ivy restaurant) and I asked whether the schedule could be changed to accommodate my pregnancy. "No problem," he said. "Have the abortion and we will start a little later." I said I intended to have my baby, to which he responded, "Do you mean to say you would rather have a baby than*

star in a picture with William Holden? Come back and see me when you are serious about this business."

WHEN THE ACTRESS DID later star in a film with William Holden and told him this story, he took her hand in both of his. "Good for you!" he said.

That, however, was not the end of the actress's experience with the unscrupulous producer. Sometime later their paths crossed again when he promised to introduce her to various producers in Palm Springs, but made it clear that he needed to get to know her better first. "Your greatest asset in Hollywood," he said, "is your social mobility."

"Social mobility" was also expected when the same actress was on a film shoot in Malta. This time a director offered to work on the script in his hotel room. No sooner had they begun than the man pushed her down onto the bed. The actress's response of bursting into laughter caused the director to become outraged, but he was cheered up when his mistress arrived the next day, and his wife shortly after. "Where would I have stood had I gone along with his assault?" she pondered. "Suppose I had been naïve enough to think he really liked me? There was a lot of wanting to have a good-looking actress for notches on their belt."

This observation is astute, as Marilyn had found herself paraded at various parties during her early career because she was beautiful. Director Elia Kazan had even written her a letter at one point, warning her to keep away from those events and the kind of people who were known to use her. The sexual harassment and abuse of actresses was not reserved for Hollywood. Behind the scenes in England, there was an abundance of fake and real producers waiting to take advantage of naïve young women. One young photographer saw more than enough during his career in the 1950s and 1960s:

> *When I come to look back at the human race, it sometimes fills me with disgust, and I suppose I've drawn a blanket over a lot of what I saw or heard in my years with show business. I know from an audience's point of view, we are all a happy lot; maybe that's how it should be. . . . We don't want to see the ugly side of things. There was one casting agent whose motto was "if they are in the business they will stag" or "hold this dear and the part is yours." He had no scruples.*

The abuse of women in the industry was frankly appalling. Marilyn was steadfast in her determination to never be taken advantage of, but she was wise to the immoral behavior, especially in the early days of living with other young hopefuls at the Hollywood Studio Club. She was certainly aware of women who thought it necessary to do nude photo sessions to further their careers, because after the discovery of her own pictures in 1952, would-be actresses openly spoke to her about it.

Marilyn was no prude and completely owned up to the fact that she had posed nude, but she worried about the next generation of actresses. Despite her image of a sexy, glamorous star, Marilyn told reporter Earl Wilson that she never approved of nudity for nudity's sake. One day she became aware of a hopeful who was obviously being taken advantage of and tried to warn her about what she was doing. The girl did not agree, and instead insisted, "But look at you!" The woman was referring to how Marilyn's career was not harmed by posing for the famous nude calendar picture, but the star was appalled that anyone would think it was this alone that had made her famous.

Marilyn told Wilson: "She didn't understand. I had to take care of bills. . . . It was to eat." She hoped actresses eager to further their careers in such a fashion knew what they were letting themselves in for. "I just say that the girl who thinks this is going to make her a success will be disappointed and disillusioned. There isn't any short cut. You may have to work harder to overcome it."

The attitude that certain men could do precisely what they wanted to women continued throughout the 1950s and beyond. It didn't exclusively apply to women in show business either. In the March 23, 1955, issue of the *Australian Women's Weekly* magazine, the letter voted best of the week was written by a Mrs. S. Moses from New South Wales. In the note, she began by saying how appalled she was by the rising number of attacks against women. However, her sympathy did not last for long, as although she did not condone sexual assault, she did admit that "I think women collectively are much to blame." According to Mrs. Moses, women just did not realize the power of their charms, and by being dressed provocatively, wearing perfume, and giving "come-hither" looks, the caveman instinct could be unleashed in even the most decent of men. These pervasive attitudes made getting ahead an uphill battle for Marilyn and other independent women.

In March 1954, columnist and friend Sidney Skolsky wrote an article entitled "Lowdown on Hollywood Women," in which he spoke briefly about the incidents women went through in the industry: "[Marilyn] just never wants to get out of her dream world. And this place called Hollywood is a dream world for the girls who come here and for those who don't. It will always be that way, in spite of the nightmares most of our Hollywood females go through, sooner or later, even though these nightmares are public gossip."

Dreamworld or not, the revelations of ex-family members and old friends, combined with the general attitude toward women in Hollywood at that time, contributed to the longing Marilyn had to escape and start anew. By 1955, it was clear: now that the actress had settled into life on the East Coast, she had no intention of leaving, at least not until she had achieved her dreams. "Marilyn looked upon New York as a shrine of culture. If only she worshipped reverently, all her dreams would come true," said one friend.

WHILE REPORTERS WERE OBSESSED by the nature of Marilyn's move to Manhattan, they were even more interested in her relationship with photographer Milton Greene. He patiently answered their questions: "I met Marilyn about a year and a half ago," he explained. "When I came out to Hollywood on my honeymoon a little while later, I introduced my wife Amy to Marilyn, and we all became good friends. I shot a lot of pictures of Marilyn—they're going to be published in a book—and I invited her to spend Christmas with us in New York and Connecticut. I introduced her to my lawyer, Frank Delaney, and she told him what was on her mind. That's how we started Marilyn Monroe Productions, her own corporation. Marilyn wants to be able to have some say in the roles she plays."

The notion of Marilyn releasing a book was another source of excitement, and Milton shared a few details about the project: "This book will show the new Marilyn Monroe," he said. "We have talked about her writing the text in the first person, but we haven't decided on that yet." In the end, the book was never written or published, though many years after her death a new edition of Marilyn's autobiography, *My Story* (based on a series of interviews with reporter Ben Hecht), would appear alongside some of Milton Greene's most beautiful photographs. Sadly, this was the closest anyone ever got to the actual book the star and photographer were planning in 1955.

Perhaps the volume did not become a reality because, at that point, the success of Marilyn Monroe Productions was paramount. "Please let me tell you why I formed my own company, seemingly so quickly," she told columnist Louella Parsons. "I am not angry with Twentieth Century Fox. I believe *The Seven Year Itch* is the best picture of my career. But I have such a deep fear of not managing my business properly and of being alone—and broke—when I am older. I've known too much insecurity in my life not to want above all else, real security against the day when they don't want me anymore."

Marilyn explained more to reporter Alice Finletter: "Technically, I'm not under contract to Twentieth Century Fox anymore. But I like the studio, and I want to make more pictures here. And I think we can work it out. I've been quoted as saying that I don't like the pictures I've been put in. I never said that. A couple of the pictures might have been better. I suggested that a very good role might be the female lead in *The Brothers Karamazov* and right away it was taken for granted that I was getting arty and wanted to play the part." Milton Greene declared *The Brothers Karamazov* rumors "a bunch of bunk. She was misquoted. A line of what she said was taken out of context."

Out of context or not, the subject was a great topic of conversation for many in Hollywood and New York City. Author of *Gentlemen Prefer Blondes* Anita Loos gave the dream her full backing. Discussing the project with actor Clifton Webb, she exclaimed that Marilyn would be "absolutely wonderful in the role of Grushenka." Webb agreed and told reporter Ernie Player that it was just the idea that was startling, not the reality. Another influential person who believed Marilyn could do it was movie mogul Samuel Goldwyn. He declared her to be perfect for the role, and Marilyn was so pleased that she cut out the clipping and carried it around in her handbag.

Marilyn actually did quietly dream of one day acting in *The Brothers Karamazov*, but for now she needed to study. Taking everything she had learned from the recent past, the twenty-eight-year-old actress gathered herself together and set about finding people who could help on her journey. It had only been a year since Marilyn fought the studio over *The Girl in Pink Tights,* and now she had walked out on her film contract and created her own production company. With eleven months of 1955 remaining, Marilyn was confident that whatever happened next, it would be completely in her control.

THE ANNOUNCEMENT OF MARILYN MONROE PRODUCTIONS seemed to anger more than just Twentieth Century Fox. Some reporters could not get their head around the fact that Marilyn Monroe—she of the wiggly walk and breathless voice—would desire to be anything other than the image they wanted her to be. Some were outwardly hostile toward her. One columnist by the name of Leonard Coulter made his feelings clear in an open letter in his "Coulter Column" for *Film Bulletin*. In it, he berated Marilyn for everything from her cooking skills to her declaration of independence and everything in between:

> *Considering the architecture with which the good Lord blessed you,*
> *I am astonished to discover that you have not learned very much*
> *about homo sapiens (no, honey; it's not something you eat. It means*
> *MAN). Thanks to Twentieth-Century-Fox, you have become a hot*
> *commercial property, and though it would be rather misleading to*
> *say you are a bone of contention, the fact remains that your own*
> *hard work and the company's exploitation genius have made a lot*
> *of people envious.*
>
> *Some of them have kidded you into believing you could become*
> *a great dramatic actress. Only the other day you said yourself that*
> *you'd like to appear in a film based on Dostoevsky's* The Brothers
> Karamazov. *Have you ever read the book? Why not choose some*
> *pleasant trifle like the balcony scene in* Romeo and Juliet? *That*
> *would be fun . . .*

One must ask if columnists such as Coulter ever chastised the male species for wanting to better their lives. It is doubtful. The fact remains that for a woman with ambition in the 1950s, life was filled with sexism and disbelief. During Marilyn's last interview, in 1962 with Richard Meryman, one of her requests was that the reporter not make her look like a joke. After being mocked during her entire career, it is easy to see why such a wish was made.

The idea of any actress—not just Marilyn—owning a production company, caused a furor in the male-dominated industry. However, a look at some statistics shows exactly why it came as a surprise. Firstly, the only mega-famous female movie mogul had been Mary Pickford, and her producing days were over by the 1950s. (Her last film was *Love Happy* [1949], which included Marilyn in a walk-on role.) A search of the phrase "female producer" in the hundreds of film magazines scanned on the Media History Digital Library brings up only nine results. None of those articles were written later than 1947. The same search in the *Los Angeles Times* and *New York Times* shows just one entry during the entire 1950s: a report entitled "Story of a Determined Lady," about theater producer Terese Hayden. Within the columns of the story, the ambitious woman is described as a "girl producer."

The phrase "woman film producer" fares hardly any better. Twelve articles appear in film magazines, with only two of those being after 1943. The same search in newspapers brings up only two results for the 1950s. While Marilyn is proof that some women were striving to be successful in the production side of filmmaking, as far as the industry was concerned, the concept was rarely spoken about and certainly not nurtured or encouraged. It was fine to look pretty in front of the camera, but to be powerful and successful behind it was a joke of magnificent proportions.

One reporter asked if Marilyn would like to be a director too and she shook her head, saying that she simply did not have enough experience. She was being a tad unfair to herself, because history has shown that she was actually something of a genius when it came to still and moving cameras. She knew instinctively how to pose to create the perfect photograph, and saw even publicity shoots as important work. Photographer Richard Avedon later said that Marilyn was always completely involved with her photo shoots and shared many ideas and thoughts, even working throughout the night if she thought the occasion required it.

Reporter Sidney Skolsky once watched as she posed for the March 1954 cover of *Modern Screen* magazine. He wrote that she began work at 12:30 p.m. and did not finish until 4 p.m. "I act when I'm posing," she explained. "Just as hard as I do when I'm playing a role in front of a movie camera. I think of something for each pose so I'll have the right expression."

A list made in her notebook shows that she made plans to attend directorial lectures by Harold Clurman and Lee Strasberg, so she might have quietly hoped to one day become a director—although after the furor caused by the revelation of her producing ambitions, she was highly unlikely to admit it to the press. Years later, during the making of *The Misfits*, Marilyn jotted down ideas on how certain scenes should be shot; she was clearly intrigued by the process.

Should she have gone down that road eventually, Marilyn would likely have been taken even less seriously than she was already. All searches for "female director" and "woman film director" in film magazines and newspapers come up with only a handful of results, and all were printed before 1943. Trailblazer Dorothy Arzner was the exception in the otherwise male-dominated industry. She started as a typist at the Famous Players-Lasky Corporation (later Paramount), but through hard work and determination had managed to become a director. By 1932, she was working independently, and in 1936 was said to be the only female director in Hollywood. In 1937, Arzner told the *Los Angeles Times* that as a lone female director, she must never raise her voice on set or act in what some might consider an unreasonable way. According to her, society still expected her to be feminine, and swearing was totally out of the question. By 1938, the *Motion Picture Herald* told readers that not one female director was under contract to any of the top fifteen producers, and by 1943, Arzner had directed her last movie.

In Great Britain, the situation was no better. The British Newspaper Archive shows no results for "female film producer" and only two listings for "female film director." Both articles are from the 1940s. Those women who dared to try their luck in the industry were met with sarcasm or disdain by the British press. An article in the *Dundee Evening Telegraph* in 1940 bore the headline "They're Doing a Man's Job" and announced that Mrs. Culley Forde was the only woman associate producer in the entire British movie industry. She could not enjoy her success alone, of course. Instead, the newspaper made sure to mention that she was the wife of director Walter Forde.

A piece in the *Sketch* from 1946 is even worse. Entitled "We Take Our Hat to Miss Jill Craigie," the newspaper celebrated Craigie's status as the only female film director in England. However, they chose to do so not with a list of her most important work, but with two pages of photographs showing her admiring her face in the mirror, laying the table for dinner, walking up the stairs, doing her hair, and reading. Of course, they also mentioned that she happened to be the wife of film director Jeffrey Dell. "Jill Craigie rightly pays as much attention to her personal appearance as she does to production details," it said.

CHAPTER FOUR

A Serious Actress

WHILE SETTING UP HER film company was momentously important for Marilyn, she also knew that if she was going to do great work, she needed a solid foundation from which to start. This meant exploring acting techniques that were new and fresh, and walking away from existing coach Natasha Lytess. In the past, the firing of Lytess has often been regarded as a cold, uncaring decision on Marilyn's part. However, before judging her action, it is important to understand the nature of the relationship and the kind of person Lytess was.

Marilyn first met the woman in 1948, during her six-month tenure under contract to Columbia Pictures. Lytess was a teacher there and was asked to help the young actress with her voice and dramatic training. She recognized straightaway how nervous Marilyn was, but instead of giving her confidence and putting her at ease, Lytess recoiled at the sound of her voice. "She was in a shell," she said. "She couldn't speak up. She was very inhibited. I had to ask her not to talk at all. Her voice got on my nerves. She'd say, 'all right, thank you, g'bye.' I taught her to let go." It is worth noting that this insulting comment was not given to the press after their association ended, but in 1952, when they were still working together. Natasha Lytess never had any qualms about telling people about her famous client, and to say she thought herself totally responsible for her career would be an understatement.

Marilyn wasn't the first or the last student who had problems with Lytess. In 1951, actor Fess Parker had an unfortunate run-in with her that was not dissimilar to the one Marilyn had a few years before. He told the *Los Angeles Times* that Lytess had asserted that he was "practically un-coachable," and while she mellowed slightly by telling the young actor that he had a certain quality, she never did explain what she meant by the enigmatic remark.

Lytess later claimed to be totally unimpressed with the young Monroe, and declared her to be not at all beautiful. In fact, she made it plainly obvious that she considered Marilyn to be beneath her in both status and talent. "Her face was as wooden as a ventriloquist's dummy. . . . She was tense and apprehensive, utterly unsure of herself. Unable even to take refuge in her own insignificance." Lytess was jealous that she had never achieved great success as an actress herself, and was somewhat obsessed with the young starlet in her care. Lytess maintained that while Marilyn insisted she be on film sets with her at all times, the coach actually felt uncomfortable to be there. This would be far more convincing if not for the fact that Lytess took over the entire set of every production she worked on, as attested by many a director over the years.

Sitting next to the director, the coach could be seen copying everything Marilyn did before the camera. Then the moment the director cried "Cut," she would often clench her fists, shout her disapproval of what had just occurred, and then rush to Marilyn's side to tell her what she had done wrong. She would also act as something of an unofficial (and unappointed) manager, who enjoyed telling reporters that they could go through her for an interview with Marilyn.

At one point the two women shared a house (along with Lytess's daughter and a maid) so that they could practice all day, every day. While in theory this was good for preparation, it also meant that Marilyn had little freedom and even less privacy. Lytess would often grow jealous and resentful of relationships Marilyn had with men, but the actress tolerated this aspect of her personality because she wanted help with her acting studies. The arrival of Joe DiMaggio in 1952, however, caused the first cracks to form in their relationship, since Lytess hated his presence in Marilyn's life and he was in no hurry to leave.

Another problem was the coach's obsession with publicity. Over the years of working with Marilyn, she would speak about her openly to any reporter who asked. Just days before the beginning of *The Seven Year Itch*, she even appeared on the television show *What's My Line* as Marilyn's coach. One must wonder if she had obtained her student's permission before signing up to do the program. By the end of 1954, when Marilyn was getting ready for her move to the East Coast, she finally took the decision to leave Lytess behind in Los Angeles. Perhaps predicting a dramatic reaction, she did not tell the coach that she was actually fired; instead, she kept quiet and hoped Lytess would figure it out for herself. She did not.

By March 1955, the drama teacher was still in the dark and columnist Hedda Hopper was eager to talk to her about it. Asked if she had been contacted by her errant student, Lytess said she had heard "not a peep." She was worried, she said, because the time was right to follow up *The Seven Year Itch* with "more fine pictures." Perhaps in a misguided attempt to create a reaction from Marilyn, Lytess was quick to tell Hopper that she was now teaching two other actors: Jeff Hunter and Virginia Leith.

Eventually Natasha Lytess woke up and realized that Marilyn was not going to come back. In retaliation, it did not take her long to contact reporters about their relationship. In an article entitled "The Storm About Monroe," writer Steve Cronin interviewed various people on the subject of how Marilyn had changed from Hollywood glamour girl to dramatic actress. One of the people he spoke to was an unnamed woman, described as "one of the few women in Hollywood who has worked with Marilyn closely for many years." Since Natasha was the only one who fit the description, it can be assumed that the quote came directly from her. "I have come to the conclusion," she said,

> that Marilyn Monroe doesn't know her own mind. I can't tell you how unhappy she was while she was married to DiMaggio. She felt closed in, a prisoner in her own house. She felt that Joe never would come to understand either her or show business. Her months of marriage to DiMaggio, despite all the fairy tales, were months of misery.
>
> When she divorced Joe, I know she felt as though a great weight had been lifted from her heart. She and Joe had nothing in common. She told me this a dozen times if she told me once. Marilyn has had very few friends in her life. Because of her sex appeal, women are afraid of her. The men she has known usually have been instrumental in helping her career. Joe was not one of these and she let him go. . . . What does all this mean? Does anyone really know where Marilyn is going? What does she want? What sort of woman has she become?

It is unrecorded as to what Marilyn's feelings were toward Natasha's outbursts, but certainly during the early months of 1955, her mind was on other matters. After she'd lived for a while with the Greenes, it was felt by all parties that Marilyn needed a base in the city as well. So it was that on January 19 she moved into New York City's Gladstone Hotel, a private space paid for by business partner Milton Greene, as per his contractual agreement. Despite the end of her marriage to Joe DiMaggio, he was seen helping Marilyn move into the hotel and then eating with her at various locations around town. Rumors swirled that the two were about to be reunited, especially when she met him in Boston while on a business trip to see a possible Marilyn Monroe Productions investor. The investment did not go ahead, but the visit nevertheless managed to garner headlines.

As the couple left a restaurant in the company of his brother and sister-in-law, journalists pounced and asked if this was a reconciliation. Joe looked at his ex-wife and asked if it was, to which Marilyn replied, "Well just call it a visit." This was obviously not the answer the baseball player was looking for, because as soon as they got away from the reporters, he dropped her off at her hotel and headed to the home of his sister-in-law's parents. The next day journalists managed to track Joe down and interviewed him on the doorstep, Joe still wearing his bathrobe. When asked again about the reconciliation, he shrugged. "There is none," he replied.

In the end, any hope of the couple getting back together was a figment of the media's imagination. Joe might have seemed rather keen on the idea, but Marilyn was adamant that she was now single and would stay that way. As happy as she was to be on friendly terms with her ex-husband, the brutal divorce and events leading up to it were still fresh wounds. For now, there would be a friendship between the pair, but it was strictly on Marilyn's terms; she was firmly in control.

On January 25, she was happy to accompany Joe to see him elected to the Baseball Hall of Fame. This meant a lot to the former baseball star, and for once he was talkative to the reporters who wanted to know about it. "You can bet I'll be there with flying colors," he said. "I'm very excited about this. And I'm especially happy because it will mean so much to my son, Joe Junior."

January 26 arrived and Marilyn gave an interview to author George Carpozi Jr. and took part in an accompanying photo shoot in her suite at the Gladstone. The chat was candid and the two ended up walking arm in arm through Central Park as Marilyn told the story of her life. Carpozi would treasure the memories of meeting the actress, and later compiled everything he remembered into a book, one of the earliest ever written about Marilyn and one she had in her own collection.

Through author Truman Capote, Marilyn was introduced to teacher Constance Collier, a British Edwardian actress who had moved to Hollywood in the 1920s. There, she taught students how to transition from silent movies to talkies and acted in a few herself. By 1955 she was settled in New York, and it was there that Marilyn became her student. At first Collier had little interest in meeting the actress because the only knowledge she had of her was through the grand buildup of publicity Marilyn had received since the beginning of her career.

She did not know how she would take to the blonde icon, but after speaking to her for the first time, Collier soon realized that Marilyn was actually a fragile talent. "My special problem" was how she described the actress to Capote. Together they studied the character of

Ophelia from Shakespeare's *Hamlet*, and when Collier spoke to Greta Garbo about it, the great Swedish actress suggested maybe she and Marilyn could work together one day. This must surely have thrilled Marilyn, since she was a great fan of Garbo as a woman and an actress.

Sadly, the relationship with Collier did not survive past a few months, since the woman's health deteriorated and she passed away in April 1955. Marilyn never forgot the great work they achieved in class, however, and attended her funeral with Capote.

CREATED IN 1947 BY Elia Kazan, Cheryl Crawford, and several others, the Actors Studio was one of the most prestigious acting institutions in the United States. A common misconception was that it was a formal acting school, but actually the studio was run in the style of a workshop and attended by actors who were required to audition in order to gain full membership. Once in the door, students could congregate, work on scenes, receive emotional guidance, correct errors, and solve problems. Most of the actors had already received some kind of training elsewhere and were now looking for a kinship, a safe place to learn emotional—rather than technical—training.

In 1951, teacher Lee Strasberg took charge of the studio, and his wife, Paula, was frequently by his side. A staunch supporter of Konstantin Stanislavski, Lee and several other teachers had taken inspiration from the System technique and evolved it into the Method, which was what the Actors Studio became infamous for. The aim was to enable actors to relax into their parts, by digging deep into their own emotions and memories. This would allow them to bring up personal episodes that would give a better understanding of the acting role.

The process was a deeply personal and even spiritual experience, and as such, it became highly controversial to those actors who preferred a more technical approach. Method director Charles Marowitz wrote about the problem in 1958, explaining that it was all just a question of balance. "No Method-man from Stanislavski onwards has ever contended that [the Method] dismisses the need for vocal and kinesthetic competence." In fact, he assured readers, Stanislavski himself said that the Method (or the System, as it was called in his day) was really there to inspire actors to develop styles and processes of their own.

Lee Strasberg actually understood that the Method wasn't a good choice for everyone, and that every actor required different tools to solve their problems. However, he was determined that the work done at the studio would be of great assistance to those who needed it. He also desperately wanted to provide the kind of support that the general American theater did not—the kind of emotional stability and variety that repertory theatre gave actors in Great Britain.

Actress and student Kim Stanley was determined that those who balked at Strasberg's techniques were merely too frightened to reveal themselves onstage. She spoke about being at the Actors Studio in 1958. "There's really no such thing as the Method," she said. "Lee Strasberg is a man gifted to see the capabilities a person really has. He releases a freedom of the spirit. It's something like psychoanalysis. You have to know yourself before you can improve. Lee has that rare ability to convince you that you're capable of more than what you're doing. If only you could attend classes for six months, you'd see what marvelous things he can do."

While actors such as Gary Cooper and Spencer Tracy denied any interest in becoming Method actors, by the mid-1950s, the membership had grown to include such high-profile names as Marlon Brando, Montgomery Clift, James Dean, and soon Marilyn Monroe. "We have made history," said Lee Strasberg in 1957, "in the sense that all over the world the Actors Studio has been thrown under a spotlight. Indeed you hardly read about an actor but you learn he is from the studio—well, I don't know when they all got in, unless it was when I was away!" While not every actor was a student there, the sheer amount of superstars choosing to become associated with the Actors Studio brought attention to a degree it had never known before.

Association with Hollywood legends was great for the studio, but it actually caused quite a stir for the actors who had fought their way in through intense auditions. The celebrities that just walked through the doors without having uttered a word in the audition process were resented by the stage actors, who all thought—quite rightly, of course—that everyone should receive the same treatment.

The negative feelings from New York City actors toward Hollywood luminaries was further complicated because for some years they had also been blamed for stealing Broadway roles from local talent. In 1956, actor Barry Nelson described the Broadway stage as dying and a phenomenon of the past. The problem, he said, was that theater managers wanted actors who were well known throughout the country, not just in New York. By employing film stars, they were almost guaranteed to sell out on opening night, and audiences were much more likely to attend a run. "As Mr. Nelson admits," wrote Eric Johns, "their presence on Broadway is decidedly detrimental to the theater and often the play itself suffers because they cannot possibly do justice to their roles. Yet genuine craftsmen in the art of acting may have been turned down or never considered because their names mean nothing to the masses."

This problem had actually worked the opposite way in the late 1920s and early '30s, when Hollywood enlisted the help of East Coast stage actors to survive the transition to talkies. The actors were brought over to California for the simple reason that they knew how to speak their lines. This left many established Hollywood actors of the silent era furious. By the mid-1950s, stage actors in New York were feeling the same way.

While still studying with Constance Collier, Marilyn met Actors Studio director Cheryl Crawford at a party. The two did not hit it off immediately, however, as Crawford was friends with Marilyn's former agent Charles Feldman and felt that he had been treated badly by the star. Marilyn stood her ground and explained that she needed somebody on her side who was not also working for Twentieth Century Fox. Crawford eventually understood the predicament she had found herself in, and the two became friends.

The story of how Marilyn actually took the final decision to become involved in the Actors Studio has often been discussed. Milton Greene was said to have given her a push in that direction, since he was friends with member Marlon Brando. Arthur Miller believed that the whole reason for Marilyn's move to Manhattan was because she desperately wanted to study there. Others believe that it was the fateful meeting with Cheryl Crawford that gave the opportunity to follow through with any fledgling plans she might have had. In truth, it was probably a mixture of all of these reasons. Marilyn had long been aware of the Actors Studio (and had told Studio director Lee Strasberg's daughter, Susan, in 1954 that she one day wanted to work with her father), so it was perhaps always inevitable that her quest to become a successful, serious actress would one day lead to the Actors Studio. Whichever path she took, this fateful decision sent her on a journey that would change her entire approach to acting.

Marilyn was introduced formally to Lee and Paula Strasberg, and they adored her from the start. They opened their home to this Hollywood misfit and made her part of their family. Daughter Susan became a surrogate sister, and Marilyn's occasional overnight stays ensured son John had to sleep on the sofa. For someone who had never enjoyed the security of living with two parents in a loving environment, Marilyn adored her time with the family and took a keen interest in their lives. John's first impression on meeting Marilyn was that she was "instinctively smart, nobody's fool."

Cynics have suggested that Lee and Paula adored the notoriety the actress brought with her. Even if that was so, there is no doubt that during those early years in New York, Marilyn relied on the family quite heavily. Paula spoke about her feelings for the actress in 1960: "Marilyn has a God-given talent, really phenomenal talent. My husband says she is a combination of Jeanne Eagels and Pauline Lord. Like them she is greatly misunderstood. Where Marilyn's work is concerned, she wants perfection and to achieve perfection in anything is well-nigh impossible. But she constantly seeks it—even at the expense of her health and peace of mind."

It was decided that Marilyn would take a variety of classes with Lee Strasberg. First there were free, one-on-one lessons that took place in the living room of the Strasberg apartment. Susan would often overhear the conversations going on in the room and noted a lot of swearing and anger from Marilyn toward Twentieth Century Fox and anyone she felt had betrayed her. Susan found these observations fascinating but also frustrating, because in all the time she had known her father, he had never once given her the kind of support that he gave Marilyn during their lessons.

Also at the Strasberg apartment were classes attended by other actors and actresses. These were more formal, fee-based lessons, and involved a series of exercises and improvisation. At first, Marilyn did not feel confident enough to take part so would sit on an easy chair and observe. Eventually, however, she started to loosen up and studied scenes with the other actors. Over the course of time, Marilyn found herself engrossed in studying *Ulysses* (she was intrigued that author James Joyce was able to get into a woman's mind through the character of Molly Bloom), as well as improvisations where she imagined herself in the role of a cat. One exercise saw the actress study animals at the zoo, where she fell in love with a lioness called June and then became worried that the big cat was lonely.

Her studies were extremely enjoyable and allowed Marilyn to open up in a way she had rarely done before. Strasberg noted that she had developed a lot of bad habits in Hollywood, but thankfully they had not affected her sensitivity or raw talent. Over time, the overemphasis on her voice—taught by Lytess—began to subside, and her true acting ability soon emerged. This new, subtle approach to her craft was perfect for Marilyn, who away from the cameras hardly wore makeup, ran her fingers through her unstyled hair, and dressed in casual clothes and no jewelry. In short, she realized that for the first time, it was perfectly okay to just be herself.

Perhaps the most notorious part of her education was when Marilyn was invited to observe work at the actual famed Actors Studio. Once again, she did not feel confident enough to do scenes there at first, so instead she sat in the crowd, made extensive notes, and watched the other actors onstage. Since Marilyn was one of the biggest celebrities in the world, the New York actors were not going to go out of their way to make her feel welcome or wanted when she walked into class. They did not greet her with hostility (not to her face anyway), but they were wary of her presence and outwardly seemed unimpressed by her star status.

Arthur Miller's sister, Joan Copeland, remembered that some of the students would whisper and ask questions such as "What the heck is she doing here?" The catty remarks would also be used to make fun of her talents, even though no one had actually seen her act onstage. Marilyn never admitted that her feelings were hurt, but Joan imagined they must surely have been. Instead, Marilyn kept quiet and tried desperately to blend into the background. Dressed down in skirts and button-up shirts or sweaters and pants, Marilyn sat toward the back of the class and, at first, rarely spoke to anyone. Her initial reaction was that the other students seemed so much younger than her, and she was intimidated by their youth and experience.

The frosty atmosphere was perhaps made no better when it became obvious to everyone that the Strasbergs absolutely adored Marilyn, and vice versa. However, over the course of time, the students began mellowing toward her, and she started to let down her guard as well. Flanked by the Strasbergs, Marilyn would attend lunch with the other students and happily took part in conversations. At night, she would often join them again at places such as Downey's on Eighth Avenue, where they would discuss art, music, and culture.

Most students kept quiet about their thoughts on Marilyn, but one unidentified member spoke to reporter Gene Houseman. The actor was keen to give a different slant on the story: "Actually nobody's being snooty with this no-talk bit," he said. "Behind it is an unwritten agreement with Marilyn. She doesn't want any publicity in connection with her attendance there, and she has placed her trust in everyone there to follow her wishes. It's really an admirable and remarkable thing that none of the students—there are about 165—has ever dreamed of violating that trust. Especially when you take into account that none of them are really bound in any way, and many of them are very poor, struggling actors who could certainly use the fast buck they might make for talking."

One of the students who remembered Marilyn coming into the studio at the beginning was Stefan Gierasch, who said that the actress sat at the back and tried not to draw attention to herself. According to him, everyone was aware that Lee and Paula Strasberg were her mentors, but he was unaware that anyone had been unkind to Marilyn; in fact, he remembered various members trying to welcome her. In comparison, actor Mark Weston said they were told never to treat Marilyn any differently than other students, and his first impression was that she was there just to take up space. This observation was somewhat unfair because while Marilyn may not have said anything at all in the beginning, she was soaking up all that the studio had to offer.

TO GET A BETTER understanding of their psyche, it was felt that students of the Method should undertake a period of psychoanalysis. Marilyn took the advice very seriously and began therapy in February 1955 with Dr. Margaret Hohenberg, a therapist introduced to her by fellow patient Milton Greene. While one may think that it was slightly unethical to treat two business partners—particularly if one had anything to say about the other—Hohenberg either did not think about this, or did not care. Documents also suggest that various business decisions were made only after consultation with Hohenberg, which was unusual, to say the least. Regardless, Marilyn attended regular sessions with the Freudian analyst, and this therapy continued with Hohenberg and others until the end of her life.

Without access to Marilyn's patient records, we cannot say categorically what happened during meetings with her psychiatrists. However, clinical psychologist Dr. L. Ruddick, who practices in Birmingham, England, has been able to shed light on the kinds of sessions a Freudian analyst could have provided:

> *Therapy is likely to start with the therapist establishing a full history from the person, including things that are important to them about their childhood, family relationships—particularly with primary care-givers—emotional symptoms, physical health, sexual relationships, important memories whether real or imagined, and events leading up to the onset of emotional/physical/psychological symptoms. The focus of the therapy is liable to have been to look at the relationship between conscious and unconscious parts of the mind (memories and fantasies), seeking to undo the repression of hidden impulses and to find alternative outlets.*
>
> *A therapist wouldn't necessarily rely on verbal information, but alongside listening would be observing the mood and the feelings to think about underlying messages. Freud used the technique of free-association at some point in his career and would just let the person talk as they so wished, free as much as possible of the influence of the therapist. Reflection was frequently used as a technique.*

There have been many discussions over the years as to whether her regular stream of therapists did Marilyn any good. It is certainly debatable. In and out of foster homes and an orphanage, Marilyn was wounded by memories of an unstable childhood, and it would perhaps have been better for her long-term health if she had dealt with it quickly and moved on. But the sustained use of therapists ensured that she was continually reminded of particular moments of her childhood that were perhaps best left in the past.

Actors Studio student Delos Smith Jr. told Susan Strasberg that Marilyn would often be conservative with the truth during her sessions with Hohenberg. Terrified because her mother had been committed to an asylum, the actress would withhold information so that the analyst would not think she required the same kind of treatment. According to Smith, Marilyn also had a fascination with suicide and spoke about it often. When he told Lee Strasberg that he feared she would die, the acting guru was furious. He believed that any negativity she harbored would be cured by immersion in the classes.

In this age of mental health awareness, it is important to acknowledge that Marilyn did have issues. She was particularly vulnerable, easily hurt, and often brought to tears or anger through perceived rejection or betrayal. Her life was always black-and-white: a person was either on her side or not, and there was simply no middle ground. She fought inner demons; she constantly looked for the truth of her life and was prone to bouts of depression. In spite of that, she still achieved great heights and never let her anxiety stop her quest for knowledge and education. For Marilyn to accept that she had problems, and to realize that in spite of them she was able to accomplish everything she did, was in itself empowering.

A private person by nature, Marilyn did not speak about her therapy sessions often, but when asked by reporter Logan Gourlay in 1955, she gave a little insight. "I'm not taking a full course," she said, before adding that she would never scoff at psychiatry and felt it useful to know what made her tick. When pressed further, she quickly changed the subject, but the question came again from the same journalist five years later. This time all Marilyn would say is that she knew nothing about psychiatrist Carl Jung, but quite a lot about Sigmund Freud. "He's the one I believe in," she said.

In 1956, Marilyn shared a little more to reporter Pete Martin. During the interview, she revealed that while previously she had felt a need to run away from her emotions, she was beginning to understand herself in a way that she never had before: "I've read a little of Freud and it might have to do with what he said. I think he was on the right track."

FEBRUARY 1955 WAS A busy month for Marilyn. In addition to her acting lessons and therapy sessions, there was a press conference to announce a charity appearance at Madison Square Garden, a birthday party for actor Jackie Gleason (attended with Joe DiMaggio), and the premiere of *East of Eden*. The film opening—a benefit for the Actors Studio—caused the most excitement, with fans queued around the block just to get a glimpse of Marilyn acting as a celebrity usher.

During a party after the premiere, it was planned for the actress to sing "Diamonds Are a Girl's Best Friend" and the event was even advertised numerous times in newspapers. However, Marilyn decided to pull out because she did not have time to rehearse and had no wish to look foolish in front of Broadway actors. Actress Carol Channing had played the part of Lorelei Lee in the 1949 Broadway production of *Gentlemen Prefer Blondes* and was urged to trap Marilyn into singing "Diamonds" with her, but she thought that a dreadful idea. "I decided it wouldn't be fair to Marilyn," she said. "I just know that I'd kill anybody who'd do it to me, so why should I do it to her?"

Away from the limelight, Marilyn, Milton Greene, and her representatives were in fevered negotiations with Lew Schreiber from Twentieth Century Fox regarding her contract. Fan mail was still pouring in to the studio and had hit an unprecedented eight thousand letters during March 1955. Many of the fans demanded to know when their favorite star would return to the screen, and, of course, that was something the studio did not yet know. After *The Seven Year Itch*, there would be no new Marilyn Monroe projects to release. Zanuck and his associates frankly could not believe that the woman they thought was no more than a ditzy blonde was actually holding them to ransom.

Marilyn, however, reveled in her newfound position. This was her way of punishing them for every bad picture they'd put her in, for every time she'd fought to read a script or even have her own dressing room. A climax of sorts came when Marilyn started returning their letters unopened. Furious, Zanuck announced that all negotiations were off and, just to add further drama, threatened to delay the release of *The Seven Year Itch*.

This might have given the studio head satisfaction, but it was all a bluff, as in reality he was campaigning to bring the premiere forward rather than push it back. Originally there had been an agreement whereby the studio would wait until the end of the Broadway run before releasing the picture. This seemed logical at the time, but in the end, despite saying that Marilyn was holding up the release, Fox paid a fine of $175,000 to the playwright and stage producers to be able to open much earlier than planned.

Marilyn may have been fighting for more money, but Fox found it difficult to believe that the ultimate aim was never to become rich. Instead, what she wanted more than anything was the right to make decisions about her own career and to express her creativity in a way that was relatable to the public. This should not have come as a surprise. Once, when Marilyn was a starlet, a member of the legal department tried to get her to sign a contract sooner rather than later. When she asked why, he told her it would save her money in the long run. "I'm not interested in money," she said. "I just want to be wonderful." She disclosed something similar to journalist and friend Sidney Skolsky: "I didn't go into movies to make money. I wanted to become famous so that everyone would like me, and I'd be surrounded with love and affection."

Marilyn ignored all threats and demands from Fox, and instead enjoyed throwing a surprise party for Milton Greene on his birthday in March 1955. She then did something rather unprecedented: she allowed photographer Ed Feingersh to follow her around New York City, going about her everyday business of shopping, riding the subway, and taking part in costume fittings. However, she was slightly concerned about her less-than-classy accommodation at the Gladstone Hotel, so by the time Feingersh arrived, Marilyn had moved into the more luxurious Ambassador.

The photographs taken during the shoot have gone on to become some of Marilyn's most iconic, and have been used on postcards and posters throughout the world. One of the most famous is a black-and-white shot showing Marilyn leaning against the wall of her balcony, wearing a simple dress and holding a cigarette. The streets of

Manhattan can be seen all around her, skyscrapers, modern and classic architecture, tiny cars and even tinier people. Everyone on the street was completely oblivious to the fact that the world's most famous woman was gazing down on them, and yet there she was.

As a child, Marilyn used to gaze out of the orphanage window and see the RKO Studio water tower. Now she was gazing onto the streets of New York City as a famous movie star. What went through Marilyn's mind during that simple but effective photo shoot? At times, she looks thoughtful, as though wondering what would become of her. At others, she is smiling broadly, her hands balancing her as she leans out over the wall, fully accomplished in mood and manner.

Other shots show Marilyn lying on her sofa, reading texts by Stanislavski and *Motion Picture Daily* newspaper. Her hair is untidy and her clothes casual, but she does not appear to care. The photos taken by Ed Feingersh that week show a person intent on success. New York had become a beacon—a strong, unmoving talisman to hold on to while she fought for her rights. Marilyn was a runaway, looking for bright lights and a positive future, and she could not return home to California without making her dreams come true first. Failure simply was not an option.

ON MARCH 30, 1955, Marilyn took part in a charity event at Madison Square Garden, which saw her sitting astride a pink elephant. As it clomped through the auditorium, fans way up in the farthest balcony cheered her name and waved furiously. Marilyn waved back and was so astounded by their support that she could not wait to tell Amy and Milton Greene all about it.

Journalists were happy to include photos of the actress riding the elephant, but some fans wondered if she had been scared. She assured them she was not. While bravery is something Marilyn is rarely given credit for, over the years quite a few photographs and stories have emerged showing her making friends with every kind of animal, from stray dogs and horses to big cats and bears. Her philosophy on her affinity for animals was simple: "Dogs never bite me," she said. "Just humans."

By early April 1955, Darryl F. Zanuck was in New York. He took the opportunity to hold a press interview to discuss the latest news from his studio, and, of course, the subject of Marilyn came up. After declaring that the company would do a major push toward finding new talent in the year ahead, he reiterated his belief that Marilyn was still under contract and their agreement was not expected to expire for another three years. Bizarrely, he then denied all knowledge of the actress's plans to produce and star in her own company's films, and stated firmly that if she did not fulfill her obligations with Fox, she might be liable for damages.

Meanwhile, Marilyn fielded other offers that came her way. One was from the Last Frontier hotel in Las Vegas to star in her own song-and-dance production. Marilyn balked at the idea and said she couldn't possibly take part as she suffered from stage fright. However, Marilyn did say yes to an appearance with Milton and Amy Greene, on the April 8, 1955, edition of Edward R. Murrow's *Person to Person*. During a meeting to discuss the television show, Murrow noted that Marilyn seemed interested but not overly enthusiastic about the interview. Then after talking for a few moments, she surprised the host by suddenly asking him about Jawaharlal Nehru, the first prime minister of India. The actress revealed that she had missed a recent show he had made about Nehru and was anxious to see it. Several days later, Marilyn arrived at Murrow's office and they watched the program together. Afterward, she said that Nehru reminded her of Charlie Chaplin because of his expressive face. Murrow was so impressed with her interest in politics that he later sent her an album compilation of Winston Churchill's speeches.

The live interview between Murrow and Marilyn, Milton, and Amy took place at the Greenes' farmhouse. Baby Joshua was put down for his sleep and the three interviewees gathered in the kitchen. Crew members from the show hurried around, setting up cameras and microphones. A few minutes before they were due to go on, one of the crew mentioned that the threesome would be appearing before millions of people around the United States. This sent Marilyn and Milton into a nervous frenzy, but Amy remained calm.

Finally, it was time to switch on the cameras. The interview started with Milton in his studio, showing Murrow his vast collection of photographs. These ranged from a snap of his son to classic poses of Audrey Hepburn and, of course, Marilyn. Waiting in the kitchen, the star of the show was sitting with Amy, wearing a casual polo shirt and skirt. Considering she was a bundle of nerves before the event, Marilyn handled herself admirably, even when listening to inane questions about what kind of houseguest she was and whether she made her own bed.

The interview was somewhat awkward at times, such as in the middle of one question when Amy Greene suddenly interrupted Murrow and instructed the group to move to the den. Just as they sat down, the telephone started to ring. Several moments later, Milton got up to rummage around the sideboard for his pipe. The open fire crackled loudly in the background, and even the dogs made an appearance, but in all, the program was interesting, especially when Marilyn was finally asked about her new life.

Explaining that it was most important to have a good director, the actress disclosed that she had set up her film company hoping to make great pictures, and that she loved New York City and Connecticut and could often go around without anyone bothering her at all. This statement received a few chuckles from Milton and Amy, who then told a story about a taxi driver who started talking about Marilyn, not realizing for a second that she was actually sitting in the back of his cab.

The full appearance, including a studio introduction, took about fourteen minutes. While Marilyn might have been the star everyone wanted to see, it was Amy who stole the show. Looking as though nothing could ever faze her, she stepped in whenever Marilyn got stuck for an answer or seemed lost for words—so much so that afterward, some viewers decided she too should be in pictures. Amy herself remained insistent that her job was to look after Milton, Joshua, and, for the present, Marilyn.

By this time, Marilyn had left the Ambassador, but she did not move into her new apartment at the posh Waldorf Astoria Towers for several days. She saw the Greenes on the day after the Murrow interview, but then promptly disappeared. Concerned, they phoned Marilyn's contacts in Hollywood to see if she had turned up there, but they had not heard from her in months. It was never brought to light where the actress had gone during her few days of absence, but wherever it was, it taught Milton a lesson. While everyone considered him something of a Svengali who kept other people away, Marilyn was more than capable of disappearing on him too.

After moving into the Waldorf, Marilyn embraced her new life. There, she entertained friends, practiced her exercises for acting class, and talked business with Milton Greene. On top of that were photo sessions where Marilyn posed in all manner of settings and situations. Milton's natural way of shooting combined with her total trust in what he could do with a camera made the photographs some of the most beautiful ever taken, and they are still among the most prized by fans and collectors today.

In her spare time, Marilyn read consistently and listened to her favorite music: Ella Fitzgerald, Frank Sinatra, and many jazz musicians. "I'm insane about jazz," she said. "Louis Armstrong and Earl Bostick [*sic*]—it just gets stronger all the time." This was not a new affection; Marilyn had loved Armstrong since her early starlet days, as well as Jelly Roll Morton, a jazz musician who had died in 1941. She also went through a phase of listening to music by composers Tomaso Albinoni and Ottorino Respighi, and she played a little piano, "The Old Spinning Wheel" and "The Long Way Home" her favorite tunes.

Away from friends and colleagues, Marilyn spent a great deal of time by herself, which she found calming and refreshing. On days like that, she would window-shop at Tiffany's; sip coffee in small, quiet cafés; and buy creams and makeup at Elizabeth Arden. Many hours were spent closeted away in bookshops, reading and buying volumes on all manner of topics. Then she would admire art in the Metropolitan Museum, or go antiquing on Third Avenue. When asked how she managed to get around anonymously, Marilyn said she merely subdued her walk, wore no makeup, and put her hair under a scarf.

Anyone coming to Marilyn's apartment hoping to find copies of *Photoplay* and *Screenland* magazines would be disappointed. When

Pete Martin went to interview her, he noted a variety of interesting books on the coffee table, notably *Fallen Angels* by Noël Coward, *Gertrude Lawrence as Mrs. A* by Richard Aldrich, a condensed volume on Abraham Lincoln (she would later become friends with its author, Carl Sandburg), and *Bernard Shaw and Mrs. Patrick Campbell: Their Correspondence* by Bernard Shaw. Meanwhile, a recording of actor John Barrymore in Shakespeare's *Hamlet* lay on the floor.

At night, Marilyn would lie in bed and listen to the sounds of the street below. The beeps from impatient cab drivers later became an observation exercise in her notebook. In the text, she pondered the idea that they were driving to support their families and go on vacation. She loved the sounds of the street outside, and the moon, park, and river were favorite sights. While appreciating natural beauty, she also wrote about nightmares in her notebooks, of strange men leaning too close to her in elevators, and a fear of being complimented, in case it was insincere.

Marilyn's anxieties and lack of confidence were always a concern. Lee Strasberg encouraged her to do exercises out of strength, not fear, and taught technical ways to become stronger within herself. She remained frustrated that whenever she tried to express herself in a sincere way, there were always those who would dismiss her ideas and instead see her as a somewhat stupid person.

Still, Marilyn's fears and inferiority complex never seemed to hold her back from trying to live her dreams and give thanks to those who had been kind to her in the past. She was forever humble, as demonstrated on April 26, when she unexpectedly attended the Banshees party for journalists at the Waldorf Astoria hotel. None of the waiting reporters knew she would be there, but everyone seemed ecstatic that she was. "Any success I've had I owe entirely to you gentlemen of the press," she announced, before Earl Wilson snapped her with his camera and *Gentlemen Prefer Blondes* author Anita Loos desperately tried—and failed—to get close enough to speak.

HER ATTENDANCE AT THE Actors Studio eventually led Marilyn to become true friends with at least one of its students—actor Eli Wallach. She had seen him playing in *The Teahouse of the August Moon* and grilled him backstage about his work and whether he thought she could ever become a theater actress. Eli had explained what was required and Marilyn listened intently.

The actor always felt that theater offered a lot more artistic satisfaction than films or television, and had actually turned down numerous movie roles in order to return to the stage. During the course of his discussion with Marilyn, it was more than likely revealed that Eli had recently hopped over the Atlantic to play in London's West End. Such freedom to move around was not something Marilyn had ever been used to in Hollywood, and it was something she would later experience as her own boss.

After seeing Eli perform in *Teahouse*, Marilyn got into the habit of seeing the play whenever she could. She would sneak into the balcony completely anonymously and spend hours soaking up the atmosphere. She also became close to Eli's wife, Anne Jackson, and would sometimes babysit their son when they wanted a night out. One day after Marilyn told Eli that she adored Albert Einstein, she was somewhat surprised to discover a signed photograph of the man in her mailbox. After phoning numerous friends to share the great news, it was revealed that Eli Wallach had sent it himself as a joke. Marilyn appreciated his humor and hung the picture up anyway.

Showing competent business skills, Marilyn also helped Eli go over a contract, instructing him on which clauses to take out and which to strengthen. An article appeared in 1955 about this very experience, and although the comment was anonymous, it likely came from Eli. "Marilyn gave me the kind of advice I'd only expect to get from a Hollywood lawyer," he said. "She knew the ins and outs and the fine-print tricks, better than an agent." Another contributor added that Marilyn knew instinctively what was good for her in terms of business.

THE CLASSES AT THE Actors Studio emphasized expressivity, and Lee Strasberg felt that an actor needed to give an emotional performance, as well as deal with the feelings that this could bring to the surface. There were breathing exercises involved, and a great deal of repetition until the sentiment was absolutely perfect. Homework was necessary between classes, and an actor had to be prepared to work on his or her own. One of the most important talents practiced at the studio was the ability to cry in front of an audience. In this regard, students were encouraged to create anything in their mind to bring up the required emotion and tears.

"Marilyn had good experience of this because of her awful child-hood," remembers actor and student Joseph Lionetti. "She could be very vulnerable in a scene and cried easily, but she was beautiful. Lee said she could be a brilliant stage actress." Indeed, at the time of Marilyn's death, Lionetti remembers that the Strasbergs were actually hoping to create a play for the actress to perform in Manhattan. They believed that with her name and the sensitivity she was able to show onstage, it could have been a sellout for at least five years.

During the New York era, Marilyn was intensely interested in theater and attended dozens of performances. She was fascinated by the whole process of being onstage and interrogated many actors about the processes involved. Just some of the plays she attended included Shakespeare's heavyweight drama *Macbeth*, *A Hatful of Rain* by Michael V. Gazzo, *Middle of the Night* by Paddy Chayefsky, and *Inherit the Wind* by Jerome Lawrence and Robert Edwin Lee. Arthur Miller's *A View from the Bridge* became a favorite, and she was thrilled to support Susan Strasberg during her run in *The Diary of Anne Frank*.

Damn Yankees—a musical comedy about a man who sells his soul to the devil to become a great baseball player—appealed to Marilyn. Intrigued by the story, the actress called a meeting between her, Milton Greene, and writer George Abbott to see if there was a possibility she could become involved. Abbott loved her voice and decided she had a special quality, but the two did not work together on the play. "Marilyn should have a show written just for her," he said. "With that personality, she's entitled to it."

Will Success Spoil Rock Hunter? by George Axelrod starred Jayne Mansfield as a Marilyn Monroe–type character. Jayne had been described as a Marilyn wannabe and rival, so it was understandable that Monroe would be curious to see the play. However, when Edwin Schallert asked her about it a few months later, Marilyn denied ever having seen it, but she seemed to know an awful lot about it nevertheless. She was aware that the main character was being compared to her, but told Schallert that if she saw the play herself, she likely wouldn't see any resemblance. The actress was steadfast in her opinion that the comparisons were probably only made because Mansfield's character does not wear underwear, a comment Monroe had been rumored to have said.

At first, Marilyn was quite happy to be photographed whenever she attended the theater. However, this came to an abrupt halt when one of her Actors Studio friends chastised her for attending the opening of his latest play. According to the student, the press only chose to write about Marilyn and almost ignored the performance completely. He claimed that the reporters' fascination with her was what cost the play a long run. After that, she would often sneak into a play with her hair hidden under a scarf so as to avoid "spoiling" any more runs.

Being recognized could often cause problems for Marilyn. Random folk would sometimes shout at her from the balcony and even insult her clothes or hairstyle. Then fans would crowd around her at the intermission to have her sign their programs. At the end of the night, they often spilled out onto the sidewalk and followed her to nearby restaurants, where they would gawk at her over their menus. Reporter Logan Gourlay witnessed this one evening when he met Marilyn after a trip to the theater. As they reached a restaurant, Marilyn whispered, "Sit down in front of me and help block the view a bit. I don't want to be stared at anymore tonight. I suppose I should be used to it by now. But I'm not." Gourlay did as he was told, but two minutes later a waiter turned up to ask Marilyn for an autographed menu.

DURING ONE TRIP TO see a play called *House of Flowers*, Marilyn went backstage to talk to the composer, Harold Arlen. There, she was overheard telling the man that she was desperate to appear on

Broadway and was considering appearing onstage before resuming film work. Just a few weeks before disclosing this, Marilyn had been approached by playwright Zoe Akins, who was working on *The Trojan Party*, a play she hoped the actress would take on as a stage production. The plans were never fulfilled, but had they been, it was sure to have been a great success. The play was intended as a follow-up to *How to Marry a Millionaire*, the movie Marilyn had starred in with Lauren Bacall and Betty Grable.

The Strasbergs continued to believe in Marilyn's talents as a theater actress and even went so far as to ask another student if he would like to act in *Macbeth* with her. During the summer of 1955, Actors Studio director Cheryl Crawford told Marilyn that she had every intention of producing a play for her. This did not come to fruition, however, and Marilyn's agent Jay Kanter believes that during this time she was far more concerned with doing good work on the screen and gaining director approval for her films.

In addition, Marilyn still suffered from an intense lack of confidence, along with nervousness in front of an audience, something she would have had to overcome if a theater career was in her future. Paula Strasberg later spoke to reporter Louella Parsons about Marilyn's nerves: "I think my husband has the solution: he says that nervousness indicates sensitivity and that's what Marilyn has, great sensitivity. And then, Marilyn is still frightened, although she is overcoming it. Lee says 'show me an actress who isn't frightened and nervous and I will say she won't go far.'"

CHAPTER FIVE

The Unlikely Feminist

AWAY FROM OFFICIAL LESSONS at the Actors Studio, Marilyn loved studying with Lee Strasberg, and the family apartment was always open to her. The couple had a magnificent library of books, and Marilyn would spend hours looking through the shelves. Almost every time she visited, she would go home with another biography to read or a play to study. The Strasbergs' home was often filled with students and creative beings, and offered a steady supply of bagels, hot chocolate, and artistic discussion.

Actress Jane Fonda later told television host David Letterman that she had been at the Strasbergs' apartment one afternoon when Marilyn walked in. The men in the room were excited to see her, but the actress immediately zoned in on Jane and spent the party with her. Jane surmised that it was because she felt safe with her; they were both young women together.

Marilyn could be shy at the Strasberg get-togethers, but she also had the ability to charm even the most ungracious of guests. Paula Strasberg saw this side of her many times, and described her as being "informed, acute, and enchanting. She has a genuine wit and is always feminine, which is becoming a lost art." Writer Radie Harris recalled a time at the apartment when Marilyn walked in wearing a particularly glamorous gown, covered with sequins. According to Harris, various other students paid Marilyn a lot of attention that evening, and one told her she would make a wonderful Rosalind, the woman who dresses herself as a shepherd in Shakespeare's *As You Like It.* "Yes, wouldn't she?" exclaimed Harris rather sarcastically. "Can't you just see Marilyn disguised as a boy?"

While Marilyn seemed happy to hang around actors at the Strasberg apartment, she was sometimes less confident at parties given by the Greenes. During one Sunday afternoon get-together, actress Tippi Hedren encountered a house full of people, all wondering when Marilyn would appear. After what seemed like hours, the actress eventually came out of her room on the second floor, looked as though she were coming down to the party, but then sat down in a corner. Nobody talked to her, and she made no attempt to mingle. After a while she disappeared, presumably back into her bedroom.

Another party given by attorney-producer Jay Julien had a similar scene. Wearing casual clothes and minimal makeup, Marilyn wandered around the room almost totally unrecognized. She did not socialize with the guests and instead ended up at a bookcase, carefully taking off volumes and leafing through each one. When a partygoer asked what she was looking for, Marilyn replied that she was anxious to find a book about the artist Francisco José de Goya. Amy Greene confirmed this kind of behavior in an article for *Photoplay*, admitting that although she would occasionally sing if someone was playing piano, Marilyn would be more likely found emptying ashtrays and picking up glasses.

From an outsider's point of view, Marilyn's attitude may seem rather aloof. However, considering the reception she had experienced at parties in Hollywood, her reluctance to freely engage is not entirely surprising. From the beginning of her career, Marilyn was invited to events merely to brighten up a table, something for the men to gaze at as they ordered dessert. "All the studios brought their top glamour girls," explained an early press agent. "I brought Marilyn and paraded her around like a horse in front of a grandstand. Jane Russell was ignored. Marilyn was the hit of the evening."

Being "paraded like a horse" is a sexist notion in today's terms, but in the 1940s and 1950s, it was to be expected for Hollywood's starlets. Songwriter Floyd Huddleston was often asked by the studios to accompany young actresses to parties to keep them safe. One evening he was asked to escort Marilyn. "He had no clue who she was," recalls his son, Huston. "She was polite and very quiet and they went to a party, but she wanted to stay outside, so they talked about Hollywood and their lives growing up. Dad thought she was very sad and though he tried to crack that surface, he couldn't."

The reaction Marilyn got from many male party guests was of a lecherous nature, but from female guests it was something else entirely. Frightened that she would somehow steal their partners, the women would keep one eye on Marilyn and the other on the men, while often discussing her motives and criticizing her attire. While the problems were confined mainly to Hollywood, they sometimes happened in New York too. This was confirmed by an unnamed friend who spoke to reporter Milton Schulman in 1956. "Marilyn's effect on high-brows is devastating. Whenever she comes to a party the men start behaving like college students. The women don't like the impression she makes on the men. They don't say much to her, but they keep watching her all the time."

During her entire career, the way some women treated Marilyn—at parties and otherwise—was frankly borderline bullying. One vocal tormentor was Joan Crawford, who made headlines in 1953 when she openly criticized Marilyn's attire at an awards ceremony. "I have never been so embarrassed in my life," she said. "The makeup of the true star is founded on talent. Miss Monroe is giving a grotesque interpretation of the artistry and sincerity that is, and has always been, behind the making of movies." Crawford said that since it was mothers who chose what their children and husbands watched at the cinema, they would never knowingly pick anything with Marilyn in it, as it "won't be suitable." When she began getting irate letters from Monroe fans, the acidic actress changed tack and said that she had been tricked into saying those words by a reporter who'd asked her "off the record."

Marilyn replied to the criticism via columnist Louella Parsons. "With all the publicity I've had and everything, I suppose it will be hard for many people to believe that I never deliberately throw my sex around, thinking 'If I do this, it's sexy—or if I look a certain way, it's sexy.'" Interestingly, Marilyn actually greatly disliked being described that way. When Earl Wilson asked if she would ever quit being sexy, she replied, "I'll never quit that! But put it 'exotic' will you, instead of sexy?"

In July 1954, *Screenland* magazine published an article on whether women as a whole liked Marilyn. The principal of a girls' school had a lot to say on the subject: "I think we've been held back by all the publicity," she said. "It was a shame that Marilyn Monroe was hailed a siren. I don't believe that women really feared her effect on men—but when the only pictures they ever saw were of Marilyn bursting out of skin-tight, low-cut dresses, it's not surprising they considered her cheap. In our school, for instance, we wouldn't let girls see her pictures. We had nothing against Marilyn Monroe, but you can't allow young and impressionable girls to think scanty clothing is the way to be popular."

By the time Marilyn moved to New York, various women's organizations had long since protested loudly over what they considered the provocative way her career was publicized. The Women's Club of Hollywood even went one step further and demanded to know what studio bosses intended to do to "curb" her. A female columnist took a swipe at Marilyn after she was photographed wearing a low-cut gown when she served as grand marshal of the Miss America contest. Later, when the actress and columnist came face-to-face at a party, Marilyn was charming and friendly to her. "Gosh," exclaimed a friend, "I thought you'd skin her alive." Marilyn smiled sweetly and replied, "It was more cruel to leave her skin as it is."

Still, Marilyn did have her fair share of powerful female admirers who were always willing to come out in support of her. One of these women was actress Faith Domergue. She took her complaints about "clubwomen or jealous movie queens" straight to columnist Erskine Johnson, who published her views. "Nobody can hurt [Marilyn]," she said. "If she stays as she is, holding her ground, being herself, she will be one of the great stars of all time. Women may not approve of an actress, but as long as they're curious, they'll come to see her films and bring their men along, too."

Lana Turner was another actress who saw nothing wrong with building up a fellow woman. When columnist Bob Thomas asked whom she would most like to encounter in Hollywood, Turner saw an opportunity to throw light Marilyn's way. "I'll tell you a girl I'd like to meet and that's Marilyn Monroe. She must be a fascinating personality, considering all she has gone through. She's taking a lot of knocks because she's on top now. I wish there were some way I could tell her not to let it get her down."

One actress shared a name with her, though not by choice. Marilyn Maxwell had become famous in the 1940s, and when she met the second Marilyn in 1948, she was stunned to hear of her desire to become a successful actress. Maxwell suggested that she should change her name to something else so that the two did not get mistaken for each other. However, Monroe had no intention of doing so, and for many years Maxwell was bombarded with fans who thought they were one and the same. In the end, Maxwell gave a standard reply: "No, I'm the Marilyn with clothes on," though no offense was meant and she actually did greatly admire Monroe. "I think she has done a great deal of good for the movie industry," she said. "She is just what the business needed—someone to put some glamour and magic back into Hollywood."

Another staunch supporter was Dame Edith Sitwell, someone who, on first glance, would not have been considered a standard Monroe fan. Sitwell was a British poet, a very posh, outspoken woman who could bring discomfort to even the most experienced of interviewers. However, underneath the fierce demeanor, Sitwell was a wounded woman who'd had a terrible upbringing at the hands of uncaring parents. Their hurtful comments had led to her running away at the age of five (she was found and returned by a neighborhood policeman), and by the time she was a teenager, Sitwell's father had all but turned his back on her. These childhood experiences alone were enough for her to identify with Marilyn, and during a trip to Los Angeles in 1953, the two were introduced. During a 1959 interview for the BBC's *Face to Face* television program, Sitwell explained that the only people she wanted to meet in Hollywood were those who were intelligent and had impeccable behavior. She saw these qualities immediately in Marilyn and warmed to her on sight. When they met, Marilyn was wearing a green dress and talking animatedly about philosopher Rudolf Steiner; the dame decided that Marilyn was an enchanting human being who had been treated extremely poorly within the industry.

Sitwell had been aware of the nude calendar pictures that were taken before Marilyn became famous, and during the discussion determined that it was as a result of those photos that Marilyn was being persecuted. As for those who had treated Marilyn terribly, Sitwell noted that they had obviously never known hunger and what it was like to need money desperately. "Well, there have been nude models before now," she said. "It means nothing against a person's moral character at all."

A downside to Marilyn's life, Sitwell decided, was that through no fault of her own, unpleasant men seemed to be attracted to her. She witnessed this for herself, but noted that Marilyn never gave these men any attention at all. In fact, she would avoid them completely and at all times behave "like a lady." After spending some time with Marilyn, Sitwell discovered just how much the woman enjoyed books and highbrow material. She told reporter William Barbour, "Of course I'd be delighted to play literary mother to her. Marilyn is a very seriously-minded girl."

After various unprovoked attacks in the media, some women began to see past the sex-symbol image and realize that Marilyn was actually a human being, flawed and easily hurt. The way she conducted herself appealed to them, and slowly their feelings began to thaw. Some women, however, had always recognized Marilyn for the intelligent, warm woman that she really was. *How to Marry a Millionaire* costar Betty Grable sent some advice through Louella Parsons: "I've taken plenty of criticism and so have other actresses. Just keep plugging. The important things are your career—and trying to improve yourself."

Jane Russell, costar in *Gentlemen Prefer Blondes,* classed Marilyn as a friend and refused all requests by the media to belittle or intimidate her. When interviewed by reporter Jon Bruce in 1953, the brunette star had this to say about her so-called rival:

Here was a girl who had the same kind of build-up that I had had, except that she was blonde while I was brunette. I wondered how that build-up had affected her, what it had done to her life, both professional and private. After I met her, I couldn't see that her publicity had gone to her head in any way. I thought she was far more beautiful, too, than I expected to find her. Her sincerity is impressive and her willingness to listen to and take advice is one of her outstanding qualities. Marilyn is wonderfully sincere in her work. She is always trying to improve and wants to do her best in every scene, yet she makes no effort to steal a scene or upstage anyone ever.

Since she was such a complex character, Marilyn found herself stuck in the middle of two different types of women: those who were disgusted or intimidated by her glamour and wanted her to tone everything down, and those who loved her look just as it was and wanted her to stop trying to be taken seriously. Marilyn shared her views on the subject in 1959: "I'd like to be known as a real actress and human being," she said, "but listen, there's nothing wrong with glamour either. I think everything adds up. I'll never knock glamour. But I want to be in the kind of pictures where I can develop, not just wear tights."

It could easily be argued that Marilyn suffered frequent frustration because people wanted to pigeonhole her into being just one kind of personality. This undoubtedly came as a result of her unique and modern outlook on life—one more fitting to the twenty-first century rather than the 1950s. She was actually a modern-day feminist, though the very idea struck the nerves of many at the time.

Feminism in the mid-twentieth century was a confusing subject, and some—women as well as men—feared that their homes and workplaces were being threatened by the bewildering attitudes of certain women. "An ardent feminist is a woman who has ambitions beyond her gender if not her talents," wrote a reporter for the *Scotsman*. As a result, many who dared claim the mantle of feminist were looked at with great suspicion and derision. Even strong women in high positions were anxious not to identify themselves in such a way.

As Marilyn had told Edward R. Murrow, she was fascinated by Indian prime minister Jawaharlal Nehru. His sister, Vijaya Lakshmi Pandit, was the Indian high commissioner and therefore a powerful woman. However, even she was loath to describe herself as a feminist. During a press conference in July 1955, a journalist asked if it was true that she did not wish to be referred to that way. "I am not a feminist!" she snapped. "I do not believe the world can be run in compartments, but by the joint endeavors of men and women as equals."

"That is exactly what a feminist is," cried the journalist. "I knew she was a feminist!" The writer was thrilled, but Pandit seethed.

In comparison, some women were happy to own the label. British Viscountess Astor had strong opinions: "I cannot understand how any woman with any imagination or understanding could fail to be a hot feminist. I was born a feminist. The more I saw of my father, the more I thought of my mother." She hated the way women of the 1950s were living their lives, especially given the fights her suffragette sisters had endured in the past. "I believe that the women of this generation are simply 'going to town' and having a good time and that they have forgotten the things that really matter," she said.

Singer Eartha Kitt was joyous to be called a feminist in 1956. "Feminism is something that cannot be put into words," she told a London luncheon. "It is something that can only be felt. You know if you are a feminist."

Although vulnerable and complex, Marilyn was a strong woman who consistently fought for what she believed in. However, because of the confusion and stigma related to the word, it is highly unlikely that she would ever have considered herself a feminist in 1955. Friend Norman Rosten further doubted that she would have joined the women's liberation movement in the 1960s and argued that in terms of economic equality, she had already proven herself.

For all of her fight, Marilyn was most definitely a woman who enjoyed flirting with men, both in manner and the way she dressed. She once told Pete Martin that while some men may prefer a woman to be subtle, she did not believe in false modesty. "A woman only hurts herself that way," she said. "If she's coy, she's denying herself an important part of life." She added to Bill Foster that she had no problems living in a man's world, just so long as she could still be a woman.

She was never offended by the attention given to her by men, but at the same time demanded respect when it came to her work. David Wayne, Marilyn's leading man in *How to Marry a Millionaire*, remembered an incident that proved just how forthright she could be in the company of powerful men. "Marilyn's one of the most phenomenal personalities of our time," he said. "One time one of the studio heads called her in. She'd turned down a picture. He roared at her, 'I've been in this business a long time and I know what's good for you.' She said, 'I've been in this business a very short time, but know better what's good for me than you do!'"

This would not have been received well by Mr. E. Rushworth, treasurer of the National Association of Schoolmasters, who gave a talk about women in 1954. He was disgusted when feminists started crying out for equal rights and pay with their male counterparts. Rushworth described the call as coming from "selfish career women, taking advantage of a delicate political balance." He surmised that feminists were looking for "an increased economic superiority over their married sisters" and warned that they were about to overturn family life as they knew it. High on his list of concerns was the bizarre concept that if women were equal to men, it would mean that the latter would have to accept lower salaries. It did not seem to occur to him that women were expecting to have theirs increased.

The look of feminism has changed dramatically over the years, especially with the coming of women such as Madonna in the 1980s and even the Spice Girls in the 1990s. They showed young women and teenagers that it was okay to be strong and outspoken while still being sexy, and "girl power" became a mantra. Today, feminism is a very individual and personal aspect of a woman's character. She can demand respect and equal rights, but at the same time be perfectly comfortable with her femininity. The popular turnout at women's marches in recent years shows that the torch has passed down through the generations and "feminist" is now a celebrated title, which has also been embraced by modern men such as Canadian prime minister Justin Trudeau and actor Patrick Stewart. The latter became a staunch supporter of women's rights after seeing his mother abused by his father when he was a boy. His dialogue about violence during a speech for Amnesty International has become a beacon for women.

It is clear that by today's definition of what a feminist is, Marilyn could undoubtedly be counted as one. Filmmaker Gabriella Apicella argues this point and agrees that, today, Marilyn is most certainly an icon for female empowerment:

> *Throughout her short life, she experienced many of the fundamental oppressions that feminism strives to free all women from, and did so within the public eye. Her life has therefore taken on a symbolic significance in terms of how important it is to ensure women are not subjugated on the basis of their gender.*
>
> *Being a survivor of child sexual abuse, receiving sexist treatment in the workplace, being challenged to sacrifice her career for marriage (causing the breakup of her first two marriages, and being an area of contention in her third), battling her employers for artistic freedom, fair pay, and respectful working conditions are all issues that many women have experienced, and continue to experience even in the twenty-first century.*

In this one woman, so many areas essential to the continual fight for female emancipation are conflated. That she overcame struggles outside of any formal feminist movement, while maintaining her characteristically gentle and feminine demeanor powerfully demonstrates one of the facets of feminism that the popular media attempts to hide: that the fight for female empowerment is in some way 'unfeminine.'

Marilyn may not be the first woman who comes to mind when thinking of feminist icons; however, as an example of a woman who was attempting to live freely, against all the odds that a repressive and abusive male-dominated society threw at her, who achieved immortality in the film industry, Marilyn Monroe deserves to be as well known for her brain and character, as she is for her face and figure."

DESPITE THEIR IMPENDING FINAL divorce, Marilyn and Joe DiMaggio continued to remain friends. Agent Jay Kanter remembers a happy occasion when he, his wife Judy, Milton, Amy, Marilyn, and Joe were all invited by Sammy Davis Jr. to attend a charity performance he was giving at the Apollo in Harlem. The singer wanted to present his famous guests onstage, so the Greenes and Kanters all walked out first. A ripple of approval echoed around the theater, and then Marilyn appeared and the audience burst into rapturous applause. Everyone was thrilled to see the actress, but when Joe DiMaggio appeared onstage just moments later, there was a near riot of excitement. "The applause was twice as loud for him," said Kanter. "He was a real hero in that neighborhood."

The Seven Year Itch premiered on June 1—Marilyn's twenty-ninth birthday—and her date once again was Joe DiMaggio. This seemed ironic, since it was this very film that had been rumored to have helped tear them apart. After the premiere, DiMaggio had organized a birthday party for Marilyn at his hangout, Toots Shor's, and the two attended together. Inside, they were seen laughing and joking with other guests, but then the evening soured and they both left abruptly and separately. Later Marilyn told author Maurice Zolotow that a rekindling of the romance was completely out of the question. When pushed further, the actress revealed that she would like to remain friends with the baseball player, but she would absolutely never marry him again.

PREDICTABLY, THE CRITICAL RECEPTION for *The Seven Year Itch* was much warmer than it had been for *There's No Business Like Show Business*. *Film Bulletin* described it as "a brilliantly produced version of the hit play, chockful of laughs and with the Monroe name insuring rousing returns in all situations. . . . Marilyn is a delight [and] everything about the film glitters." *Motion Picture Daily* was just as complimentary: "The big achievements in humor come from the tour de force acting job turned in by Ewell and the infectious, polished performance of Miss Monroe. In this picture she has grown up a good deal as an actress and her natural beauty is enhanced as a result."

Another positive review came from the *Harrison's Reports* journal. It described *The Seven Year Itch* as "a top-notch sophisticated comedy, based on the highly successful stage play of the same name. . . . Marilyn Monroe, aside from her obvious physical attributes, is exceptionally good as the curvaceous blonde, a naïve yet knowing character who is sociable without being designing, but whose natural sexiness plays havoc with Ewell's vow to remain a faithful husband during his wife's absence. It is the best role Miss Monroe has had to date, and her deft handling of the characterization proves her ability as a comedienne."

To celebrate the release, Twentieth Century Fox installed a fifty-two-foot-high cutout of Marilyn in the skirt-blowing scene in Times Square. There to unveil it was none other than TV star Roxanne, the same actress who had spectacularly criticized Marilyn to Earl Wilson in 1954. Passersby were asked what they thought of the photo, and while some expressed a desire to look just like Marilyn, others thought the whole thing was vulgar and in bad taste. The actress herself tended to agree with the latter, not because Marilyn was in the least bit ashamed, but because it was exactly the image she was trying to walk away from.

Knowing that was the case, it is not out of the question to think that possibly the executives at Fox were deliberately trying to provoke her, by displaying the giant cutout in the city Marilyn had "escaped" to. She must surely have been buoyed a few days later, though, when a poll was released that named her the tenth most admirable woman in the world. Whatever Fox thought of her, the men and women of the United States classed her inspirational enough to be on a list that included Queen Elizabeth II, Eleanor Roosevelt, and Mamie Eisenhower.

Several days after the installation of the huge cutout, builders were seen taking it down again, and people wondered if the mixed reaction was the cause. Not so, the workmen told reporters; it was merely being replaced by a photo that was more flattering. That may have been the case, but staff at Loews Theatre admitted to reporters that various complaints had been received from people who thought the picture to be in questionable taste. Whether any of these individuals was Marilyn was never revealed.

Theaters around the world thought up fun and innovative ways of publicizing *The Seven Year Itch*. In Miami, one cinema manager staged a contest to find the best Marilyn look-alike, one wearing the customary white dress blown around by a wind machine. The winner received an all-expenses paid holiday "at a swank hotel." F. J. Bickler, manager of the Fox Wisconsin Theater in Milwaukee, decided to give his customers what he called a "lie detector test." In the foyer, staff asked customers if they intended to see *The Seven Year Itch*. If they said no, they were then handed a small folder complete with photos of the skirt-blowing scene on the cover. The notion was that if you smiled at the photo, you'd enjoy the movie too. It was a somewhat half-baked idea, but it created just the right publicity to get an audience into the auditorium.

Many theaters used large cardboard cutouts of Marilyn to advertise the film, including the Criterion in Oklahoma City, which installed a huge, forty-foot example. But the manager of Loew's Poli Theatre in Worcester, Massachusetts, went one better. Taking an actual white skirt, he glued it onto the lower half of the cutout and used a fan to blow it skyward. The cutouts worked well until one cinema in Englewood, New Jersey, reported that theirs had been kidnapped from the foyer. It was never found, and skeptical movie magazines claimed the story was a publicity stunt.

Another theater in Portland, Oregon, allowed Marilyn fans to place their footprints in cement, just as she herself had done several years before. For fans who wished to be just like their idol, a photo of Marilyn's footprints was there for comparison, while a radio commentator lay on the ground to record it all for posterity. In yet another cinema's competition to find a Marilyn Monroe look-alike, the winner was given the job of riding up and down the sidewalk in a boardwalk stroller, handing out back scratchers to the public—presumably to cure their own "seven-year itch."

Another—almost unbelievable—story came from Yankton, South Dakota, where theater manager Clyde Crump made the decision to send his customers sugar pills in little envelopes. Once opened, a note revealed the words: "Little Pills for All Your Ills! Your pill should dissolve in water for two and a half hours, during which time visit the Yankton Theater. When you return throw the pill away, because you won't need it after seeing Marilyn Monroe in *The Seven Year Itch*!"

The vast and varied ways of publicizing the film were exciting for the studio and press alike. "Every day, in every way, exploitation gets better and better," wrote a reporter for the *Motion Picture Herald*, "when good men use their heads, hearts and hands, to obtain results."

It wasn't just exhibitors who saw an opportunity, however. One enterprising tradesman decided to cash in on the scene between Marilyn and the plumber, where she gets her big toe stuck in the bathtub faucet. Teaming up with the manager of a Lexington, Kentucky, theater, George Pridemore set up a makeshift bathroom in the lobby, complete with a real-life model with her toe jammed up the faucet. Audio pumped into the venue declared, "If this ever happens to you, like it happens to Marilyn Monroe (of all people!) in *The Seven Year Itch*, starting tomorrow at Schine's Kentucky, call George Pridemore Plumbing!"

Newspapers also serialized the story of the film, long after its initial release, and Sam Shaw's photographic book, *Marilyn Monroe as The*

Girl, helped draw in even more fans. While Marilyn would not live long enough to know it, *The Seven Year Itch*—along with the white, halter-neck dress she wore during the subway-grate scene—would go on to become the most iconic of all her films. Pictures of the actress standing on the grating are still used on everything from clothing, mugs, clocks, and key rings to compact mirrors and storage boxes.

Back in 1955, the publicity campaign paid off considerably. "Weekend business of Twentieth Century Fox's *The Seven Year Itch* at Loew's State was reported to have topped the house record," reported *Motion Picture Daily.* "The picture pulled $50,000 for the three days, it was said, with early morning lines forming at the theater's box office."

The excitement surrounding the film helped the studio, theater managers, and plumbers alike, but the person most thrilled was Marilyn. While she was still anxious to never play a fluffy role again, the success of the movie gave her power and confidence like she had never had before. She was determined, therefore, to use her leverage to its full advantage.

FOR MARILYN, 1955 WAS a year for making or renewing friendships with great people. Gone were the Hollywood hangers-on, and in came a variety of writers, theater actors, poets, and even fans. Authors Truman Capote and Carson McCullers were gossip buddies, while lenswoman Eve Arnold discussed great literature while snapping her photograph.

Marilyn herself was somewhat astounded that highbrow and creative people were anxious to get to know her. When Earl Wilson told her that Lawrence Langner, founder and director of the Theatre Guild, had begged him to get her autograph, Marilyn was shocked. Not only was Langner involved with the guild, but he was also an established playwright and producer in his own right. The literary great was not too embarrassed to tell Wilson that the last time he'd asked an actress for her autograph was in 1908. He then wrote a beautiful note. "Dear Marilyn: We need you for our Shakespeare Theatre. Yours admiringly, Lawrence Langner." He then suggested that perhaps Marilyn would act in *A Midsummer Night's Dream*. "What a dream!" he wrote. Langner wasn't the only unlikely fan. Poet Robert Frost and author Aldous Huxley were desperate to meet Marilyn, and John Steinbeck, Pulitzer Prize–winning author of *The Grapes of Wrath*, wrote to her in April 1955. His mission was to request an autograph for his nephew, Jon, but it was clear that after meeting her in person, he was just as impressed by Marilyn as the young fan was.

One group of admirers consisted of six youngsters who followed Marilyn wherever she went: in and out of taxis, going to the theater, walking home, going shopping—if Marilyn was doing it, they were recording it. These fans became known as the Monroe Six and christened the actress Mazzie as a term of endearment. The photographs taken by the group are remarkable. Because they were amateur snappers, there is no trace of the polished pictures so often posed for by the star. Instead, they reveal a real human being—a messy-haired, dressed-down actress, going about her life. Whereas Los Angeles provided no real opportunity for the fans to have daily access to Marilyn, Manhattan provided the polar opposite, and as time went on, she came to love the Monroe Six as her walking companions. Marilyn told columnist Hedda Hopper that the group even sent her flowers when she was ill and cut out articles for her scrapbooks.

Her fans provided a particular kind of friendship—a safety net of sorts while making her way around the city—but Marilyn also craved companionship of people with a shared interest. This was given to her by way of a rainy Manhattan day when she was out for a walk with photographer Sam Shaw. Shaw had known and photographed Marilyn many times, and she was comfortable in his company. When he suggested sheltering at the home of friends, she trusted his judgment and happily went along. When the door was opened into the apartment of Norman and Hedda Rosten, a cold and wet Marilyn was quickly introduced as Marion and shown to the living room to dry off. Over the course of the afternoon, the Rostens and their visitor spoke about poetry, the couple's daughter, their lives, and finally careers. Marilyn explained that she was an actress, but even at that point in time, neither Hedda nor Norman recognized her. It was not until "Marion" told them her stage name was Marilyn Monroe that they finally realized it.

The friendship between Marilyn and the Rostens grew quickly, and they would often spend the weekend on Long Island together, talking about books, playing badminton, drinking champagne, and enjoying each other's company. Marilyn also attended various events with Norman and Hedda, either alone or together, such as a performance by pianist Emil Giles at Carnegie Hall. On that particular occasion, Norman and Marilyn went alone and at the intermission they spoke to Giles himself. He seemed enamored of her and insisted that one day she must visit Russia. Marilyn assured him she would and then they spoke about Dostoyevsky.

When Rosten adapted Joyce Cary's book *Mister Johnston* into a play, Marilyn volunteered straightaway to become an investor. It wasn't a huge success, but it gave actor Earle Hyman the vital stage experience he needed to become a member of the Actors Studio. There, he encountered Marilyn and she took him under her wing, welcoming him warmly and even raising her hand to defend his talents when another actor criticized him. "I thought she was extremely brave to stand up and say that and I never forgot it," he said.

The friendship of Norman Rosten and his family was quite significant to Marilyn. The Rostens provided security, welcomed her into their home, and genuinely cared about her. The actress adored the happiness her New York friends brought into her life: "For the first time I felt accepted, not as a freak, but as myself," she said. The fact that Norman was a poet was an added bonus. For many years, Marilyn had enjoyed writing poetry, and although it was a deeply personal subject to her, she had spoken briefly about it in 1951: "You get such wonderful thoughts and ideas at night when you are alone. I like to let my moods come and go then—and that's when I like to write poetry." In another interview from the same period she admitted, "My poems are kind of sad, but then so is life."

During small gatherings at the Rosten house, there would sometimes be impromptu poetry readings. Rosten remembered that Marilyn once read a W. B. Yeats poem titled "Never Give All the Heart." The words seemed to mesmerize her:

Never give all the heart, for love
Will hardly seem worth thinking of
To passionate women if it seem
Certain, and they never dream
That it fades out from kiss to kiss;
For everything that's lovely is

But a brief, dreamy, kind delight.
O never give the heart outright,
For they, for all smooth lips can say
Have given their hearts up to the play.
And who could play it well enough
If deaf and dumb and blind with love?
He that made this knows all the cost
For he gave all his heart and lost.

She read it slowly and with great thought to every word. When she had finished, the whole room was quiet, and the actress looked to be in a world of her own.

Marilyn knew that Rosten would never laugh or criticize her own attempts at writing poetry, and she would often send him rough drafts through the mail or show them to him in person. Looking at the pieces today, her words are prophetic and often heart-wrenching. In one titled "Life," the actress ponders her place in the world, telling the reader that she somehow remains down but is as strong as a cobweb in the wind. In another, she describes the colors of the sidewalk, seen from the heights of her apartment. Some of the more lighthearted poems rhyme, such as the one written about hospital gowns revealing her bare derriere. Others are more like notes—the observations of a woman, an actress, and a human being.

In addition to writing and reading poetry, Marilyn was also deeply interested in art. She admitted to one interviewer in the mid-1950s that she had gone through a Michelangelo period and currently had an obsession for Francisco José de Goya. "I know just the monsters he paints," she explained. "I see them all the time. And if Goya sees them too, I know I'm not out of my mind." She wrote about these monsters in her private notebooks, describing them as her most steadfast companions that came out of the darkness as she tried to sleep.

She remained forever intrigued by Goya, and when a script about the artist was sent to Marilyn a few years later, she considered taking a role. However, the producer planned to push the moral boundaries and introduce a nude scene. Marilyn told Earl Wilson that she did not think the nudity was relevant, so in the end turned it down.

Marilyn greatly admired artists and was an occasional but keen sketcher herself. The pictures she drew and painted throughout the mid- to late 1950s show varying moods and sometimes a playful nature. All are abstract and often feature just a single color: red. In one, Marilyn draws a catlike woman, dancing and smiling broadly, with long eyelashes and a hat or elaborate hairstyle perched upon her head. In another deeply contrasting piece, there is a small girl in a plain dress, with short, curled hair and one sock falling down.

A wispy picture with great swirls and flair is titled *A Cat Watching Its Own Tail Move*. *Viewed from a Night Table* shows a variety of items, including a glass, what looks to be a part of a headboard, and a book of poems. Some of her artwork includes tiny, delicate features, but most are done with a sweeping, passionate hand. One of the most intriguing pieces of art that Marilyn created is titled *Jumping into the Frying Pan from the Fire*. It shows the profile of a woman with full lips, long hair, and arms sprawled out behind her. She is nude from the waist up, but her lower body is covered with fishnet stockings, flames lapping at her feet.

While Marilyn might never have exhibited her work, she relished the hobby. In 1958, she took her interest further by enrolling in a correspondence course with the Famous Artists School of Westport. Recently sold at auction, the letters show that the school was recommended to her by her friend Jon Whitcomb and her course of choice was painting. Alas, it is not known whether she ever submitted her work for critiquing, but that certainly did not affect the value of her portraits. One titled *Lover Watching His Love Sleep* sold in 2016 for $25,000, while a nude study drawn for Broadway set designer Boris Aronson went for $75,000 in 2015.

It wasn't just painting that interested Marilyn. While she never attempted sculpture herself, there were several pieces that greatly intrigued her. One day she visited the Metropolitan Museum of Art with Norman Rosten, and he later recalled how she was spellbound by a work by Auguste Rodin titled *The Hand of God*, which depicts an entwined Adam and Eve emerging from marble in the hand of God. According to Rosten, the actress spent a long time walking around the sculpture, totally transfixed by it. Years later she bought a similar piece for display in her home.

When biographer Maurice Zolotow visited Marilyn in New York during the mid-1950s, she was just returning home with a statue of Queen Nefertiti. When asked what had intrigued her about the piece, the actress replied that somebody had once told her that she looked like Nefertiti. Interestingly, when Marilyn was a model in the 1940s, her boss, Emmeline Snively, kept the same bust in her office to show starlets that beauty was not a new phenomenon. The item was always a conversation piece, and so the likelihood of it being Snively who told Marilyn that she and Nefertiti looked similar was—no matter how bizarre—quite high.

CHAPTER SIX

Inspirational Woman

DURING THE MID-1950S, MARILYN'S fan mail averaged around five or six thousand letters per month. She received all kinds of correspondence. Young men would send marriage proposals and requests for signed photographs, while teenage girls would say how they too wanted to become an actress when they were older. One older lady fan even sent in underwear, just in case she was cold when wearing such skimpy clothing.

Of Marilyn's fans and detractors, director Billy Wilder had the following to say to Pete Martin: "There are two schools of thought about her—those who like her and those who attack her, but they both are willing to pay to watch her." Young film fan Maureen Brown was definitely one of the former. She remembers the days in the early 1950s when she first discovered the woman she has now admired for over six decades:

> *I first became aware of Marilyn after seeing her in cinema news-reels. She was so beautiful, so vibrant. Since I was a skinny, dark-haired twelve/thirteen year old, I wanted to be her! . . . I had seen*

quite a few of her early films, but it was seeing her in these newsreels that made me love her before she was even a big star. I would buy film magazines—mostly Picturegoer *and* Photoplay*—with my pocket money and pin pictures and newspaper cuttings all over my bedroom walls.*

For a time I also had photos of Jayne Mansfield, Diana Dors, and Brigitte Bardot, but they were soon replaced by new ones of Marilyn, as she became more famous. I loved all the pinup pics of her when she was a model. In fact, I loved everything about her! Most kids had Elvis or Cliff Richard inside their desk lids, but not me. I had Marilyn! I was so excited when she came to England because by now we had television and she was in the news constantly. My love for her has never diminished and in fact it has grown even stronger over the years. Marilyn was way ahead of her time in so many ways and I was devastated when she died. If I had one wish, it would be that I could have known her in real life, but I'm grateful that I was able to know her through film and television during the time she was alive.

Maureen is a true example of the kind of teenager who was fascinated by Marilyn as a person and image, but not everybody was enraptured. One young fan remembered being forbidden to see her films because his mother considered the actress to be a bad influence on young girls and boys. When his friends arranged a trip to see a Monroe film, he went along anyway, praying that his mother would never find out. Of course she did, and within minutes of taking his seat, he was dragged out of the cinema, disappointed to be caught and embarrassed to be shown up in front of his friends.

It wasn't just middle-aged women who did not particularly care for her. Virginia Nicholson, author of *Perfect Wives in Ideal Homes*, remembers Marilyn being famous when she was a little girl: "Like everybody else, I watched and enjoyed her films. But I never had any aspirations to be like her, as although she seemed beautiful, funny, and sexy, in the world I grew up in, she was really the personification of the 'dumb blonde.' We all much preferred Greta Garbo, who seemed way more mysterious and sophisticated! Yes, obviously, Marilyn Monroe was very much a 1950s 'type': ultra-feminine, aspirational, with all the wily pseudo-submissiveness and glamour that was unfortunately expected of women at the time. Her personal story is also deeply sad. I have always thought of her as a very damaged human being."

Virginia's recollection of Marilyn being the personification of a dumb blonde is an important one, because it reflects exactly what the studio chiefs wanted the public to think. It also illustrates just what the actress was fighting against during her rebellion and beyond. Feminist author and advocate Gloria Steinem had similar feelings. She actually walked out of a screening of *Gentlemen Prefer Blondes* because she was embarrassed and believed that Marilyn was a joke—someone who was the complete opposite of everything Steinem wanted to be in her life. It wasn't until the women's movement some years later that she realized what had been going on in society and Marilyn's life during that time and wondered if she could have saved her, given the chance. Steinem's original negative feelings were forgotten, and in the 1980s, she contributed text to accompany George Barris's photos in the book *Marilyn: Norma Jeane*.

While Marilyn was campaigning for acceptance and her rights as an actress and a woman, she was unknowingly starting a ripple effect that would filter down through the decades. Fans inspired by her determination and revolution sometimes go on to have creative lives themselves. Madonna and Mariah Carey are perhaps the most famous examples of how much Marilyn inspired subsequent generations, but they are far from the only ones. Filmmaker Gabriella Apicella finds strength and encouragement through being a fan:

Quite simply, I do not believe I would be working in the film industry if it were not for Marilyn Monroe. When I first saw her, I was only a child, skipping through television channels, and alighting on a fragment of a documentary. The clip on-screen was her performing "Diamonds Are a Girl's Best Friend." As a child of the '80s, I thought at first it was a clip of Madonna's "Material Girl" video. While I looked and saw that this was not Madonna, but someone else, I was instantaneously hooked.

She was magical to me. I could not believe at first that she was a real person who had actually existed! (In some ways I still catch myself feeling that way!) The following day, my mother bought me a second-hand copy of Marilyn Among Friends *by Sam Shaw and Norman Rosten. It so happened that this was during some difficult changes in my home-life, and while chaos reigned around me, I sought solace in images and films of Marilyn. I became immersed in her world as much as I could, covering my walls with every image I could find.*

As I grew older, I wanted to read what she read. I watched the other films of the directors she worked with, and actors she knew, or respected, or performed alongside. I read plays and books that she admired. All of my knowledge of film history is a spider web with Marilyn Monroe at the core.

When I went to university and discovered Italian neo-realist films, I was elated to discover that the iconic director of Bicycle Thieves—*Vittorio De Sica—was on Marilyn's list of approved directors. As a new dimension of understanding about film and its history opened up to me, Marilyn was still there in the heart of it all!*

As a screenwriter, I am fixated on visual storytelling, and how the language of cinema has the power to translate emotions through the screen to millions via nuance, gesture, and behavior. Marilyn taught me this in Bus Stop, The Misfits, The Prince and the Showgirl, Gentlemen Prefer Blondes, *and* The Seven Year Itch. *The tremor of lips, a wink, a raised eyebrow. . . . In cinema, these convey more than words can hope to.*

Because Marilyn Monroe made me feel so very much through the power of film, I know in every cell of my body that cinema is the most powerful art form on earth. While I spent a long time keeping this world at a safe distance while working in office jobs, never risking my dreams seriously enough to see if I could succeed as a filmmaker, I am now a few years in to my own magical journey, and will always thank Marilyn for her inspiration from the very beginning.

ON JUNE 12, 1955, Marilyn gave a short but revealing interview to NBC's David Garroway. During the chat, she revealed that she kept a journal; did not mind if she fell from the top of show business, as long as she could be a great actress; was grateful to be famous but missed her anonymity; and when she retired, she would like to move to Brooklyn. The last revelation raised laughs from Garroway, but

Marilyn insisted that it was true—that she loved walking the streets, meeting the people, and looking at the view of Manhattan.

While this might have been the case, Marilyn's affection for Brooklyn might also have come as a result of a new, unexpected love. Arthur Miller was the famed playwright of such theatrical works as *Death of a Salesman* and *The Crucible*. He had met Marilyn some years earlier, when she was still a starlet and he was hoping to sell a script to Hollywood. She was mourning the loss of her agent and lover, Johnny Hyde, after his death in December 1950, and Miller gave her a shoulder to cry on. They also found a lot to talk about, and spent hours discussing great works of literature. Miller realized that Marilyn was far more than the image she portrayed on-screen, while she discovered that in addition to being a great writer, he was also a skilled carpenter, tennis player, and could strip down a car engine just as well as a mechanic.

However, Miller was married at the time, and fearing that he'd fall in love with the starlet, he'd quickly fled from Hollywood and headed back to New York. The two kept in touch for a while, exchanging book lists and notes, but there was no romantic attachment. Interestingly, in 1954, when asked by *Pageant* magazine to name ten men who interested her, the current Mrs. DiMaggio gave Arthur Miller a glowing report:

> *He is one of the few contemporary playwrights who has found a way to successfully mirror our times. Like in* Death of a Salesman. *Or, he's also adapted Ibsen's* Enemy of the People. *Like in his new play, about a witch hunt. In his plays, he has a way of waking people up with what he says. I know there are wonderful things to come from him still. Yes, I've met him. He's very attractive personally. I think*

his play that meant the most to me was Death of a Salesman, *but the thing I liked most was a book he wrote, called* Focus. *It was about anti-Semitism. I wish he'd write more books. It was a very serious, wonderful book.*

While she may have raved about him in 1954, it wasn't until a year later, when Marilyn was in Manhattan and Miller's marriage was crumbling, that they reintroduced themselves properly. This time, he did not run away. Instead, he became even more estranged from his wife and fell madly in love with Marilyn. Because the DiMaggio divorce was not yet final, and Miller was still living in his marital home, the romance remained a closely guarded secret. During this time, whenever asked if there was any relationship in her life, Marilyn always—without exception—told reporters that there was nobody and she wished there was.

This period of secrecy must surely have been difficult, but somehow the couple managed to carry out their romance with just a few rumors here and there. Together they explored Brooklyn, met in friends' homes, and went to offbeat restaurants and on bike rides to districts not known to be frequented by fans or press. The relationship was so secret that even her hairdresser, Peter Leonardi, was surprised when it was eventually revealed. "I was with her morning, noon, and night during this time, and I never even heard the name Miller," he said.

Years later, the actress told Louella Parsons about her admiration for the playwright: "I am in love with the man, not the mind. When I first met Arthur, I didn't even know he was the famed writer of plays and the Arthur Miller I became attracted to was the man—a man of such charming personality, warmth, and friendliness. I won't say that later I didn't fall more in love with him after I grew to know him and to appreciate his great talent and intellect. But I would have loved him for himself without his fine achievements."

IN EARLY SUMMER 1955, Milton and Amy Greene left on a trip to Europe to try to find suitable projects for MMP. This revelation intrigued and amused columnist Hedda Hopper, who quipped that they would surely need Zanuck's permission before purchasing anything for Marilyn herself. In any case, Milton asked if the actress would like to go with them, but instead she decided to stay in New York to study and spend time with Arthur Miller.

While the Greenes might have been anxious to find work for the actress, she was being inundated with scripts and potential offers. The Jean Harlow biopic surfaced again, and there were *The Girl in the Red Velvet Swing*, *Bus Stop*, and *The Blue Angel*. Marilyn was also rumored to be interested in purchasing the rights to a civil war story called *The Smiling Rebel*. But work was not on the immediate agenda, and at the end of July, Marilyn spent the weekend in Connecticut, relaxing with Cheryl Crawford.

In early August, she attended the centennial celebrations in Bement, Illinois. Promoted as a day dedicated to President Lincoln and the arts, Marilyn was thrilled to take part, especially since she had long been an admirer of the former president. Photographer Eve Arnold captured the Bement trip with her camera, and the photos reveal a tired but determined woman, anxious to do her best and make people happy. Marilyn worked hard that day, and the residents greatly appreciated her taking the time to speak to them. A highlight came when she was asked to judge a competition to see who had the best beard in town. This had little to do with culture, but Marilyn went along with it in good humor, telling reporters that some of the beards were longer than her hair.

An obvious hit in Bement, days later Marilyn was invited to a Soviet embassy reception in Washington, DC. The aim was to meet Soviet agriculturists who were touring the United States, but the actress turned the organizers down, blaming a prior commitment. Shortly before the invitation, the delegates had viewed *There's No Business Like Show Business* and gave their approval. "It seems to me she's not there for the sake of the motion picture," said one delegate, "but instead the motion picture exists for her."

The summer continued on a calm and happy path. She spent a weekend with the Rostens and also took up residence with the Strasbergs in their summer house on Fire Island. While there, residents got used to seeing Marilyn on the beach, wearing jeans and no makeup, her hair uncombed and her feet bare. Beside her always would be a stack of books, several of them volumes of poetry. Most people stared quietly from afar, but there were those admirers who got a little too close. One day on Fire Island she was mobbed to such a degree that the police had to be called. A few weeks later, during a trip to Port Jefferson, Marilyn and Norman Rosten were forced into the sea by a crowd of fans and literally had to swim for their lives.

One person who saw a lot of Marilyn during her vacation time was Lee and Paula's daughter, Susan. She was still a teenager, but shared a room with the actress and suffered equal amounts of jealousy and happiness while in her company. She cared for her surrogate sister, and the two would often gossip about all manner of subjects, including their love lives, makeup, and clothes. However, Susan was still insecure about the amount of time and attention the actress received from her parents and found it hard to accept that after searching for a father all her life, the one Marilyn actually found was Susan's.

On October 20, 1955, Marilyn made the pivotal decision to officially say a firm good-bye to Los Angeles by having her belongings shipped to the East Coast. When they eventually arrived, she moved everything into her new apartment on Sutton Place. Then on October 27, her divorce from Joe DiMaggio was finalized. Earl Wilson was eager to hear if she had been in touch with him in recent months. "No," she said. "At least I haven't made any appointments to see him." When Wilson asked if she'd like to be married again, Marilyn refused to give anything away. "I do, but it's not as simple as that and I don't see any time for that now." She also assured Wilson—falsely—that there was no man in her life. When the same reporter caught up with DiMaggio and asked about the failed marriage, he shrugged and replied, "I never think about that anymore."

In November 1955, rumors swirled that not only was Marilyn close to negotiating a new contract with Fox, but she had also secured herself a magnificent role in a new film called *Bus Stop*. This story was treated with caution by Marilyn, but she did speak to columnist Edwin Schallert about her immediate plans for the future. During the chat, Marilyn revealed that she would embrace the freedom of acting onstage, had every intention of staying in New York indefinitely, and wanted to continue her studies at the Actors Studio.

"The public deserves its money's worth when I appear in a picture," she said, before adding that was precisely why she wanted the best directors and training. When asked a little later which directors had been beneficial in her career, Marilyn showed no hesitation, listing John Huston, Billy Wilder, and *How to Marry a Millionaire*'s Jean Negulesco. However, while she certainly appreciated Negulesco's direction, the film itself was not a favorite, and she saw the character of Pola as a gimmick and not at all genuine.

On December 12, Marilyn attended the premiere of *The Rose Tattoo* with actor, friend, and occasional love interest Marlon Brando. The performance doubled as a benefit event for the Actors Studio, and Marilyn seemed to revel in posing for pictures for Milton Greene and other photographers. She grew shyer, however, when a radio reporter pounced on her, Marlon, actor Sid Caesar, and playwright Tennessee Williams. Brando seemed to take over almost the entire fifteen-minute chat, and at one point he and Caesar were so busy talking and asking questions that the female journalist seemed irrelevant to the proceedings.

It was clear that out of the four people standing in front of the reporter, it was Marilyn she most wanted to speak to, but getting past Brando was quite a task. When she was able, Marilyn confirmed that she attended the Actors Studio twice a week, participated in Lee Strasberg's private classes also twice a week, and then additionally observed at others. When questioned by Brando about the nature of her studies, the surprised actress revealed she was studying *Ulysses* and improvisation.

Once Brando and the others had gone, Marilyn further explained that she hoped her next film would be *Bus Stop*, and that acting on the stage was a definite plan for the future. At that point, Helen Hayes, the "First Lady of the American Theater" joined the conversation and Marilyn seemed rather shy in her presence. The veteran actress confirmed that the two had met just days before when they were both at the Actors Studio, but offered no further comment. At that point, Marilyn managed to find a way to escape and the radio interview was brought to a swift finish.

No doubt if the reporter had asked Marilyn about her stage plans while Marlon Brando was still nearby, he'd have had a lot to say. The actor greatly enjoyed working in theater and spoke about his feelings just a few months before *The Rose Tattoo* premiere: "On the stage there is a feeling of integration within the company, which is lacking in films. On the stage you're dealing with art, pure and simple."

IT HAD NOW BEEN a year since Marilyn walked out of Hollywood and into her new life. While it had been one of learning, making friends, and exploring the city, there had also been moments of frustration because of her ordeal with Fox. Marilyn mentioned this to Maurice Zolotow: "My fight with the studio is not about money. It is about human rights. I am tired of being known as the girl with the shape. I am going to show that I am capable of deeper acting."

Milton Greene spoke about Twentieth Century Fox in an interview with John Gold: "They were pretty tough on Marilyn at times. Some of the things that were said came pretty close to intimidation. It took courage for her to sit it out all those months and not give way. But Amy and I told her we would win in the end—and we did."

Milton was correct. On December 31, 1955, Marilyn finally signed a new contract with Twentieth Century Fox. After continuing to receive thousands of demanding fan letters over the past year, the studio bosses knew that they really had no option but to bow to her demands. Spyros Skouras was a seasoned businessman, and he knew that Marilyn was good for the studio, even if Darryl F. Zanuck refused to admit it. For a long time the two men argued about how many rights the actress should have, but Skouras was adamant that the contract needed to be finalized without any further delay. Eventually Zanuck conceded, gave in to the actress's demands, and the feud came to an end.

The contract Marilyn and her associates were able to negotiate was nothing short of revolutionary. Gone was the clause that insisted she must work solely for the studio. Instead, she would have to shoot just four Fox movies in the space of seven years and would be allowed the freedom to make films for Marilyn Monroe Productions too. In addition, she could perform in a number of television and radio programs. The script, choreographer, and cinematographer of each film would be approved by her, but more importantly, the directors on her handwritten list were now the only ones she had to work with. These included Billy Wilder, George Cukor, Elia Kazan, Joshua Logan, William Wyler, Joseph L. Mankiewicz, Alfred Hitchcock, David Lean, John Ford, John Huston, Vittorio De Sica, Fred Zinnemann, Lee Strasberg, George Stevens, Vincente Minnelli, and Carol Reed.

Marilyn had won a huge battle both for herself and for other actors who wished to have some creative freedom. She spoke about the deal to reporter Earl Wilson: "What I have settled for is a compromise. It is a compromise on both sides. I do not have story approval, but I do have director approval. That's important. I have certain directors I'll work for and I have trust in them and will do about anything they say. I know they won't let me do a bad story. Because, you know, you can have a wonderful story and a lousy director and hurt yourself." Normally loath to discuss money, Marilyn was anxious for Wilson to know that her contract was worth $100,000 a picture. "The same

$100,000 that they said I walked out on before!" She did not add, however, that there were several bonuses and other clauses that gave her the opportunity to earn much more than that.

Around the same time that the new contract arrived, a decision was made to relieve company director Frank Delaney of his duties within Marilyn Monroe Productions. After Marilyn's death, he told her former business manager, Inez Melson, that he felt that Marilyn and others in the company could not wait for him to go. He regretted any negative feelings toward him, however, since he felt perhaps he could have helped in her future career.

To biographer Maurice Zolotow, Delaney revealed that by the time the new contract was signed, Marilyn had piled up a huge amount of expenses, all of which had been paid by Milton Greene. The money had become such a concern that if the contract had not been executed, he would surely have gone broke.

Ironically, just two months after the end of Marilyn's standoff with the studio, Darryl F. Zanuck was accused of walking out on his own contract when he announced that he wished to step down from the helm of Twentieth Century Fox. In echoes of Marilyn's battle, he then left Hollywood—only he moved to Europe, not New York—before coming back to negotiate a new contract for himself as an independent producer. He eventually returned to take control of Twentieth Century Fox in 1962.

ON JANUARY 2, 1956, the *New York Times* carried an announcement that Marilyn was to act in the screen adaptation of Terence Rattigan's play *The Sleeping Prince*. Scheduled to be shot over

ABOVE: This photograph is a perfect example of how Marilyn felt during the early 1950s: glamorous, but bored with how her career was progressing.
Courtesy Photofest.

LEFT: Marilyn arrives in New York in September 1954 to do location shots for *The Seven Year Itch.* During time off, she took the opportunity to meet with future business partner Milton Greene and plan her escape from Hollywood.
David Wills Collection.

The "Heat Wave" number in *There's No Business Like Show Business* was a turning point for Marilyn. Not only did it thoroughly appall her husband, but it cemented her idea that she simply must move on from such frothy roles.

The white dress worn during the subway scene in *The Seven Year Itch* has become iconic in its own right. It is known the world over as the "Marilyn dress" and is a staple of any look-alike's wardrobe. *Courtesy Everett Collection.*

ABOVE: The scene that created an icon. The attention that came from Marilyn's skirt blowing over a subway grate ended her marriage but gave the actress the strength to reinvent herself as a trailblazing businesswoman. Photo by Kas Heppner. *David Wills Collection.*

LEFT: Marilyn is seen here with her *Seven Year Itch* costar, Tom Ewell. Ewell played the part of Richard Sherman on Broadway as well as in the film, and it became his most famous role.

ABOVE: One of the funniest scenes in *The Seven Year Itch* comes when Richard Sherman (Ewell) imagines seducing The Girl (Monroe) to the sounds of classical music. In reality, they accidentally fall from the piano bench during a rousing chorus of "Chopsticks." *David Wills Collection.*

LEFT: The stairs in *The Seven Year Itch* play a pivotal role when The Girl (Monroe) takes up the floor of her apartment to gain access to Richard Sherman's home downstairs. "We can do this all summer!" she says. *Courtesy Photofest.*

LEFT: Billy Wilder found working with Marilyn on *The Seven Year Itch* to be a challenging experience. However, despite the stress, he recognized her talent and directed her again in 1959's *Some Like It Hot.*
Courtesy Photofest.

BELOW: October 1954: Marilyn appears at the Santa Monica Courthouse to obtain a divorce from Joe DiMaggio.

LEFT: To the outside world, Marilyn and Joe DiMaggio were the ideal couple. However, while he was a genuine and faithful friend, he could be a controlling husband. The pair separated, though remained friends until Marilyn's death. They are seen here at the premiere of *The Seven Year Itch* in June 1955.
Courtesy Photofest.

BELOW: Drama coach Natasha Lytess tried to control Marilyn's life on and off set. The actress dropped her after the making of *The Seven Year Itch* and a bitter Lytess never forgave her.
Courtesy Everett Collection.

Marilyn saw her New York years as an adventure. Her arrival at the famed Actors Studio was met with scorn from some of her fellow students, but when she performed a scene in class, they gave her a round of applause.

Despite rumors to the contrary, Marilyn was not a dumb blonde. Her book collection was extensive, her taste varied and often highbrow. Here she is seen reading at home during her early career. *Courtesy Photofest.*

British poet Dame Edith Sitwell became a staunch supporter of Marilyn, and the two met on several occasions. Sitwell thought that Monroe was a true lady who had been unnecessarily persecuted as a result of her nude calendar photos.

Reporter and society hostess Elsa Maxwell adored Marilyn and thought she had great talent. "She had the courage to challenge the big movie moguls," Maxwell said. "She has the ambition to want to know and work with fine artists." *Courtesy Photofest.*

LEFT: Over the years, Marilyn was photographed with many animals, including monkeys, birds, wild cats, and—seen here at a 1955 charity event—an elephant. Her philosophy on her affinity for animals was simple: "Dogs never bite me," she said. "Just humans."

BELOW: The premiere of *The Rose Tattoo* was held in New York on December 12, 1955. That evening, Marilyn was interviewed about her plans for the future, including her hopes of acting onstage.
David Wills Collection.

LEFT: Marilyn, *Bus Stop* director Joshua Logan, and costar Don Murray. Murray would go on to be nominated for an Academy Award for his role as Bo, but Marilyn was, shockingly, overlooked.
Courtesy Photofest.

BELOW: Happy times with business partner Milton Greene and Warner Bros. executive Jack Warner. They had just agreed to a distribution deal for *The Prince and the Showgirl*, which was to be made under the banner of Marilyn Monroe Productions.
Courtesy Everett Collection.

The 1956 press conference for *The Prince and the Showgirl* caused a sensation. Marilyn stole the show when her dress strap broke, while Laurence Olivier seemed out of his depth and somewhat aloof. *Courtesy Photofest.*

LEFT: Marilyn's arrival in London in July 1956 caused a frenzy. She is seen here with new husband Arthur Miller, who eventually drove a wedge between his wife and her business partner, Milton Greene.

Courtesy Photofest.

BELOW: While Marilyn made few friends in England, she did become close with Oscar-winning cinematographer Jack Cardiff. Here, they are seen between takes on the set of *The Prince and the Showgirl.*

Courtesy Photofest.

LEFT: Marilyn was thrilled to work with Laurence Olivier, but the decision for him to direct as well as act in *The Prince and the Showgirl* proved to be traumatic. The British actor had no time for Method acting, and by the end of production the stars were barely speaking to each other.

Courtesy Photofest.

BELOW: Marilyn's image was used as inspiration for many businesses during the 1950s. Here, a group of young women take part in a look-alike competition in Hastings, England.

Mirrorpix/Courtesy Everett Collection.

ABOVE: Marilyn and Montgomery Clift in her last finished film, *The Misfits*. They had great respect for each other, and Clift described Marilyn as "the most gifted actress on the American screen." *Courtesy Photofest.*

LEFT: Marilyn on the set of her last, unfinished movie, *Something's Got to Give*. Despite any problems in her private life, she never stopped studying and striving to better herself. *David Wills Collection.*

the summer months, the film would apparently be directed by John Huston and costar legendary British actor Sir Laurence Olivier.

Dubbed "an occasional fairy tale," the play was set in 1911 and revolved around the Grand Duke Charles, who invites a young American showgirl called Elaine Dagenham (who later reveals her real name to be Mary) to have dinner with him at his private residence. Unbeknownst to her, it is strictly a dinner for two, though the duke's attempts at seduction do not go far, particularly when his eccentric wife turns up and takes a shine to Elaine, asking the young woman to accompany her to the king's coronation. A thread running throughout the tale is Elaine's theory that the duke does not have enough love in his life. By the end, both parties have decided that they love each other, though circumstances prevent them from continuing any further with the relationship.

The play opened to great applause at London's Phoenix Theatre in 1953 and starred Laurence Olivier as the duke and his wife, Vivien Leigh, as the showgirl. Having played various American roles in the past, Leigh was eager to turn the part into a British one instead. However, being American was essential for the role, since there is a pivotal scene where Elaine reveals she has specific political opinions related to her country. Leigh relented, and according to *Theatre World* magazine, audiences "gave Vivien Leigh the most enthusiastic welcome of her career."

Vivien declared Olivier to be her favorite leading man, though critics did sometimes question the partnership. "One wonders," said a columnist for *Theatre World*, "if there might be some disadvantage in a leading lady having her husband for a leading man." The same anonymous reporter did have to admit, however, that "by knowing each other so intimately in private life, they are bound together by a mutual understanding that enables them to communicate ideas to each other on the stage without so much as a suggestion of sign language."

The play was brought to Marilyn's attention by Charles Feldman in 1954, and later by Milton Greene, who was eager to purchase it for MMP. By the time Marilyn became interested in it as a vehicle, director William Wyler was in the running to buy the property, but the moment he withdrew, MMP stepped in and won the deal. Much was said about the fact that Vivien was dropped from the starring role, with some suggesting the harsh cinema lighting made her too old to play the part. There is possibly some truth in that theory, though more likely is the fact that with Marilyn's company producing the material for the screen, she was certainly not going to pass up the opportunity of starring in it herself.

In early February 1956, Laurence Olivier and Terence Rattigan arrived in New York to meet with Marilyn and attend several other business meetings. It was not the first time she had met the actor; the two had been introduced during her starlet days, when she was in the company of agent Johnny Hyde. However, even Marilyn doubted that Olivier had actually remembered such a meeting, so when the two finally did get together, it was regarded as a brand-new experience for both.

Marilyn's agent, Jay Kanter, remembers that the actress was enamored by the prospect of working with Olivier, and he was given the task of meeting both the actor and playwright at the airport. According to Kanter, the plan was to take them to a hotel and Marilyn would meet them there, but New York City was suffering a particularly awful downpour and as the car sped from the airport, Olivier announced,

"No, let's not have her out in the rain." Instead, he wanted to meet at her Sutton Place apartment, so as soon as he could, Jay called Milton to let him know what was going on and to alert Marilyn.

After freshening up in the hotel, Jay took the men to the apartment, where they were met by Milton Greene. "Come in," he said enthusiastically, and proceeded to serve them food and drink while Marilyn readied herself in the bedroom. Unfortunately, she took so long to get ready that everyone was left wondering whether she would ever come out at all. An hour went by and finally Jay told Milton that both Rattigan and Olivier would need to leave for another meeting fairly soon, which prompted the photographer to go see what was going on.

When he returned, Milton announced that it wouldn't be too much longer, but after more time passed, Jay ended up going into the room himself. The actress was sitting in front of her dressing table mirror. "Marilyn, they're waiting and have to leave soon," he told her. Jay recalls that she was scared to death of meeting the English heavyweight, but finally got up and went into the living room. The two were introduced and Olivier was "so gracious and she was very silent but in total awe of him."

Olivier charmed her throughout the meeting, to the point where Marilyn came away thinking that he really was the greatest actor in the world. The relationship had gotten off to a fantastic start, and this was cemented when Marilyn and Olivier attended a performance of *The Diary of Anne Frank* together. Unfortunately, a trip backstage was not as positive as it could be, after Susan Strasberg asked the actor what he thought of her performance as Anne. When Olivier criticized her, Marilyn without hesitation jumped to her friend's defense.

Even this early in their relationship, there were rumblings of trouble. Olivier had attended a lesson at the Actors Studio and witnessed Lee Strasberg berating a student he believed to have many faults. Olivier thought the episode was a form of bullying, and he told Strasberg so, in the most polite way he could. He was not, however, the first to witness such behavior. Writer James Roose-Evans wrote in 1957 that Lee easily lost his temper with those refusing to take criticism. To one actress he was heard complaining, "I wish you would use some of that emotion in the scene. You waste my time, our time, and I'm insulted."

Laurence Olivier did not support the Method, but he had actually read Stanislavski and found his teachings interesting. What he did not appreciate, though, was anyone who brought the man's ideas and actions onto a film set. In his opinion, if one was to study Stanislavski's System or Strasberg's Method, one should do so at home and then leave them firmly at the studio door.

In addition to acting methods, there was also the problem of directorial credit. While Marilyn was extremely happy with the idea of costarring with Laurence Olivier, she had not initially thought about him as a director. That was why it had been originally announced that John Huston would take the job, because the director had already been in negotiations with Rattigan before the project was confirmed. Olivier had directed the play, however, and when Huston dropped out, the British actor was soon given that job on the film production too. Marilyn went along with the decision, but according to Susan Strasberg, her father Lee was not the least bit happy about it. To complicate matters further, the film would be released under the banner of both Marilyn Monroe Productions and Laurence Olivier Productions.

A press conference was called to announce the project, but it was all rather stilted and formal. In fact, some reporters felt that Olivier answered most of the questions as if he were the prime minister, such was his rigidity and politeness. However, they were all intrigued by the announcement that the film would mean Marilyn moving to England for four months. Then when her dress strap broke in front of the entire room, the reporters went wild and the normal chaos of a Monroe press conference ensued.

When Olivier was due to leave the States, newspapers were filled with gushing quotes between the new business partners. "Marilyn is an expert comedienne and therefore a good actress," he was quoted as saying. "Olivier has always been my idol" was her reply.

On his arrival at London airport, Olivier told reporters that he had adored spending time with Marilyn. "She is very sweet, very charming, very talented and very easy to get on with," he said. "I am not in the least surprised to be playing against Miss Monroe. I am delighted. It seemed a very good idea to make a film with her."

Even Vivien Leigh was quoted as saying she was thrilled that the part she had played onstage had now gone to Marilyn. "I cannot think of anyone better than Miss Monroe," she said, before adding that the actress was more than welcome to live with her and Olivier in London. Anyone hoping that the *Gone with the Wind* star would laugh at Marilyn's acting talents was left severely disappointed. Instead, Leigh expressed her belief that she was "an absolutely brilliant actress" and was sure that she could act in any Shakespeare play she wished to.

The teaming with Laurence Olivier seemed to bring out a new way of thinking toward Marilyn not only as an actress, but as a revolutionary too. Alan Brien from the *Aberdeen Evening Express* was first to recognize that she was undoubtedly leading a revolt of Hollywood actors against the studios. Noting that stars such as Jane Russell and Burt Lancaster had also taken up the fight in the past six months, Brien said that Marilyn was winning the battle and had achieved in one year the freedom it had taken Orson Welles and Laurence Olivier a lifetime to secure.

OLIVIER AND RATTIGAN BEGAN the mammoth task of changing elements of *The Sleeping Prince* to suit the screen. Out went the name Elaine Dagenham/Mary, and in came the prettier Elsie Marina. Then the part of the duke's eccentric wife was changed into a vague and brusque mother-in-law. Along with the name change, Elsie's character was also softened slightly, since in the play she was something of a political philosopher. "You can hardly expect Marilyn Monroe to depict a political theorist," said Rattigan. "Shall we say that, as played by Miss Monroe, she will be a girl whose thought processes do not work quite so fast."

When casting began, many of the actors who had appeared in the stage version were now enrolled to appear in the film. These included Richard Wattis as Peter Northbrook, Jeremy Spenser as King Nicolas, and Paul Hardwick as majordomo to the duke. While Vivien Leigh would not have a part in the film, her presence was everywhere apparent, particularly since Terence Rattigan never made any secret of the fact that by the time he had finished writing the original play, it had been her he was specifically writing it for.

During their time working on the stage production, Leigh and Olivier had rehearsed their parts for hours, and they shared secret keywords between each other to have perfect timing in every scene. Then after each performance, the couple would sit down to discuss how they could experiment with their parts to make them even better for the next evening. One scene when the duke makes a phone call while the showgirl eats caviar made a huge impression on audiences and critics alike. "Perhaps only a husband and wife would have the patience and endurance to rehearse that scene as frequently as the Oliviers did," said *Theatre World*, "often at home, long after rehearsals were over at the theatre."

It was clear to everyone that Marilyn had taken on a monumental task by optioning the project, and that through natural loyalty to Vivien and the story, it would be exceptionally difficult to win over the original theatrical cast.

OLIVIER'S TRIP TO NEW York happened to coincide with a momentous event in Marilyn's life—that of changing her name legally from Norma Jeane DiMaggio to Marilyn Monroe. The significance of changing her name at this juncture in her life cannot be understated, particularly as she had used the stage name for almost ten years and had not taken any steps to change it legally before. She felt comfortable in her skin and with her name, and in February 1956 the time was ripe for her to officially own the identity of Marilyn Monroe.

She was proud of what was happening in her life, and every day led her further and further away from the dumb-blonde sexpot. She was planning for her future. Just a week after the name change, Marilyn drew up her first will. In it she left most of her money to Arthur Miller and then split the rest between Lee and Paula Strasberg, her doctor

Margaret Hohenberg, Michael Chekhov's widow, the Actors Studio, Norman Rosten's daughter, and the health care of her mother. With the legalities of the name change and will now in place, Marilyn was free to continue with her creative work.

So far, she had been classed as an observer at the Actors Studio, but on February 17, 1956, Marilyn acted in her very first scene, from Eugene O'Neill's play *Anna Christie*. Perhaps the biggest surprise about the event was that despite her nerves, she actually volunteered to do the part. Nobody had pushed her, nobody had forced her into it; it was merely something that Marilyn herself finally felt happy and brave enough to attempt.

The scene was performed with actress Maureen Stapleton, and together they rehearsed furiously to make sure it was absolutely perfect. One evening, after many hours of going over the scene, the two women shared a cab home, but as Marilyn was to get out first, she offered to pay something toward the fare. Stapleton did not wish to take her money, and the two began a discussion as to who was right and who was wrong. At first it was somewhat lighthearted, but when Stapleton realized that Marilyn was not going to leave without giving her money, she lost her temper. "If you pay that driver, I'm finished with you and the scene!" she said. Marilyn kept her money and got out of the cab. Stapleton regretted being so forthright and intended phoning Marilyn as soon as she got home. However, Marilyn phoned first and it was clear that the taxi situation had really upset her. Because of Stapleton's forceful tone, Marilyn had convinced herself that Stapleton did not want to act the part or appear onstage with her. It took a lot of consoling to convince the actress that that wasn't the case at all. The two made up and rehearsals continued.

So as not to attract unwanted attention from those not normally due to attend class that day, Marilyn chose not to put her name on the board of upcoming scenes. Of course, word soon leaked out and the studio was packed with just about every student imaginable. "Believe me when I say that Marilyn got out there and did her scene in front of one of the toughest audiences in the world," said Arthur Miller's sister and fellow student Joan Copeland. It was certainly a harsh crowd, especially since many of the students still hadn't forgiven Marilyn for being such a huge star.

Just before the two actresses were due to go onstage, Marilyn suffered a severe bout of nerves, which she later said had rendered her unable to remember a single word. Still, when Stapleton suggested they place a script on the stage as they performed, Marilyn was horrified. She would do this scene if it killed her, and there would be no script to help her along the way!

Despite her anxiety, in the end the scene was remarkable and the normally brutal audience gave Marilyn a round of applause. Fellow actress Kim Stanley recalled that it was the first time she had ever heard clapping in the Actors Studio and afterward felt obliged to tell Marilyn just how much she admired her. Joan Copeland described the performance as beautiful. "She displayed—you know—the kind of talent it was hard to believe she had." Marilyn, she recalled, was absolutely thrilled when the students who had shown a definite dislike toward her actually came up afterward to say how good she was.

Still haunted by feelings of inferiority and a lack of confidence, after the class Marilyn cried to the Strasbergs because she felt that her performance had not been as good as it could have been. Later she told reporters that she did not have any feelings toward the performance at all, because it had all passed in a blur. She may have had reservations, but nobody else did. The scene went down in history as one of the most important and influential ever performed at the Actors Studio, and was still being talked about long after her death.

ON FEBRUARY 22, 1956, Marilyn did a unique and beautiful portrait sitting with famed photographer Cecil Beaton. From the beginning, the actress's informal style—mussed-up hair and hardly any makeup—made a huge impression on Beaton. He later wrote that he was a little startled by her at first, and mistook her joyful manner for exhibitionism. However, he soon realized that it was merely a case of exhilaration, "like an over-excited child asked downstairs after tea."

Marilyn greatly enjoyed working with the famous photographer, and one portrait of her, lying on a Japanese tapestry with a chiffon scarf ruffled around her shoulders, became her favorite. In the picture, she is holding a carnation to her breast, looking deeply at the camera, with her hair swept upward. Marilyn was fascinated with the piece. She bought prints for friends and told a reporter from the *Los Angeles Times* that the look actually reminded her of when she was a little girl.

CHAPTER SEVEN

Performance of a Lifetime

LIKE *THE SEVEN YEAR Itch* and *The Sleeping Prince*, *Bus Stop* was a play long before it was made into a movie. Starring Kim Stanley, the Broadway production was a smash hit, though the actress refused to accept all the glory, claiming that the other actors in the play were just as good as she was. "Nobody believes it now that they have seen Miss Stanley in action," wrote Mawby Green for *Theatre World*. "For she is contributing the best comic characterization since Judy Holliday fractured the town in *Born Yesterday*, stopping the show on several occasions merely with her delivery of a line."

It was reviews like this that made Marilyn a little hesitant to take on the role. Hearing just how much audiences and critics alike enjoyed Miss Stanley's performance was daunting. However, among all the praise there were a few who—while admitting it was a slick show—complained that perhaps the depth of performances in the play as a whole was somewhat lacking. This gave Marilyn hope that she could bring something more to the film than had been given onstage.

The play *Bus Stop* was written by William Inge and revolves around a group of bus passengers who are stuck in a diner during a snowstorm.

Over the course of one night, the characters all reveal their hopes and fears, until the snow has cleared and their lives can return to normal. Among the passengers is a nightclub singer named Cherie, who has been "kidnapped" by a cowboy named Bo intent on marrying her. At first she has no interest in this bully and instead is desperate for a man who will respect her. During the course of the play, Bo proves that he can be that man, and she unexpectedly falls in love.

The film—written by *The Seven Year Itch*'s George Axelrod—carried far more action than was portrayed on the stage, and as a result, some of the original characters were removed and new scenes added, among them one of Cherie singing "That Old Black Magic" in a nightclub and major parts shot on location at a parade and rodeo. Director Joshua Logan later explained to William Inge that as the main plot revolved around the love story of characters Bo and Cherie, the deletion of some secondary characters made way for a better exploration of their own personal tale. He did not explain, however, that some longer speeches had been deleted because Marilyn had told George Axelrod that she had a problem with long lines. Years later, the writer would remember Marilyn as "a unique work of art, manufactured (flaws and all) in an edition of one. Afterwards they broke the mold. Later they broke her, too, but that's another story."

To prepare for the role of Cherie, Marilyn worked closely with Paula Strasberg, who also agreed to go with the actress on location. There were countless hours spent discussing the project with Milton Greene, and together they deliberated over everything from what makeup Cherie should wear (pale because she spends most of her time indoors) to the state of her fishnet stockings (ripped and darned because she doesn't have much money).

Behind the scenes, teacher Lee Strasberg wrote to Joshua Logan to tell him that he believed Marilyn to be one of the greatest actors that ever came through the doors of the Actors Studio. It was this comment that made Logan finally commit to the project, and by the end of filming, he completely shared Strasberg's view. For the rest of his life, whenever interviewed he would say that Marilyn was a combination of Greta Garbo and Charlie Chaplin. He wholeheartedly believed that she was one of the most extraordinary actresses that ever lived. This was fine praise indeed from a professional who had worked extensively on Broadway and had just directed the Academy Award–nominated film *Picnic*.

Bus Stop was to be a pivotal role for Marilyn, not just because it was an extraordinary part, but also as it required her to go back to Los Angeles for the first time in over a year. When she left after the making of *The Seven Year Itch*, the actress had been adamant that she would only return when she received positive answers to her demands. Critics had laughed, but now she was going back as the president of her own company, an Actors Studio protégée, a friend of poets and intellectuals, and most important of all, armed with the best contract of her career. The critics remained perplexed, but at least they found it harder to laugh now. Marilyn had taken on Hollywood and won; only a fool would make fun of that.

THE RELATIONSHIP BETWEEN ARTHUR Miller and Marilyn had become extremely serious, and he had finally moved out of his family home. The couple continued to see each other secretly, but if there was any hope of long-term happiness, it was clear that Miller would have to obtain a divorce as quickly as possible. Marilyn's trip to Los Angeles gave him that opportunity, and he made arrangements to travel to Nevada while *Bus Stop* was being filmed.

The closeness between Miller and Marilyn came at a price. Ever since her arrival in New York, she had listened to the advice presented by Milton Greene and his associates. She didn't always take their suggestions, but her attention was in their direction. After the appearance of Miller, however, this began to shift. He had a long career in theater, he read scripts and plays with an unfaltering eye, and he knew a lot about the business. Marilyn listened to his views and agreed with his opinions on politics and literature. Despite being touted as complete opposites (or the "Beauty and the Brain," as the press liked to call them), the pair actually had a great deal in common, and this inevitably threatened to jeopardize the relationship she had with Milton, since she now looked to Miller for support before her business partner.

Still, away from romantic entanglements, there was work to be done. In that regard, the last week of February 1956 and the first few weeks of March were extremely busy. After flying into Los Angeles on February 25 with Milton, Marilyn was met at the airport by dozens of reporters all intent on getting an exclusive. They wanted to know about the new Fox contract, what it was like to be back in Los Angeles, and whether she was happy.

Marilyn took it all in her stride and assured everyone that she was thrilled to be back in her hometown. She wasn't enraptured, however, when she attended a court appearance to sort out the 1954 charge of driving without a license. During proceedings on February 29, Judge Charles J. Griffin enjoyed reprimanding the actress, while she smiled sweetly and promised not to do it again. Afterward, Marilyn appeared on the court steps and declared that the judge had made the right decision by penalizing her. "I don't really believe in ignoring traffic citations," she said with a grin.

On March 1, a *Sleeping Prince* distribution deal with Warner Bros. was announced. The event created a lot of publicity, and at a press party Marilyn was seen posing ecstatically with Jack Warner and greeting actor and fellow Warner Bros. associate James Stewart. This was an extraordinary moment for Marilyn, and it seemed as though everyone was thrilled with her success. However, one person quietly waiting for her to fall was former teacher Natasha Lytess. She had tried unsuccessfully to contact Marilyn since her dismissal at the end of *The Seven Year Itch*, and on hearing that the actress was back in Hollywood, the scorned woman was prompted to try to reunite once and for all.

After receiving no reply to her phone calls, Lytess turned up at the Beverly Glen home Marilyn was sharing with the Greenes and demanded to see her former pupil. She was sent away by agent Lew Wasserman, and as she walked down the path, turned back to look at the house. Marilyn was standing at an upstairs window, but did not wave or smile. Afterward, the actress instructed her agents to put a stop to the unwanted attention and Lytess went away—for a while.

SO WHAT BECAME OF Natasha Lytess? The drama coach never forgave Marilyn for her dismissal, and in 1960 she wrote a fairly stern but sanitized version of their relationship with researcher Jane Wilkie. Wilkie did not particularly like Lytess and complained bitterly that, despite her best efforts, almost all the manuscript was a complaint against Marilyn. It remained unpublished.

Several years later, Lytess wrote another memoir, only this time it was filled with every sordid, degrading, and scandalous story she could muster. In 1962, Marilyn's press agent received word that Lytess had sold it for $10,000 to *France-Soir*, the owner of a magazine called *France-Dimanche*. The agency asked how much it would cost to buy it back, but the publisher refused, explaining that they had world rights to the piece and therefore were on course to make a lot of money. They also disclosed that the story was so intimate that they probably wouldn't be able to publish it in its entirety. Lawyers were consulted, but the agency was told that until the article actually appeared, there was nothing that could be done to stop publication. For now, all everyone could do was wait.

While the agents concerned themselves with its possible release in *France-Dimanche*, the story suddenly appeared in London's *Sunday People* newspaper. As predicted, the piece left absolutely nothing to the imagination. The first installment boasted the horrendous title "Marilyn Monroe: Her Secret Life, I Made Her—Body and Soul." In the article, the embittered teacher told readers all about her first meeting with Marilyn—how the starlet was dressed like a "trollop" who had dyed yellow hair and a petulant mouth. She said Marilyn's voice was "like a knife clattering on a cafeteria plate."

Natasha's foul-mouthed tirade was utterly without compassion toward her former pupil and disclosed everything she could possibly think of to blacken Marilyn's name. Some of the less intrusive stories involved Marilyn having a romance with millionaire Howard Hughes when she was still a starlet. During that time, he apparently flew her and the drama coach to Palm Springs and delivered yellow roses to the house every single day. Natasha boasted that she went along for the ride and received flowers too, but even she had to admit that hers were just out of courtesy, not romance.

Natasha Lytess was completely and utterly obsessed with Marilyn's sex life, as evidenced thoroughly throughout the articles. Mostly her stories concentrated on the actress's lack of knowledge about kissing and intimacy. According to Lytess, she had to explain what the word *sensual* meant, and Marilyn then bought manuals to study the subject. The fact that the actress had already been married and knew the basics of sex long before she met the teacher was completely ignored by Natasha.

The complaints that Jane Wilkie noted in her unpublished manuscript are everywhere apparent in the articles, but there were times when Lytess had to confess that Marilyn was actually a good person. One story involved a millionaire who wanted to give the actress a car in exchange for sex. She turned him down and the vehicle was returned. Then Lytess fell behind on her mortgage payments, so to help her out Marilyn sold a mink coat given to her by agent and lover Johnny Hyde. These small, heartwarming memories were rare, however, and for the most part Lytess's story was one of utter vitriol.

It is bad enough that the teacher went after her former student in such a brutal and coldhearted manner, but it is especially distressing to know that the first three articles were published on July 15, 22, and 29, 1962—also known as the three weeks leading up to Marilyn's death. The next one—published on August 5, 1962, the very morning the world woke to the news that Marilyn had passed—detailed the star's turbulent relationship with Joe DiMaggio. The series should have ended there, but in light of Marilyn's passing, Lytess was happy to write one more article, published on August 12, 1962. Was this last installment to be an apology? A declaration that the other articles had been mean-spirited and unkind? No, not at all.

Aside from describing her as "my poor Marilyn," the final article was much the same as the rest, only this time Lytess compared an apparent suicide attempt from the early 1950s to Marilyn's real death the week before. She had already written about this episode, but now wanted to share more to shed light on why Marilyn had ultimately died. She was sure—she claimed—that Marilyn would want the world to know all about it, although she had chosen not to disclose the words previously because "some confidences must be kept until death." In the form of a conversation between herself and the actress, Lytess described Marilyn's reason for the first suicide attempt as being because men only wanted one thing from her. Then, in order to pass some blame to the public who adored Marilyn, Lytess claimed that because the star had been admired by the world for her body, it had given her a complex about sex, which had been ever-present in her mind.

To finish it all off, the teacher then spoke about Marilyn's marriage to Miller, and added a dubious conversation that supposedly happened between Lytess and Monroe after the marriage had broken down. According to the coach, she spotted Marilyn at Schwab's drugstore in Los Angeles, where she supposedly poured her heart out about Miller and—once again—her sex life.

If Lytess felt in any way sorry for the loss of Marilyn's life or the articles leading up to it, she certainly never showed it. Instead, she remained embittered about the relationship until her own death on May 12, 1963, less than a year after she had penned the vicious editorials. While it was clear that the teacher felt abandoned by Monroe, it should not have come as a surprise. After the limits she tried to impose on the actress's life and career, it was only a matter of time before Marilyn rebelled and took back control. The way Lytess handled events afterward was nothing short of deplorable, and to continue the slander even in the week after Marilyn's death was proof that not every woman was on her side and the actress made the best decision by letting her go.

IN SPRING 1956, A press conference held at Marilyn's rented Beverly Glen accommodation brought out the silliest of questions from reporters who were just happy to have Marilyn back in Hollywood. Thomas Wiseman, a reporter for the *London Evening Standard*, must surely have been an object of jealousy, however, since he was able to garner a private audience with the actress.

Flirtatious and playful, Marilyn wore a low-cut dress with a white rose tucked into her neckline, until she suddenly pulled it out and tossed it aside. "If I keep it there much longer," she laughed, "it is liable to wilt." She then commented on a variety of topics, including how the house furniture was not to her taste, her belief that men were helpless creatures, and the notion that her ideal man must be a poet, "though that doesn't mean he has to write poetry." At one point the star briefly lay on the floor and kicked her legs in the air. "That would make a good photograph, wouldn't it?" she asked. "Sell a lot of papers."

When the topic moved to the fact that during the whole interview she had not received any telephone calls, Marilyn grew pensive. She ceased the leg kicks and sat quietly on the sofa. There then followed a rather touching conversation where Marilyn explained that she never had any real friends while living in Hollywood, and that her move to New York had finally enabled her to find some. She then defended her studies and stressed that her move was no publicity stunt. She did not want to rid herself of the Marilyn Monroe character, she said, but stressed that while it was part of her personality, it certainly wasn't the whole part.

Another reporter who interviewed Marilyn during this time was Elsa Maxwell, and the two chatted about a variety of subjects. The one she most wanted to mention, though, was the rumor of a romance with Arthur Miller. With other reporters, Marilyn had denied the relationship so much that it was beginning to look as though she didn't know Miller at all. However, with Elsa she opened up slightly: "I like Arthur very much. And I'm proud to have such a great playwright for my friend. I've had very few friends in my life, as you know." When Elsa said that the two should get married, Marilyn laughed and replied, "You're wonderful! Unfortunately we haven't reached any such serious stage—yet. . . . I don't say I won't marry him. But I tell you, honestly, I have no plan to marry him—now."

Life at the Beverly Glen house was hectic, with the Greenes, their son, Joshua, and numerous staff and colleagues mulling around. To gain a little privacy, Marilyn rented a room at the Chateau Marmont hotel. There, she spent time with Arthur Miller, who sneaked in and out of Los Angeles during his Nevada divorce residency.

The schedule for *Bus Stop* was relentless. Preproduction had begun on February 27, and by March 8 Marilyn and costar Don Murray (acting as Bo) posed for photographs on the Fox lot. The production then headed to Phoenix on March 15 for location shots at a parade and rodeo. After that, filming moved on to Sun Valley, Idaho, before returning to the stages of Hollywood shortly thereafter. Unfortunately, exhaustion, coupled with all the old insecurities that had plagued Marilyn during her years in Hollywood, soon returned, and her anxieties often reached mammoth proportions. Having Paula Strasberg on set proved beneficial to the actress, but as with Natasha Lytess before her, she seemed to fall into the role of second director, which none of the cast and crew particularly enjoyed. Eventually Logan asked her to stay in the dressing room until the day's scenes were completed.

Despite this being the first time Joshua Logan had ever worked with the actress, he seemed to understand Marilyn better than any other director. He later told Laurence Olivier that he had never worked with such a talent before, and that she was a "tremendous actress." If she understood a direction, she would achieve such heights that Logan was often completely taken aback. If she did not understand what he wanted her to do, he would gently repeat the request and then Marilyn would give it everything she had.

Her main problems on set were all related to the anxiety of whether she was giving a good performance. Logan noted straightaway that Marilyn would sometimes forget her lines, not because she hadn't learned them but because she was too busy thinking about the way she had delivered a line prior to the one she was now speaking. With her mind still on something they had shot ten seconds before, it was impossible for her to remember what she was supposed to be doing now.

He noticed that Marilyn was highly critical of herself, so he spent a great deal of time reassuring her that everything was perfect. It was a hard task, though, as the actress was so nervous on set that she would often break down and declare herself terrible. At those times, no amount of reassurance would convince her that she was actually giving a magnificent performance.

Instead of growing impatient like so many directors before and after him, Logan used a simple but effective technique of asking his assistant to repeat the words to her whenever she stumbled. That way he could continue shooting the scene and Marilyn would get back on track quickly. He then edited the scene later so that it appeared flawless. Another trick was to shoot as many angles as he possibly could, because even when she made a mistake, other parts of the scene would be perfect and usable.

Logan also got into the habit of leaving the camera rolling even when the scene had finished. That way, if he sensed that Marilyn was in a particularly good mood, they could do the scene again immediately, without any interruptions. If he shouted "Cut" after it was finished, she would cool off considerably and it would take a while for her to warm up again. The technique of keeping the camera rolling whenever possible proved invaluable for actor/director relations, as well as for the final edit, but another tactic was stressful for others on set. Because Marilyn was rarely happy with the way she had played a scene, Logan started printing every take she approved of, or was word-perfect in. This meant that it did not matter what kind of performance her costars gave during that scene, if Marilyn was good it was going in the can anyway. As a result, other cast members felt unnecessary pressure, trying to remain flawless during each and every take.

By April 1956, the shoot was almost halfway through. However, Marilyn fell ill with a bronchial infection and was admitted to Cedars of Lebanon hospital in Los Angeles. Whenever the actress became ill during a film shoot, there would inevitably be some talk as to whether she was being genuine. However, in Joshua Logan, Marilyn met a staunch ally, and in a letter to George Axelrod he made clear his belief that she was genuinely unwell. In another note written on the same day to William Inge, the director expressed his view that Marilyn was perfect for the character of Cherie; he loved her accent and thought she was adorable.

While she recovered from the infection, two of the film's actors— Don Murray and Hope Lange—were married. Lange had been lucky to be cast as a young waitress, since Marilyn was paranoid about having another blonde on set and had previously asked for her to be removed. She was not, however, and her performance, with slightly darker hair, complimented Marilyn's perfectly.

After the excitement of the Murray wedding, the company busied itself by shooting scenes that didn't involve Marilyn. Several of these took place on the bus heading toward Grace's Diner, and saw Bo and his friend Virg (Arthur O'Connell) having a conversation about women and, of course, Cherie. Joshua Logan loved Don Murray's performance as Bo, and predicted that *Bus Stop* would make him a big star. He was right, as while the actor perhaps didn't reach the heights of Marlon Brando or other contemporaries, he worked regularly from then on, and was still making movies into his seventies.

Marilyn returned to work and shooting continued, but now Don Murray was unwell with pleurisy. However, because of Joshua Logan's careful eye toward any problems Marilyn might have, the filming of *Bus Stop* was easier than it could have been. This did not mean that there were no problems, though. Logan was a patient man, but even he had his limitations. During one outdoor scene, the company had a tiny snippet of time to get the shot in a perfect light. Marilyn knew this and yet continued putting on her makeup, oblivious to everyone clock-watching outside. When she eventually walked onto set, she did so just as the magic light faded. Logan was so incensed with her behavior that he jumped up and down in front of hundreds of spectators, swearing furiously.

Another problem arose between Marilyn and Murray. During one scene where Bo tries to stop Cherie from walking away, he tugs on the train of her show costume and is shocked when it comes off in his hand. She flies around, shouts at him furiously, and grabs the tail from his grasp. During one take, Marilyn shocked Murray when she turned and went at him with her fists. He braced for impact and the actress bounced off him and straight onto the floor.

As Murray picked her back up and apologized, Marilyn stayed in character and delivered her line. This time, though, instead of just grabbing her tail, she whipped it across the actor's face and he was left with a cut just below his eye. As she ran off set, Murray stormed after her, intent on telling her off. It was Logan who eventually managed to persuade him not to, fearful that it would create more drama.

Even scenes that had already been shot caused controversy at times. One proved more bothersome than others due to the possibility of nudity and sexual connotation. During one part of the story, Bo visits the guesthouse where Cherie is staying, gets past her landlady, and proceeds to barge into her bedroom. Flinging open the curtains, he demands that she get up to join him at the parade, but then ends up on the same bed as Cherie, stroking her naked shoulder and getting rather carried away with himself.

Murray told columnist Earl Wilson that Marilyn was totally naked underneath the sheet, and he did his best to make sure she stayed completely covered during the scene. However, as she moved around, the sheet kept coming off, and he would have to move quickly to pull it back on. On May 16, 1956, *Bus Stop* producer Buddy Adler received a letter from Fox colleague Frank McCarthy, who had queried the problems that could come from such a scene. While everyone agreed that the camera operator had made sure Marilyn looked covered at all times, a difficulty arose because Logan changed the scene slightly to have it dissolve at the crucial moment. This new development could lead viewers to think the couple had sex when the camera turned off, and Fox could not risk this happening.

McCarthy was happy for the scene to stay as directed, but knew that the company needed to protect itself against any misunderstandings. On hearing the initial concerns, Adler proposed a change that could work for everyone: the landlady would be seen in Cherie's bedroom, walk to the door, but not actually leave. Throughout the conversation between Bo and Cherie, the camera would then cut away to the landlady, particularly when his hands were on Marilyn's body.

McCarthy approved this angle and then added a point of his own: the landlady should say that she runs a respectable establishment and then vocally refuse to leave the room until Bo has gone. In the final film, there was a compromise. The landlady does leave the room as Bo talks to Cherie, but she makes sure the door is open so that she can hear what is going on. As the couple are about to kiss, the landlady returns, this time to interrupt proceedings by telling Bo he'll be late for the parade.

The Travilla-designed "snake costume" (nicknamed that way because the pattern looked a little like scales) that was worn during much of the film—including the nightclub scenes and one on the bus—was another center of concern. McCarthy told Adler that he would be on set when the costume was used, though in the end it was approved and got past the censors.

Another scene that just scraped through was the kissing one between Bo and Cherie, toward the end of the film. First, because it was believed that Marilyn's mouth was far too open to be decent, and then after reshooting it several times, they had problems because saliva could be seen as the couple's mouths parted. It was also a problem when Marilyn's face was leaned against her arm in despair. As she raised her head, a stream of wet could again be seen. The censors were dismayed, but the actress fought for the spittle to be left in, claiming that it would not be realistic if it disappeared. She won her battle and the scenes stayed intact.

One scene that was not so lucky, however, was where Cherie is trying to escape the attentions of Bo. She plans to head to Hollywood to make her dreams come true, but when filming a suitcase-packing scene, Marilyn leaned over and her dress fell away from her breasts. McCarthy knew it would never be approved so suggested a cutaway shot of Cherie's friend Betty instead. In the end, even this wasn't enough, and in the finished scene, it is Betty who is seen packing the case, not Cherie.

On May 17, 1956, the action moved to a scene where Cherie and Bo talk in a shed outside the nightclub where she works. During this part of the movie, he insists on pronouncing her name as Cherry, much to Cherie's chagrin, but in spite of that, her initial reaction is one of intrigue and warmth. Joshua Logan was blown away by her performance and that day sat down to write a letter to George Axelrod. In it he described another impressive scene where Marilyn's character tells her friend all about her life's direction and her ambitions for the future. The director thought she had played it charmingly, and he was sure that all who watched the movie would fall instantly in love.

On May 29, 1956, *Bus Stop* wrapped production and Marilyn presented Joshua Logan with a portrait of herself in a silver frame. Then several members of the cast went to the home of film producer William Goetz to see his art collection. That evening, Marilyn posed thoughtfully for Logan's camera, in front of paintings by artists including Honoré Daumier, Édouard Manet, Paul Cézanne, and Pablo Picasso. A bronze statue of a fourteen-year-old dancer by Edgar Degas seemed to catch the actress's imagination, and Logan captured her gazing wistfully at it.

The interest in this particular piece is revealing. While Marilyn might not have been a professional dancer, she took many classes during the years and starred in various movies that enabled her to dance on-screen. However, her love of the art went far deeper than that, and in her vast library of books she had several volumes of related texts. Among those acquired over the course of her lifetime were *The Thinking Body* by Mabel Elsworth Todd and *Dance to the Piper* by Agnes de Mille. The former was a physiology study of how psychological processes affect movement of the body, while the latter was the autobiography of dancer Agnes de Mille. This book would have been particularly stimulating since the author had struggled against adversity to achieve her dreams, just as Marilyn did her entire life.

On June 1—Marilyn's thirtieth birthday—a party was given for her at the Beverly Hills Hotel. Thrown by Joshua Logan, the star appeared to have a wonderful time and was thrilled to meet Indonesian president Sukarno. After Marilyn left the event, Logan's wife, Nedda, discovered that the actress had left her purse behind. A huge Marilyn fan who loved her performance in *Bus Stop*, Mrs. Logan made sure the bag was returned to her several days later.

Despite the one blowup between actress and director on set, Marilyn had gotten along with Joshua Logan remarkably well. Even in the middle of *Bus Stop*, Logan told reporters that he was desperate to work with Marilyn on a play, and was prepared to direct her in any future film she wanted him for. Unfortunately, there was one problem that Marilyn was not aware of at the time of shooting: the film was just too long. On May 17, Logan mentioned to George Axelrod that he was worried about how he could ever bring the film to under two hours. This remained a concern throughout the entire production, and as it reached the editing stage, it became clear that some scenes would have to go.

In the end, Logan and editor William Reynolds trimmed so much off that *Bus Stop* came in at around ninety-six minutes. They achieved this by editing tiny pieces here and there, right through to huge chunks of otherwise perfect scenes. By July 5, 1956, it was almost finished, though producer Buddy Adler still wished that more cuts could be made. Logan's wife, Nedda, also became involved when she revealed that her favorite shot was that of Cherie putting on Bo's coat in the final scene of the film. In honor of her, several more feet were added to the shot, making it longer than originally planned.

Marilyn had been looking forward to seeing the film, especially since it was the first she had made since she began her work at the Actors Studio. However, she came away outraged after discovering that one of her major scenes—talking to Hope Lange on the bus— was cut so dramatically that some of her best lines had completely disappeared. She became so incensed about it that when she later bumped into Logan during the making of *The Sleeping Prince*, she slammed a door in his face and refused to speak to him. She did not attend the premiere either, and told fellow actors that she did not like the way she looked in the movie.

Thankfully, the tension between Logan and Marilyn did not last forever, though they never did work together again. He later told Lee Strasberg that he had loved directing her, before adding that the actress's presence in the movie gave it a distinction that would have certainly been absent without her.

While Marilyn may have complained about the way *Bus Stop* had been edited, the critics seemed to enjoy it mightily. Alan Dent for the *Illustrated London News* appreciated Don Murray's performance, and exclaimed that Marilyn as Cherie had progressed a stage on her acting journey. According to him, *Bus Stop* showed that she "has some talent." However, he was unfairly critical about Marilyn's close-up shots, declaring that she showed no expression or emotion whatsoever while Murray's character was speaking to her. To even the most casual observer, this comment seems totally unfair, for Marilyn's tearful eyes reveal one of the most soulful performances of her life.

Thankfully, the *New York Times* was steadfastly on Marilyn's side and acknowledged her performance as confirmation of her being a genuine actress, as opposed to a sex symbol. They told readers that while the film was a good one, Marilyn was certainly the best part of it. The *New York Herald Tribune* thought similarly and gave the actress great acclaim as a "New Marilyn." *Bus Stop*, it said, "fools the skeptics about her ability as a serious actress. Her work had beauty, action, mobility and was very touching."

This would have greatly pleased Marilyn. Shortly before the release of the film, she spoke about being known as a glamour girl. "If that part about my being a symbol of sex is true," she said, "it ought to help the box office, but I don't want to be too commercial about it. After all, it's a responsibility . . . being a symbol I mean."

While not naming the film directly, actor James Mason was thoroughly impressed with everything Marilyn had to offer to the world of acting. "[She is] the only phenomenon of the old fashioned glory of the movies that is left," he told reporters in New York, explaining that she was "strides ahead of other young actresses with the possible exception of Gina Lollobrigida."

One person who did not see the film however, was Kim Stanley, the actress who had played the part of Cherie on Broadway. When asked why this was, she replied, "I didn't avoid the film because I thought [Marilyn] would ruin the part, or because I was afraid she might have done it better. But frankly, it's possible she could do it better than I could—especially on close-ups. Marilyn has that wonderful child-like quality that is explosively sexy. Because she's a fine actress, Hollywood couldn't have made a better choice for the part."

While the play's leading lady might have been reluctant about the film, its writer William Inge was more than happy to take a look. Joshua Logan and screenwriter George Axelrod were both apprehensive about what Inge would make of the movie, considering a lot of his work had been cut out. However, a phone call from his agent, Audrey Wood, put all nerves to rest. Wood greatly enjoyed the film, and a follow-up telegram from Inge confirmed how well Logan and Axelrod had done. Logan admitted that it wasn't quite the film Inge would have hoped for, but given the time restraints and deadlines, he felt they'd all done a fine job.

Perhaps the saddest part of the *Bus Stop* legacy is that while Don Murray was nominated for an Academy Award for his part as Bo, Marilyn was completely overlooked. In her entire career—performing in a variety of comedic, musical, and dramatic roles—not once was the actress ever nominated. For someone who fought so hard to gain success in cinema, it is a tragedy that she was forever ignored. Perhaps if she had been nominated even once, her legacy would have the critical support it merits.

CHAPTER EIGHT

The Woman Who Impacted the World

IN 1952, MARILYN HAD complained bitterly when her nude calendar photo suddenly began appearing on trinkets such as ashtrays and glassware. At the time, she was quoted as saying, "I don't know exactly what rights I have, but it seems to me I should have some say in the way my picture is used." By 1954 onward, however, Marilyn's appeal had taken on an entirely new form. Now instead of just a picture on a plate or cup, her image became a way of introducing discussion, keeping delegates' attention in meetings, enabling fans to dress like their idol, and even more.

In May 1955, Dr. Robert Williams spoke at a meeting of the American Society for Clinical Investigation. His talk was to show how statistical graphs and charts could be too complicated to understand. Projecting a giant photo of Marilyn in her famous nude calendar pose, Dr. Williams used a beam of light to follow the curves of her body in the picture. "Notice the kind of curves that are quickly understood and appreciated," he said, while the room burst into applause. "Do I make my point?" he asked.

At the Grantham and District Young Farmer's Club meeting in the United Kingdom, one member asked what kind of woman would make a perfect wife. "She should be a cross between an African farmer's wife and Marilyn Monroe!" was the reply. This wasn't the only time Marilyn was mentioned by British agriculturalists. In 1956, a meeting was held by the National Farmers Union, at which the discussion was how to boost sales of beef. County councilor Mr. J. W. Irvine-Fortescue told delegates, "The thing that always takes the trick nowadays is sex. Let us 'fee' Marilyn Monroe to advertise farm products on television, saying that British beef is best." Many delegates agreed, but the idea was ultimately scrapped when another member of the council decided he'd prefer his steaks to be advertised by British bombshell Diana Dors.

In Washington, plans for a Marilyn Monroe supersonic fighter plane were revealed, much to the amusement of newspapers around the United States. To the disappointment of fans, however, the aircraft did not have Marilyn's famous features painted on the side; instead, it sported an hourglass shape. This design gave it a smaller middle, which was said to reduce drag on the aircraft by 15 to 25 percent. Then in 1956, the US Navy announced that the crew of the atomic submarine *Nautilus* had hung a poster of Marilyn on the inside to boost morale.

The British North Western Gas Board saw an ingenious way of using Marilyn's image to promote its annual report. Wanting to be sure that readers would actually look at the journal, a photograph of a swimsuit-clad Marilyn was sent out with each of the twenty thousand issues. "Figures are dreary if presented in the ordinary way of an annual report and accounts," said a spokesperson. "But they are not half as dreary if presented in conjunction with another kind of figure—the kind belonging to Marilyn Monroe."

Even schoolboys saw Marilyn as an opportunity to make money and gain street cred. In Los Angeles during 1953, a nine-year-old boy started a business whereby he sold the actress's phone number to school friends for five cents. He made quite a lot of money, until Marilyn married Joe DiMaggio and his business went bust. His mother laughingly told reporters that it was she who had provided the much-sought-after phone number, but it was actually the general line for the Beverly Hills Hotel.

Marilyn's influence reached far and wide. In Great Britain, her image was used to illustrate the point of many talks and discussions, including one given to the Luton and District Industrial Safety Association. Talking about eye protection, the speaker lightheartedly added, "With Jane Russell and Marilyn Monroe to be seen, it is up to you to protect your eyesight!" If the rest of his speech failed to get the attention of the audience, the mention of Marilyn most certainly did.

In Portsmouth, Councilor S. H. Monard thought Marilyn's name might swing the vote in a campaign for safety at a children's playground. "I don't know whether you have fallen on concrete," he told county council staff. "If you have, it is not funny. Falling on tarmac or bitumen compared with falling on concrete is really like a caress from Marilyn Monroe." While his comment might have excited his colleagues, he did not win his case and the playground was installed with concrete instead.

For those who could not act but still wanted to be like the star, there were classes to help them fulfill the ambition. American choreographer Arthur Murray created a dance called the Marilyn Monroe

Mamba, while several British teachers offered lessons in the art of perfecting the Monroe walk. An article about moving with grace singled her out as a perfect example. "Marilyn Monroe is a good walker," said teacher Liljan Espenak. "She has perfect coordination." Reporter Ed Weisman commented that this was great news, "if only that a woman has something nice to say about Marilyn."

In 1957, designer Christian Dior released an uplift panty girdle, which reviewers quickly dubbed the perfect item to give women a Marilyn Monroe walk. New York reporter Olga Curtis was keen to try it for herself, so spent a day wandering around the city in the item. While it was comfortable, she ended the experiment declaring that she still didn't look anything like Marilyn. "But what can you do?" she wrote. "The Marilyn Monroe walk can be had only if you've got the Monroe-type of natural resources to start with."

For those able to perfect the Monroe look and walk, there were look-alike competitions to enter. It would be fair to say that most young women wanted to win one, including a seventeen-year-old skater involved in an ice show in Weymouth, Dorset. When she heard that they were having a Marilyn look-alike competition on the promenade, Penny Wilson pulled off her skates, changed into a bikini, and then ran down to the seafront. She won the contest and then returned in time to complete the second half of the skating show.

In Steger, Illinois, a little girl named Cheryl Ooms dressed up as her idol and won first prize in the age-seven-to-twelve category of the local fete. Meanwhile, in Atlanta, Georgia, twenty-year-old Joan Ferchaud entered and won a Marilyn look-alike competition. Her prize was the opportunity to act in a local play and have her photograph in the newspaper. That was fun but nothing compared to the prize Pauline Spanos won when entering a tribute contest in Lowell, Massachusetts, in 1959. The lucky woman was flown to New York, where she stayed at the famed Plaza hotel, then attended the premiere of *Some Like It Hot* before appearing on the Jack Paar television show.

It wasn't just young women who won prizes. In Lovington, New Mexico, a hen called Marilyn Monroe tied for third place in a competition to see how many eggs could be laid in the space of a month. "Marilyn" laid twenty-one in total, but was beaten by winner Mary Jane, who won a sack of Purina mash for her efforts. "Mary Jane Beats Marilyn Monroe in Egg Contest" screamed the *Lovington Leader* newspaper.

At Queen's University in Belfast, students had a discussion about the charms of Marilyn versus those of cookbook author Mrs. Beeton. The actress—described as "the ultimate triumph of alliteration"—won the debate, though some university lecturers complained about the subject, claiming that there was a great deal of "ill-mannered and boorish behavior from certain sections of the audience." The subject was classed by some as "flippant and infantile," though the students themselves seemed to thoroughly enjoy it.

Marilyn even found herself discussed in the House of Lords, during a debate on the effect that television could have on the British film industry. One Lord admitted that he knew nothing about techniques such as 3-D or Cinemascope, but "then there are other phenomena, such as Marilyn Monroe, which is much easier for most of Your Lordships to understand." Chuckles were heard echoing around the House.

Not every club, organization, or distributor was pleased to be associated with Marilyn, however. In August 1954, the Italian magazine *Epoca* arrived on the shores of Malta. Government officials checked the issues to make sure there was nothing salacious inside and then proceeded to clip out photos of Marilyn, before taking them to be burned. When asked why they had done it, the censors replied, "They're indecent."

In November of the same year, many scenes from *Gentlemen Prefer Blondes* were cut by censors in New Delhi. The reason for this, they announced, was because of the sight of Marilyn and Jane Russell's thighs. The "Diamonds Are a Girl's Best Friend" number did not fare well, and instead of just a trim, the authorities cut the entire sequence.

Just as the New Delhi censor had finished trimming *Gentlemen Prefer Blondes*, another problem arose, this time in Vienna. A magazine editor there made the mistake of publishing a nude photograph of Marilyn and found himself hauled into court, charged with "arousing temptation to lasciviousness." The poor man was eventually found not guilty when the judge told the court that "it cannot be assumed that the photograph would cause such temptation."

A similar story appeared when the US Post Office banned the Star of Fire Gem Company from selling drink coasters featuring the famous nude calendar photo. Claiming that the items were indecent, the issue was taken to court and Judge William M. Byrne took the side of company boss Eddie LeBaron. According to Byrne, the pictures were not obscene and could be sent after all.

In January 1956, Trinidad film censors banned posters of the subway-grate photo, as they felt them to be "unseemly." Local distributors responded by sticking the posters up anyway, but with the underwear section blacked out. Censors demanded they be taken down immediately, and when asked why, they said that the blacking out of the panties made the posters even "more unseemly." Another controversy happened when it was reported that some Japanese women had stopped wearing underwear after hearing that Marilyn did the same. The Japanese underwear industry worried that their companies would be shut down if the women continued following Marilyn's supposed example, though it turned out to be just a phase.

But for every man, woman, or business that thought negatively about Marilyn's influence, there were countless others that remained inspired and delighted by her. During the mid-1950s, she was everywhere, as witnessed by one spectator walking through a Wiltshire park. As the man approached two boys on their way to school, he overheard one tell the other that his friend had been asked in English class to write down two words that were frequently said in his home. "And what did he put?" asked one boy. "He wrote Marilyn Monroe," said the other.

IN LONDON, LAURENCE OLIVIER was busying himself with preparations for Marilyn's arrival. Just as the adaptation of *Bus Stop* had caused headaches for screenwriter George Axelrod and director Joshua Logan, now the script of *The Sleeping Prince* was keeping Olivier up at night. Having acted in the stage production himself, the actor knew that the play was two hours without intermission. While writing the film script, he complained that the story had gained a mind of its own, therefore making the screenplay even longer than the play.

After chopping it down as far as he could, Olivier managed to get the script to two hours ten minutes, but even that was over the standard film time. In something of a panic, he telephoned Warner Bros. mogul Jack Warner to discuss the problem and was somewhat relieved when the executive said the length would be fine. Unaware yet that

Marilyn hated his edits, Joshua Logan recommended that Olivier not worry about the length of the script, and instead delete any unwanted footage at the end of filming.

Having sorted that out, Olivier turned to the subject of Marilyn herself. While he had greatly enjoyed being with the actress in Manhattan, he realized that spending a few days with her off set would be nothing like spending four months on. On June 8, the actor/director went to bed wondering if he should write to Joshua Logan for more advice. Quite astonishingly, he woke up the next morning to a letter from Logan himself, offering help on how to handle working with Marilyn.

The director explained the kinds of techniques he had used to get the best performance from the actress, as well as how to calm her fears and anxieties. Probably thinking about the evening he shouted at her, Logan recommended that Olivier not go in that direction. When the actor later replied, he said that he'd never imagined that anyone would ever yell at Marilyn, though he understood how hard it was to achieve the patience required on set—especially when acting as well as directing. He promised that he would take a break if ever he felt stressed.

Olivier read the letter over and over again, underlining passages and sentences he thought would be particularly useful. Although Logan warned him not to allow Paula Strasberg on the set, Olivier was surprisingly thrilled to hear that she would be accompanying Marilyn to England. He had recently worried that she would have no friends in the country and had actually enlisted the help of his friend Bunny Bruce to become a companion, should the need arise. He also took great comfort in the fact that Logan described Marilyn as being very passionate while working. He could cope with almost anything, he decided, except a lack of enthusiasm.

When Olivier wrote back to Logan on June 9, he did so with great animation. Over the course of six pages, he went over many of the details that the director had shared, and reassured him that everything had been digested. He even went so far as to describe the letter as being a bible not just for him, but for his colleagues too. Time would tell, however, just how much—or little—of Logan's advice he was actually willing to take.

On June 11, 1956, Arthur Miller received his divorce in Nevada and returned to New York. Now that he was free, the playwright discussed a possible marriage with Marilyn, and the two spent time with his parents. There is some discrepancy as to when the family was formally introduced, but they had certainly seen Marilyn during a performance of Miller's plays. Whether they ever thought of her becoming part of their family is questionable, so when Arthur did reveal that they were to be engaged, his parents were intrigued but cautious.

Despite initial worries, the actress won them over quickly and they both seemed to like her; in fact, his father—Isidore Miller—was particularly fond of and remained close to Marilyn for the remainder of her life. Marilyn even trusted him enough to read her poetry, and while it wasn't all to his taste, Isidore sensed a great need for his approval. "When Arthur's parents told me, 'Darling, at last you have a father and a mother,' this was the most wonderful moment of my life—next to marrying their son," Marilyn said.

DURING LOCATION SHOOTING FOR *Bus Stop*, Marilyn had been invited to "a political whing-ding and hamburger fry," hosted by the Speaker and Democratic members of the Arizona House of

Representatives. Despite a plea from her press agent that her presence there would be good for business, Marilyn refused the invitation, and admitted that she had no interest in becoming embroiled in politics. She would soon come to regret saying that, however, when Arthur Miller dragged her into his own political affairs in the weeks and months ahead.

June 21 came and Miller made a much-publicized court appearance. It was the time of the McCarthy witch hunt, and the House Un-American Activities Committee had decided that Miller was worth investigating due to his attendance at a so-called communist meeting in the 1940s. During the appearance, the playwright asked for the return of his passport and the court demanded to know why he needed such a document. Miller replied that he would soon be going to London with the woman who was to become his wife. When questioned as to who that might be, the playwright confirmed it was Marilyn Monroe.

A huge mass of reporters was waiting for Miller outside the courtroom, and once again he announced that Marilyn was to become his wife. This set off a firestorm of attention, and within minutes she was besieged by reporters in the foyer of her Sutton Place apartment building. During the awkward, impromptu press conference that followed, Marilyn tried her best to answer the reporters' questions, but it was difficult since the couple had merely spoken about an engagement in the past. They had not—as far as she was concerned—actually agreed on timing of a wedding. In fact, when discussing the subject of marriage, Miller had previously wondered if they should do it on his birthday, which was four months away. Out of everything that had happened in the past two years, the unexpected announcement of the Miller marriage was the first time Marilyn had felt utterly out of control. It was to be a feeling she would repeat in the weeks ahead.

When the House Un-American Activities Committee stated that the playwright would probably face contempt of Congress for not naming names, some of Marilyn's friends and colleagues worried that she would be dragged into the fray. Of course, Fox president Spyros Skouras was first in the queue and begged Miller to cooperate. He refused, and Marilyn was exceptionally proud of his decision. When the studio asked her to step away from the drama for fear of black-listing, she rebelled and stated that they had no right to tell her what to do. Marilyn fully intended to stand by her fiancé, and there was nothing anyone could say to stop her.

Fox executives weren't the only ones worried. By now, the presence of Arthur Miller was presenting tension for the Strasbergs too. During a meeting between Marilyn, Miller, and themselves, the topic of blacklisting came up once again. After they tried to give some advice on the subject, Arthur made it clear that he did not appreciate their involvement in his affairs. Paula had good reason to be concerned, since blacklisting had happened to her during her early years in Hollywood. However, Arthur immediately became suspicious of the couple's intentions.

Marilyn and Miller appeared outside Sutton Place on June 22, 1956, and had numerous photos taken by the reporters camped on the sidewalk. Marilyn assured everyone that it was "the happiest day of my life," while Miller said he was determined to claim his passport. "I'm sure everything will work out all right," he said, "but even if I don't receive a passport we'll be married as planned." Shortly thereafter, they left Manhattan with Miller's mother and headed to his home in Roxbury, Connecticut.

On June 29, 1956, Marilyn and Arthur applied for a marriage license and were then driven back to his Connecticut home by a cousin, Morton Miller. Behind them were a number of reporters, all desperately trying to catch an exclusive. Unfortunately for *Paris Match* correspondent Mara Scherbatoff and photographer Ira Slade, the car chase ended in unexpected tragedy. As the cars sped down narrow, winding lanes, Scherbatoff's vehicle missed a corner and smashed straight into a tree. The journalist was thrown into the windshield.

The car was totally wrecked and debris was sprawled all over the road. Hearing the commotion, the Millers' car ground to a halt and everyone—including Marilyn—went running back to see if they could help. Mara was laid on the grass and assistance was given to the other injured party. Miller was seen running through the woods for help, while a visibly shaken Marilyn was taken to the house. Reporters heard her shouting, "There's been a terrible accident!" as she entered the home, and shortly afterward an ambulance was dispatched to the scene. Unfortunately, while Ira Slade could be treated for his injuries, nothing could be done to help Scherbatoff, and she passed away.

Almost directly after the accident, Marilyn and Arthur Miller held a scheduled press conference and were photographed with his parents. Everyone was on edge after recent events, and Marilyn and Milton Greene were seen furiously whispering to each other shortly before the questions began. When it was indicated that there should be some kind of statement regarding the accident, nobody was able to decide exactly how it should happen. "Somebody should question you," Marilyn told Miller, and a journalist stepped in to tell the couple how they would normally work under the circumstances. "Who is going to question him?" demanded Marilyn, and when given the answer, she snapped, "Okay, fine!"

"Well, we just had a terrible accident on this road," started Miller, "as a result of the mobs that have been coming by here. I knew this was going to happen; at least I suspected it was because these roads were made for horse carts and not for automobiles." He continued by saying that the whole reason for requesting a press conference was so that the tragedy that had just played out could have been avoided. Marilyn looked terribly pale and nervous, but despite the horrendous events she had just witnessed, managed to keep herself together.

Perhaps realizing that Marilyn was not in a position to go into great depth during the interview, the reporters aimed most of the questions at Miller. Some were connected to his trial, while other journalists were more obsessed with finding out exactly when the marriage would take place. "You saw what happened today," Miller replied. "If we make an announcement now, it might get worse."

On hearing that there probably wouldn't be a wedding anytime soon, the press returned to their New York offices. This gave the couple an opportunity to sneak off to White Plains to be married in a small, intimate ceremony. The only guests in attendance were Miller's cousin and his wife, and Milton Greene. The bride wore a pink sweater and simple black skirt, while the groom dressed in a blue linen suit, white open shirt, and no tie.

Afterward, a spokesperson made the announcement of the marriage to the press, though he was met by a barrage of frustrated questions. "It's as much a surprise to us as to anyone else," he assured them. "They certainly pulled a neat one." Not being able to get a statement from the couple, some journalists tracked down the police chief in White Plains to see what kind of security had been put in place during the ceremony. He assured them that "there was no question of controlling onlookers because it was all done so quickly." When that wasn't quite exciting enough, reporters contacted Miller's mother, who had only a few words to add. "I guess they suddenly decided to go through with it without telling me," she said.

At that point, the media seemed to give up on gaining any exclusives and went back to reporting the death of Mara Scherbatoff. The story ultimately made headlines around the world, and Miller was summoned to give evidence at the hearing. This was done in the form of a written testimony, and the couple was found to be completely innocent of any blame for the reporter's death. Instead, it was decided that the driver of the car was solely responsible. Still, Marilyn believed that the death was a terrible omen, and never forgot the trauma of what she had seen.

Several days after the civil ceremony, another wedding was performed—this time Jewish in nature and with many friends and family in attendance. The bride—who had recently converted to Judaism—looked happy and beautiful in a tight gown with a small veil, while the usually gloomy-looking groom appeared contented in his surroundings. Amy Greene later said that Marilyn had cold feet before the wedding and wondered if she should go through with it at all. However, any sign of those nerves was long forgotten by the time photographs were taken, and she seemed completely at ease on the arm of her new husband.

Joshua Logan and his wife, Nedda, put a lot of thought into a wedding present that would be totally unique. It consisted of Marilyn's favorite Cecil Beaton picture in a three-paneled silver Cartier frame, with the signed print in the middle and a handwritten description of Marilyn by Beaton himself on either side. Marilyn absolutely adored the gift and kept it with her for the rest of her life, often showing it off to friends who visited her Manhattan apartment.

On May 1, 1969, nearly seven years after her death, the Museum of the City of New York put on an exhibition of Beaton's work. In March of the same year, Nedda Logan wrote to Lee Strasberg—by that time caretaker of the Monroe estate—to ask if the gift could be used in the exhibition. Lee Strasberg wrote back nearly a week later to explain that Marilyn's estate had still not been settled and the work remained in a warehouse. It was eventually released some thirty years later, and sold at Christie's auction house for $145,500.

While the Logans were clearly ecstatic to see Marilyn and Arthur married, not everyone was overjoyed. Amy and Milton Greene were skeptical about whether it was the right decision for their friend and remained uncertain about their feelings for Arthur Miller. This was made even more apparent when the playwright voiced concern that Marilyn's career was being mismanaged. While making *Bus Stop*, letters had gone back and forth between the couple, which discussed several arguments the actress had had with her business partner. Miller—perhaps unconsciously at first—wanted to help with that side of Marilyn's life, and as a result, cracks started to appear in the working relationship between her and Milton Greene.

Because of what Miller regarded as interference in his affairs, he did not care much for Lee and Paula Strasberg either. Susan Strasberg believed that they actually had much in common, but their problems were based on a power struggle over Marilyn's affections. However,

Paula seemed quite tolerant, at least in the beginning. While speaking to reporter Vernon Scott, the drama coach described how Marilyn became "awakened intellectually when she married Arthur," before going on to say that Marilyn's initial move to New York had completely changed her life. "Instead of the Hollywood crowd and press agents, she is in the company of writers, critics, and creative people," she said.

CHAPTER NINE

The Power Struggle

MARILYN AND ARTHUR MILLER arrived in London on July 14, 1956. They were met by hundreds of photographers, reporters, and fans at the plane itself, and by Laurence Olivier and Vivien Leigh inside the gate. The next day a press conference was held at the Savoy Hotel, where Marilyn was asked about the kinds of roles she would like to play in the future. "I would like to do *Pygmalion*," she said. "As far as Shakespeare is concerned, I would like very much the part of Lady Macbeth, but at present that is just a dream."

After a few days of press conferences, it was time to start work. Unfortunately, even at this early stage, it was clear that the making of *The Sleeping Prince* was not going to be smooth sailing. First of all, Marilyn disliked rehearsals intensely, whereas Olivier seemed to relish them. Then while introducing her to the rest of the cast and crew, the actor appeared to talk about Marilyn as though she knew nothing about acting at all—or certainly not the way they all knew it to be done. This was not a positive first impression, and the actress became guarded from the outset.

Circumstances were made no better when Olivier's way of

directing came across as patronizing and abrupt. After the sympathetic and calming way Joshua Logan had worked with her on *Bus Stop*, this was a shock to Marilyn, especially since *The Sleeping Prince* had actually been bought for her own film company. Marilyn's reaction was to rebel against his orders, and she was often late on set. In return, Olivier decided she was awkward and unprofessional, and the relationship got off to a dismal start.

Another—much less surprising—area of discord was the fact that Laurence Olivier had absolutely no interest in the Method. In fact, it would be fair to say that a dislike of the practice was widespread among many British actors during the mid-1950s. "To espouse the Method in London," wrote theater director and playwright Charles Marowitz, "is to preach paganism in the heart of Vatican City. People will not stand for it." He concluded that the Method was "the mid-twentieth century's favorite running gag, and as long as its emblem is a torn T-shirt and an actor picking the fuzz out of his navel, it will remain that way." The problem was made worse when opportunistic, London-based "teachers" of the Method began advertising their services purely because they had read Stanislavski's books *An Actor Prepares* and *Building a Character*. This was controversial since they had never actually practiced the technique in their lives but thought themselves qualified to take students' money purely through reading about it.

Olivier was never going to support or appreciate Marilyn's acting technique, but one person who did was Dame Sybil Thorndike, who had been hired to play the eccentric mother-in-law. She was a magnificent and highly successful actress who turned seventy-four years old during the making of *The Sleeping Prince*. Despite being rather a dominating figure, she showed great patience with Marilyn and supported her on many occasions. "She is quite enchanting," Thorndike said in September 1956. "There is something absolutely delightful about her. She is not at all actressy."

Marilyn adored Thorndike, and even though she rarely spoke to anyone on set, she found it easy to engage with the matriarchal figure. One day the thirty-year-old actress asked her older colleague just how she had so much energy. Thorndike said it came through being happy, in love, and working, while at the same time making sure she was never separated from her husband.

Once when Olivier was complaining about what he classed as Marilyn's poor behavior, Thorndike interrupted, telling the actor that Marilyn was the only member of the cast who knew how to act in front of a camera. Marilyn found out about the intervention and was immensely grateful; she couldn't quite believe that someone as respected as Thorndike had spoken up for her in such a manner. Actually, Thorndike was no stranger to the differences in acting techniques, and had actually talked about it two years before she began work on *The Sleeping Prince*:

Apart from closing theatres and causing an overcrowding of the acting profession, the advance of mechanized entertainment has considerably changed the style of acting. The influence of the screen has tended to make it more naturalistic. The heroic flourish associated with Irving, Tree, and Bernhardt finds no place in the theatre of today. It belongs to another age. On the other hand, there is a higher degree of sincerity. Neither actors nor audience are content with stage tricks. They both prefer them to be hidden and the resulting realism gives the impression that actors live their parts.

Out of everyone on the set of *The Sleeping Prince*, it was the eldest woman who seemed to understand Marilyn the best. While this astonished the actress herself, it really shouldn't have. Dame Sybil Thorndike was always extremely interested in young people, and her grandchildren educated her on the kinds of plays currently in fashion. Within her work, she was always first to help any actor who needed guidance. Actor Henry Kendall later recalled that everything he knew about acting had come from working with Dame Sybil in the theater. As a result of her open mind and modern ways, Thorndike was much more qualified handling Marilyn than Laurence Olivier could ever hope to be.

In fairness to him, Olivier was not the only person who did not appreciate Marilyn as a fully formed actress. Just days after her arrival in London, Mr. G. R. H. Nugent, joint parliamentary secretary to the Ministry of Agriculture, Fisheries, and Food, gave a talk to delegates at the National Whaling Commission in London. He announced in the most sexist way imaginable that Marilyn Monroe had arrived: "She has obviously come to England to dispute the saying of our great literary man, Dr. Johnson. He adjured us never to believe in round figures. One has only to take one look at her to see the truth that round figures do exist. Even without the assistance of a by-product of your industry, which has helped ladies' figures." The delegates cheered and laughed at the remarks, which were even translated for those who did not speak English.

At least one of *The Sleeping Prince* cast members was happy to make fun of the star. Intrigued by the way Marilyn walked, actor Richard Wattis decided to do an impression of her at Pinewood Studios. "I tried to walk like her down the corridor one day," he told a reporter from the *Aberdeen Evening Express*, "but the only attention I attracted was from two policemen—who were not impressed."

In a strange country and surrounded by people who seemed to be largely unfriendly, Marilyn decided to spend all her off time in the company of Arthur, Paula, and Milton. She then insisted on eating her lunch in the dressing room, which caused further friction between herself and Olivier. Staff at the Pinewood Studios restaurant stepped in to promise a menu of anything she wanted, but Marilyn still refused and instead a stove was installed in her suite of rooms and a private chef called in.

When publicist Alan Arnold asked studio staff what they thought of Marilyn, he was told she was "a bit stuck-up, but nevertheless sweet and charming." He also claimed—or exaggerated—that no matter how hard they tried, nobody could remember a single word she had said, and this aloofness caused a great deal of tension. Actress Vera Day remembered overhearing some of the studio girls being catty about Marilyn's appearance and claiming that they too could look like her if they wanted. "I'm telling you, they couldn't," said Day. "They could not." Even Marilyn's British bodyguard publicly announced that he thought Mr. and Mrs. Miller were boring, and that when they asked if he would go back to the States with them, he immediately said no. "It was dull working for them," he said.

But Marilyn's admirers still loved her. When she gave the press conference at the Savoy Hotel, it was noted that most of the five hundred fans outside were teenage girls and women. Even singer Alma Cogan was keen to express her admiration for the star. When asked who she might like to be if not herself, she responded, "Marilyn Monroe! I am not kidding. I think she is a great actress and she seems to have a wonderful sense of humor."

Irish dramatist Seán O'Casey was excited to learn that out of everyone in England, the two people Marilyn most wanted to visit were Dame Edith Sitwell and himself. "I would love to see her," he told *The Stage* newspaper, "and I would like to meet her husband, Arthur Miller, one of the greatest American playwrights." Laurence Olivier actually invited the author to visit with him and Marilyn in London, but the Devon-based O'Casey declined the offer. He did, however, come to regret the decision, especially on hearing the news of the actress's death some years later.

While in the end Marilyn was unable to meet O'Casey, she did follow through with her plans to visit Dame Edith Sitwell, whom she had previously met in 1953. When asked about the meeting in 1959, Sitwell explained that she had been visited by both Marilyn and Arthur Miller. Unfortunately, they could not talk for long as there were many people milling around outside and interfering with the meeting. Sitwell was concerned that the hangers-on might make up stories about the visit after the event, so it was cut short and postponed until their return to New York.

Other luminaries were able to meet Marilyn at a party given by Terence Rattigan. These included Sir John Gielgud, Anthony Quayle, Sir Terence and Lady Nugent, Sir Hartley and Lady Shawcross, Dame Edith Evans, Douglas Fairbanks Jr., and the Duke and Duchess of Buccleuch. According to writer Radie Harris, the excitement from those wishing to speak with Marilyn was incredible.

THE HARD AND PAINFUL work done on the set of *The Sleeping Prince* meant that Marilyn had little time for anything else, but she was able to make occasional day trips into London and Brighton. Her quest for culture was always apparent, and she spent hours studying art in the National Gallery or buying books of poetry and literature from Foyles, London's premiere bookstore. There were also many trips to the theater, including one with her husband to see *The Caucasian Chalk Circle* by Brecht. True to form, afterward the press mocked Marilyn by saying that she could not understand the German language in the play and had to turn to her husband for guidance. Not so, said Arthur Miller. "The truth is she was very interested and I don't speak German and she'd been talking to a lot of people about Brecht in New York and knew what it was about."

OFFERS OF WORK BEGAN flooding in months before Marilyn even arrived in England, and included stints such as standing for election as Lord Rector of Glasgow University, visiting a clothes man-ufacturer in Scotland, and opening a nightclub in the seaside town of Skegness. Any invitations were politely but firmly turned down.

However, while it was easy to say no to the nonacting jobs, it was far harder to say no to the BBC, particularly as they offered Marilyn what could have been a thrilling role. *Lysistrata* by Aristophanes was an ancient comedy play that revolved around an intelligent woman's efforts to stop a war by persuading women to withhold sex. The idea being that if the men were denied their most primitive desires, they would eventually be forced to negotiate peace. Before that happens, however, a battle of the sexes prevails.

The story had interested Marilyn for some time, and she had actually been invited to play the role on US television earlier in the year, but nothing came of it. Now, in summer 1956, the BBC's Third Programme radio service obtained the rights to a translation by Dudley Fitts and was anxious for Marilyn to take on the title role. The thought of playing such a part must have excited Marilyn greatly, but she ultimately turned it down. "I am familiar with *Lysistrata*," she explained, "and I think it has a wonderful title role. I would certainly like to play it someday, but my commitments in *The Sleeping Prince* make it impossible to consider at the moment."

It wasn't the first time Marilyn had turned down a part she was fascinated by; she had done so at least twice in 1955. In August of that year, executive producer Albert McCleery offered her the prized role of Grushenka in NBC's television adaptation of *The Brothers Karamazov*, but she did not sign on to the project. Then, after hearing that she had wanted to play Adelaide in the film version of *Guys and Dolls*, an invitation was extended by actress Vivian Blaine to have Marilyn do a guest appearance—or longer if required—in a Las Vegas stage version. This too came to nothing, likely because at that time the contractual issues with Fox were still being fought.

By summer 1956, there were no such worries, and yet sadly she also turned down the opportunity of starring in the Paul Osborn play *Maiden Voyage*. Sent to her by Miller's friend Kermit Bloomgarden, the piece was due to be produced for Broadway in the winter of 1956. Marilyn was thrilled to be asked, but Miller explained to his friend that she would be too exhausted to do it. Undeterred, the man sent her a copy of the play, which was a satirical story based on Greek mythology and inspired by the poem *The Odyssey* by Homer. Bloomgarden explained that he wanted the actress to play Athena after she had greatly impressed him over dinner one evening. The project didn't go ahead, but Marilyn still read the play and made various notes inside. Interestingly, while Bloomgarden wanted her for Athena, Marilyn's jottings seem to suggest that she preferred the role of Hera, wife of Zeus.

It remains a baffling question: why Marilyn was so vocal about doing particular kinds of roles, and yet when presented to her, she was loath to actually do them. Nerves certainly played a part, and so too did a lack of confidence—the fear that once again she would be laughed at or mocked by the media, other actors, or both. Elsa Maxwell described the situation well in an article she wrote during the summer of 1956. "[Marilyn] had the courage to challenge the big movie moguls. She has the ambition to want to know and work with fine artists. But she's also like the scared young thing who stays on and on in the powder-room to postpone everything she has worked for and looked forward to."

WORK CONTINUED ON *THE SLEEPING PRINCE,* but tensions between Marilyn and Olivier grew worse as time went on. By the middle of production, she confided in cinematographer Jack Cardiff that she was unsure if the actor was really the genius she once thought he was. In Cardiff she found a firm friend, and he photographed her not only on set, but in her Surrey home too. So comfortable was she in his presence that Marilyn shared her artwork with him. "It was remarkable," he said. "It revealed all her innate restlessness. I felt a great sympathy for her. I wanted to protect her from so much human weakness. Love should protect her but it doesn't seem to be quite enough."

There were various anxieties to contend with on set. Despite Logan's advice to keep Paula Strasberg away, Olivier had allowed her presence and came to deeply regret it. Not only did Marilyn look to her for advice far more than to her director, but the coach would often whisk the actress away to discuss script problems and teach hand exercises between takes. When publicist Alan Arnold asked if the exercises had been learned from Olivier, Strasberg snapped, "Definitely not. We have our own set."

Strasberg always insisted she was only there as Marilyn's friend, though she became something of a laughingstock during the filming of the coronation scene when overheard telling the actress to think about Frank Sinatra and Coca-Cola as her motivation. Susan Strasberg later wrote that her mother unfairly shouldered the blame for much of Marilyn's behavior, even though she was the one desperately trying to get her on set—prepared and on time. To try to calm matters, Lee Strasberg flew to London for a few weeks but became so anxious with all the drama that he spent much of his time trawling museums and longing to go home.

Milton Greene had accompanied the Millers to London, and for the most part it appeared that he and Marilyn were still working happily together. One day he brought an expensive Jaguar car on set, and Alan Arnold had an idea to take publicity photos of Marilyn, the car, and some soldiers. Associate director Anthony Bushell refused to allow her to do the shoot, however, claiming that the actress needed to rest. He bizarrely suggested that Laurence Olivier pose instead, but at that point Milton and Arnold insisted that it looked like rain and called the whole shoot off.

Marilyn and Milton might have still been on speaking terms, but Arthur's distrust of him was growing ever more apparent. He suspected that the MMP vice president was buying antiques with the company's money, and drew Marilyn into the argument by telling her all about his theories. Tension between Milton and Arthur was the last worry she needed, and the situation became even more heated when she read an entry from Miller's journal, berating her behavior on set. She was furious that Miller appeared to be on Olivier's side and could not believe he had left the book for her to find. Paula stood on the sidelines, wondering why Miller was becoming involved in Marilyn's professional life in the first place.

Alan Arnold was asked by Olivier to release three photographs from the set, to stop reporters trying to break into the studio. He did as he was asked, and when one of the photos appeared in a newspaper the next day, he innocently showed it to Marilyn. She was furious. "What a terrible picture!" she cried. "Who put that out?" The shocked man mumbled something about thinking she already knew and then left as soon as he could.

Marilyn took her complaint about the photos straight to Olivier. However, instead of the director making sure that nothing would be released in the future without her authority, Alan Arnold was reprimanded and told never to show the actress any pictures again. This kind of secretive behavior was totally unacceptable, but sadly nobody but Marilyn seemed to think it warranted any further discussion.

Eventually, a major disagreement came when Olivier made the catastrophic mistake of telling Marilyn to be sexy. She objected bitterly to such a direction and walked off set, much to the director's chagrin. If he had done more research, however, he would have discovered that such a request would always cause friction. Less than a year before the England trip, Marilyn spoke openly to reporter Logan Gourlay: "When a director says, 'Marilyn, give us some of that old Monroe sex appeal in this scene,' I just don't know what to do. I really don't." She then added that the fuss surrounding her sexy look was frankly embarrassing, and that she was fed up with being referred to as an international sex symbol. "I just want to be called an actress," she said.

There wasn't a lot to be happy about, but a high point of the England trip came when Marilyn was able to meet Queen Elizabeth II. She had made no secret about wanting to visit the queen, and publicist Alan Arnold found the request on his to-do list on a frequent basis. Olivier had found out about the desired invitation and told him to strike it off, but Marilyn won in the end and was presented not only to Queen Elizabeth, but her husband and sister too. Photos were beamed all over the world and the actress was thrilled.

MARILYN COULD NOT WAIT to leave England and return to the States, but the trip actually proved beneficial to Arthur Miller. Banned in England because of homosexual references, his play *A View from the Bridge* was able to finally open thanks to a loophole in the censorship rules. In 1952, a membership organization called the New Watergate Theatre Club was formed, which aimed to show those plays deemed too racy for British audiences. This was done by selling tickets exclusively to club members, therefore giving the play an equivalent of an X rating in movies.

In 1956, the society chose to showcase Miller's play at the Comedy Theatre, in what *Theatre World* described as "the most interesting event for the London Theatre during the past months." Marilyn attended with her husband, dressed in a red velvet gown and towering platform shoes. Those in charge of dressing her for the evening were appalled when Marilyn asked for a red gown, and told her it would be far more fitting to wear black. Incensed, she replied that Miller's favorite color was red, therefore that's what she would wear. Inevitably, while the play received good reviews, it was Marilyn who stole the headlines.

Talking to reporter Thomas Wiseman while watching rehearsals, Miller explained that he had no worries that his work would suffer as a result of his new marriage. He also revealed that despite any disagreements on set (which he emphasized as completely normal), *The Sleeping Prince* was the best film Marilyn had ever made in her career. He also spoke quite openly about the adulation received by his wife wherever she went. Describing her as "a very warm person who loves people," Miller admitted that some of the fascination was unfortunate "and unhealthy. Like fitting people into categories. Making me in all situations behave like an intellectual, and making her behave how Marilyn Monroe is expected to behave."

Probably the most fascinating part of the interview was when Miller was asked about the life he and Marilyn would lead on their return to the United States. "We shan't live in Hollywood," he said. "We shall live in my house in Connecticut. Marilyn will only make one film in every eighteen months or so, which will take her about twelve weeks." What about the rest of the time?, asked the reporter. "She shall be my wife," Miller replied. "That's a full-time job."

IF *THE SEVEN YEAR ITCH* showed Marilyn how much she wanted to flee the position of wife and embrace an acting career, *The Sleeping Prince* sent her in the totally opposite direction. Marilyn had forgiven Miller for writing about her in his journal, and during the last few weeks of filming, he was almost constantly on set. Sometimes he would not make his presence known and instead hide behind the set until Marilyn finally looked over and saw him. "You!" she would cry and then jump into his arms. Cast members noted that the two would laugh and hug, completely oblivious to anyone who was around them.

This affection was in complete contrast to the way former husband Joe DiMaggio had behaved on movie sets. Susan Strasberg witnessed him standing in the shadows during the "Heat Wave" number on *There's No Business Like Show Business*, looking like "an Italian marble sphinx." When Marilyn tried to rush into his arms, he became completely closed off, causing her to stop dead in her tracks and give him a small peck on the cheek instead.

When Marilyn and Arthur left England on November 20, 1956, they were accompanied to the airport by Laurence Olivier and Vivien Leigh. Reporters were anxious to know if there had been any truth to the rumors of fights and drama on set, but Marilyn would not say anything against her costar. Instead, she smiled patiently and told journalists that "[Olivier] is the greatest actor I have ever worked with. [There were] no rows, just the kind of agreements and disagreements one always gets. I have no idea how the stories of rows got about."

When asked what she intended doing once back home, Marilyn honestly replied, "I have nothing lined up for me right now except being a wife. We are going home to New York, where I want to be a wife, where I will be Mrs. Arthur Miller."

AFTER RETURNING TO THE States, Marilyn was impressed by her ability to survive the London ordeal and went back to classes at the Actors Studio. Unfortunately, after deciding that Milton was too sympathetic to Laurence Olivier during *The Sleeping Prince*, their relationship had soured considerably and Marilyn wasn't sure she still wanted him in her company. The warning signs had actually been publicly revealed on November 13, 1956, when a British-based version of Marilyn Monroe Productions was registered in London. With a capital of £100 in £1 shares, newspaper reports of the formation were revealing. Whereas the announcement of the original MMP had come with a glamorous press conference and much fanfare, this time it was done quietly, with little attention at all. A statement was released to the press that disclosed that the British version of the company was designed to make movies in England that may or may not star Marilyn in the main role. "She will be president," the release said, "and Mr. Milton Greene who is Vice President of Marilyn Monroe Productions Inc. the American company, will also serve in the British company, but in what capacity we do not yet know."

By 1957, Arthur Miller's feelings toward the Greenes were still as negative as ever, and Marilyn found herself in the middle of their squabbles. The relationship had crumbled irretrievably, and she accused Milton of mismanaging her company, making secret business commitments, and not informing her about the contents of particular contracts. After much bickering, she eventually fired Milton from the organization.

The shocked photographer retaliated by releasing a statement that said he had given up his photography career for the star and although he was going to hire lawyers, he did not know exactly what the problem was in their relationship. "He knows perfectly well," Marilyn retorted. She then fired lawyer Irving Stein as well, and he threatened to sue for failure to pay his salary.

Before *The Sleeping Prince* was released, the title was changed to *The Prince and the Showgirl*. Milton's proposed position of executive producer came under fire when Marilyn's representatives told Laurence Olivier that they did not wish him to be billed this way. The actress told reporters that she had not been aware that Milton had promoted himself to this position, and accused him of having a false credit, which she would not be party to. Whether this was true is questionable. Certainly, when Olivier was working on the script, he had been advised that Milton had production ambitions. The actor told Joshua Logan that most of the work would be done by the time Milton arrived in England, but that he planned to talk about it as soon as he could.

The feud regarding the credit became an enormous, unwanted pain for Olivier. Letters went back and forth until eventually the actor demanded that they sort it out themselves and he made no further comment. When the film premiered, Greene's name did appear in the credits, though seeing it there must surely have been a bittersweet experience for him. Their troubles rumbled on for months, until finally the two former partners came to a mutual understanding. Expecting Milton to go after a huge compensation deal, Marilyn was shocked when he left with only the money he had originally invested. According to Amy Greene, both business partners cried when saying good-bye and neither fully recovered.

The Prince and the Showgirl was not a huge box-office success, but it did receive some positive reviews and Marilyn gained critical acclaim. Viewers could clearly see that despite everything, the actress was spectacular, and she went on to win a David di Donatello—the Italian equivalent of an Academy Award—for her performance. Even Laurence Olivier had to admit that Marilyn was a charming presence on-screen, despite everything they had been through.

CHAPTER TEN

The Human Being

THROUGHOUT THE MID- TO late 1950s, Marilyn continued to take her roles as an actress and a wife extremely seriously. Together with Miller, she split her time between a Manhattan apartment and a farmhouse in Connecticut. She grew flowers and tended a vegetable patch, and often told reporters how happy she was to be a caring wife to Arthur and stepmother to his children. While she was sincere in her comments, friends wondered if she was trying to prove to the world that she too could be a "normal" housewife of the 1950s. Susan Strasberg noted that the determination to be a contented wife "sounded like an ad for a woman's magazine—nice but not her."

It is true that while she did appreciate being Mrs. Arthur Miller— at least at first—at the same time Marilyn still wanted to be recognized as a successful human being in her own right. She continued to enjoy the company of interesting women, and was thrilled when Danish writer Karen Blixen asked Carson McCullers to introduce them. However, the idea of female support and empowerment remained alien to many, and chauvinism was a plague that continued to be witnessed by women in all walks of life.

In 1957, actress Elizabeth Sellars had seen enough sexism in the industry and took her complaint to *Theatre World* magazine. They printed her feelings in a profile of the star: "Miss Sellars wonders why plays and films by British writers invariably have better parts for men than women. Maugham and Coward wrote wonderful parts for actresses in the past, but in recent years she considers most British dramatists put their best writing into the men's parts."

In October 1958, a reader of *Modern Screen* wrote in to the questions page, asking, "Does Marilyn Monroe have much money of her own, or is she dependent upon her husband for support?" "Dependent upon her husband, playwright Arthur Miller" was the reply. The fact that Marilyn had worked far more than her husband during their marriage was completely irrelevant to the magazine writer. In Marilyn's day, so long as a woman was married, she would forever be dependent upon her husband, as far as society was concerned.

Marilyn suffered two miscarriages during the relationship with Miller. Her heartbreak, coupled with several failed operations to help her carry a child, led to added strain on the marriage and an increased reliance on prescription medication. Marilyn had long suffered from insomnia, and rumors of an addiction to barbiturates were ever present. Even during 1956, publicist Alan Arnold disclosed in a newspaper article that the star was seen receiving pills on the set of *The Sleeping Prince*. Unfortunately, the addiction grew only worse as the years progressed and nobody seemed able to help conquer it.

Marilyn's body became so used to the pills that at times they wouldn't work at all. During those occasions, she would telephone friends and often appeared at the Strasbergs' house in the middle of the night, groggy and in need of help. In situations like that, she would sometimes take more pills than prescribed, and despite assuring friends that she was always in control, her reliance resulted in several overdoses. Friends and family became desperate for Marilyn to come off the medication completely, but night monsters and insomnia made that an idea too impossible to comprehend.

Problems with Miller's contempt-of-Congress trial rumbled on until finally he was acquitted in summer 1958. Marilyn told reporters that she knew he would win, as she had been studying Thomas Jefferson and according to his work, the case could have no other outcome. Throughout the marriage, she tried to be a contented wife, but memories of her unhappy childhood, coupled with depression and anxiety, sometimes made it challenging. In spring 1959, Marilyn spoke to reporter David Lewin on the subject. "It is getting used to it—happiness and belonging—that is difficult. I'm not satisfied with myself—no one ever is. What I'd like . . . what I'd like is to have more freedom within myself. Freedom to be really happy. I'm still a little scared of it all."

Arthur Miller shared his view with the same journalist: "What people don't realize about Marilyn is that she is a perfectionist. . . . She is a complete realist about everything—she estimates any situation on the basis of the sternest realities. My wife is always the girl on the outside."

Marilyn completed only three more films after *The Prince and the Showgirl*: *Some Like It Hot* (1959), *Let's Make Love* (1960), and *The Misfits* (1961). In the last, Miller wrote the part of Roslyn for his wife, but the character was so close to her own personality that she found it hard to cope. "It really didn't start out that way when I was writing the screenplay," Miller claimed at the time. "But she has such a strong personality I just couldn't escape it."

When asked by reporter Erskine Johnson if she likened herself to the character of Roslyn, Marilyn gave a cryptic reply: "No one ever knows how one looks at or upon another, especially if they're close—do we?" In the same interview, she revealed that during the four-year marriage to Miller, there were times when he had forgotten her birthday and their wedding anniversary. "I couldn't resist reminding him," she said.

The band of actors cast in *The Misfits* included childhood idol Clark Gable and friends Eli Wallach and Montgomery Clift. During a break on set, Clift was asked by Johnson to talk about Marilyn's acting skills. "You know what I think about Marilyn?" Clift asked. "I think she's the most gifted actress on the American screen. Here's real proof of how I feel about her. I'm jealous when I watch what she does on the screen." Then he jokingly added, "She's so good an actor, I hate her."

While shooting scenes at Paramount Studios, director Henry Hathaway encountered Marilyn pacing up and down outside. The two walked together, and during the course of conversation, she cried and revealed the frustration of constantly "being" Marilyn Monroe. She told Hathaway that she had believed the marriage to Arthur might enable her to leave the character behind, but that hadn't worked out at all. By this time, the Miller marriage was in complete turmoil, and immediately after Marilyn made *The Misfits*, the couple separated. "Arthur taught me a lot," Marilyn said. "I was his pupil and he was a wonderful teacher. But that is not a sound enough basis for a successful marriage."

Despite previously saying he had no interest in Marilyn's business life, the playwright had been added to the board of directors of Marilyn Monroe Productions, but on November 23, 1960, he offered his resignation. Tellingly, although Marilyn was the president of the company, Miller addressed the note "Dear Sirs." He then went on to marry a photographer he'd met on the set of *The Misfits,* and the two achieved what Marilyn had been unable to—the creation of a family.

Marilyn never again made a film for Marilyn Monroe Productions, though she continued her classes at the Actors Studio. While her performance in *Anna Christie* had taken the studio by storm in 1956, fellow student Joseph Lionetti remembers a later scene from *The Seagull* by Anton Chekhov. "She was absolutely wonderful," he said. "She was prepared and had worked hard on it. Lee was very pleased with the scene and liked it very much. He gave some critiquing as he did with everyone but he was very pleased."

Over time, Marilyn studied a variety of other scenes, both at the Actors Studio and in classes at Strasberg's home. Lee harbored hopes of seeing her onstage as Natasha in Anton Chekhov's *Three Sisters,* and in the meantime, the much-admired part of Grushenka from *The Brothers Karamazov* was performed in the Strasberg living room. Having met Anna Sten—star of the 1931 movie *The Murderer Dimitri Karamazov*—at the Actors Studio, Marilyn questioned her intensely about the story and what made the characters tick. Although *The Murderer* was filmed in German, the actress had seen it several times and thought it wonderful. Sten came away from the conversations knowing that if Marilyn ever had the opportunity to act in *The Brothers Karamazov* on-screen, she would be absolutely fascinating. She thought Marilyn to be a profound individual who was determined to discover everything she could about Grushenka and the story itself.

Despite previously dismissing Somerset Maugham as too cynical, Marilyn planned an elaborate television performance of *Rain,* with

Lee as her director, but illness and other issues ensured that this did not ultimately happen. However, no matter what was going on in her life, the actress continued to study. The part of Lorna in Clifford Odets's play *Golden Boy* was researched over two pages in her journal, and then other notes concerned a scene from Tennessee Williams's *A Streetcar Named Desire*. She went on to act out a scene from *Streetcar*, playing the part of Blanche while actor (and son of Paula and Lee) John Strasberg took on the role of a young messenger. Marilyn walked into class laden down with a variety of props so that the scene would be as authentic as she could possibly make it.

"At the Actors Studio they're letting me try more mature scenes, [like] the prostitute in *Damaged Goods*," Marilyn said. "I've got an idea on that. I've never seen a prostitute played the right way—as someone scared." This scene was eventually performed with actor Delos Smith Jr., and then another from *Breakfast at Tiffany's* was acted with Michael Pollard. Both scenes were met with great admiration from her fellow students, but Marilyn always knew there was more to do. "I've still a lot to learn about acting," she told Logan Gourlay in 1960. "That's what I look forward to. That's why I don't worry about growing old and losing my looks. I won't fight it. I'll be a character actress like Marie Dressler. Wasn't she just great?" Marilyn adored Dressler, but another actress she greatly admired was Eleonora Duse, an Italian performer known as one of the greatest actors of all time. Visitors to Marilyn's home would be surprised to discover a framed photograph of Duse on her sideboard. Others would be even more shocked to learn that she knew absolutely everything about her life.

While her own existence was not always a positive experience, Marilyn endeavored to be warm and encouraging to the people she encountered during her day-to-day life. Supporting causes she believed in was something the actress was deeply sincere about, and during her lifetime she helped with charities such as the Milk Fund for Babies and the March of Dimes. She also gave time to the orphanage she had lived in during childhood. Although intensely private, Marilyn spoke briefly about this to columnist Louella Parsons in 1952: "I want to lead a drive to do something personal for orphans—not just the usual thing of sending dolls or food to an orphanage. I mean something intimate, actual contact with the children. It's the most awful thing in the world to feel that you have nobody to love you."

Another charitable endeavor happened on the set of *Let's Make Love* when Marilyn discovered that the studio coffee vendor had been told his services were no longer required. Furious, the actress took her complaint to Fox executives, who eventually relented and allowed the seller to return with his refreshments cart. Marilyn showed further support by gathering costars Yves Montand and Gene Kelly to have photos taken with the vendor and his drinks. Afterward, she signed a photograph: "Sid, there is nothing like your coffee." Marilyn's former father-in-law, Isidore Miller, later explained that she was exceptionally charitable, but the sheer number of people she supported would never be known. Marilyn, he said, helped people because she wanted to, not because she desired glory or gratitude.

To supplement his studies at the Actors Studio, Joseph Lionetti worked with Kenneth Battelle, one of Marilyn's hairdressers. On one particular day, the actress arrived at the salon and Joseph was given the task of washing her hair before having it styled by Battelle. The next day Marilyn returned and requested her hair be washed out, as she felt it had been "teased" a little too much. By this time, Kenneth had gone out of town, so Joseph offered to wash and style it himself. "She was shy. Very delicate and introspective," he remembers. "She was quite lovely but hard to win over. I don't think she would have let me do her hair if not for the fact that I'd helped with Mr. Kenneth." Joseph was just a young man at the time and desperate to leave a good impression. Marilyn, sensing a deep pride in what he had done, whispered in his ear afterward that she thought his work was even better than the famed hairdresser's.

"I once met her outside a restaurant," Joseph recalls, "and she arrived with a washed face—no makeup—wore a kerchief on her head and very ordinary clothes. During lunch we discussed our work at the Studio. Acting was vitally important to her. She had a wonderful combination of joy and sadness, all at once—about where she came from and what she had achieved. She was a survivor."

UNFORTUNATELY, DURING 1961 MARILYN disclosed to her therapist, Marianne Kris, that she had gone through a period of great depression after the death of *Misfits* costar Clark Gable. Offered a chance to recuperate in the hospital, Marilyn unexpectedly found herself in a secure ward for mentally deranged patients—a place she would never have willingly agreed to go. Always anxious that she would end up in the same kind of institution as her mother, Marilyn cried out for her friends to help. After Marilyn wrote letters to the Strasbergs and ex-husband Joe DiMaggio, the latter arrived at the hospital and demanded her release immediately.

After the pain of her last divorce, coupled with the stay in the psychiatric unit, Marilyn decided that a break from Manhattan was necessary. She went home to Los Angeles, but she did not give up her East Coast dreams. "All I know is that I'll be back in New York soon," she told reporter Jonah Ruddy, "and I'll go on with study at the Actors Studio and private classes with Lee Strasberg. The classes have been terribly helpful to me and I enjoy them."

By 1962, Marilyn had hired a Los Angeles–based psychiatrist, bought a small Spanish-style house, and returned to work at Twentieth Century Fox, on a comedy called *Something's Got to Give*. It didn't look to be a fabulous role, but Marilyn went along with it, if only because it led her one step closer to finishing her contract. However, frequent illness and absence from the set caused a great many problems, and circumstances were made no better when Marilyn took time off to return to New York to sing "Happy Birthday" on the occasion of President John F. Kennedy's forty-fifth birthday. When she became sick shortly afterward, the actress was fired, and lawyers for Fox announced their intention to sue for $500,000, claiming breach of contract.

Marilyn was devastated but also incensed. She gave a forthright statement to her press representatives. In it, she admitted being ill but said there were still scenes to be written that did not require her attendance on set. Furthermore, Marilyn felt that Fox executives had fired her because they were panicking after overextending themselves financially on Elizabeth Taylor's movie *Cleopatra*. In the following days, Marilyn's statement was not reported in the press. Instead, it was claimed that she had made no comment at all.

Hollywood tried to silence Marilyn, but the defiant actress wrote to each of her costars, begging them to believe that the shutdown of production was not her fault. Marilyn then let the lawyers deal with Fox, and despite feeling fragile, she undertook photo sessions, berated the studio system in interviews, and began making plans for the future. These exciting proposals would have involved finally breaking free from her old studio, making another movie with Billy Wilder (likely *Kiss Me, Stupid*), working on a musical with Gene Kelly, going back to Manhattan in the fall, and setting up a second production company. Of course, there was always time for reading too. During the summer of 1962, Marilyn became engrossed in *To Kill a Mockingbird* by Harper Lee and *Captain Newman, M.D.* by Leo Rosten. The latter was loosely based on the military experiences of her new therapist, Dr. Ralph Greenson.

East Coast friends continued to play an important part in Marilyn's life. She entertained Norman Rosten during a trip to California, continued to share a close bond with her former father-in-law (Isidore Miller was even her date for the president's birthday party), and thanks to the involvement of Amy Greene, she was once again speaking to Milton. The two looked forward to seeing each other in the months ahead. Joe DiMaggio was firmly back in Marilyn's life, and they enjoyed frequent and enjoyable times together when she wasn't busy gardening at her new home or traveling to buy Mexican furnishings.

Sadly, while Marilyn did try desperately to regain control of her life during the summer of 1962, a combination of her pill intake and the constant going-over of her early life through therapy sessions was more than her body and mind could bear. Marilyn never had the chance to fully move away from the traumas that had haunted her, and while she did have a fairly optimistic approach to her future, in the end it proved not to be enough. All her projects, adventures, and escapades came to a tragic end on the evening of August 4 into the early morning of August 5, 1962, when Marilyn passed away at the age of just thirty-six.

After investigating the matter, officials decided that because of previous overdoses and bouts of depression, her death was the result of a probable suicide.

IN THE DAYS FOLLOWING Marilyn's death, various friends and colleagues paid tribute to her. Billy Wilder—who had directed *The Seven Year Itch*, the film that was the catalyst for Marilyn's New York adventure—headed the remembrances: "Maybe she was tough to work with. Maybe she wasn't even an actress. But it was worth a week's torment to get those three luminous minutes on the screen."

Dame Edith Sitwell said she was aware that Marilyn seemed lost and without any real friends, while actor and admirer Clifton Webb was left heartbroken. "I was deeply, deeply fond of her," he said. "I am so shocked. People should have been more tolerant of her." Perhaps the most surprising of all the comments came from Laurence Olivier. Forgetting the disastrous relationship for a while, he blamed Hollywood for Marilyn's final undoing, and added, "She was difficult to work with, but she could be incredibly sweet, most tenderly appealing, and very, very witty."

Ex-husband Arthur Miller decided not to go to the funeral, but gave his thoughts to reporter Robin Stafford. "It was a tremendous shock to me," he said. "But I still maintain it was not deliberate," adding that it would not be like her "to do the other thing." In a letter to Joshua Logan, he reiterated that he believed the death to be an accident, but told the director that she had always lived close to death.

This was also felt by Susan Strasberg, who later wrote that Marilyn saw death as a friend and she was not afraid of it.

From the patio of the Connecticut home he had once shared with Marilyn, Miller told reporter John Gold: "If she was simple it would have been easy to help her. One must have humility and respect for the mysteries of life. She could have made it with a little luck. She needed a blessing."

Joe DiMaggio and Marilyn's half-sister, Berniece, were on hand to organize the funeral and make sure that Marilyn was remembered in a positive way. In that regard, only a handful of friends and colleagues were invited to the service, where Lee Strasberg spoke about Marilyn's tremendous love for acting and his belief that she could have become a great theater actress. No fans were invited, but a statement was released by Marilyn's agency, advising how they could best remember the star. Instead of flowers, the agency suggested donations should be made to the Los Angeles Orthopedic Foundation or a children's hospital.

Since Marilyn had such an affinity with children, this suggestion seemed completely in keeping with how she would want to be remembered. That was fifty-five years ago, and yet her legacy still helps children around the world today. Hollygrove—the children's home where Marilyn lived for a while as a child—continues to this day. Kathleen Felesina, director of fund development there, shared a few words on how Marilyn's life and legacy have helped and inspired everyone who is associated with the center:

The spirit of Marilyn/Norma Jeane is felt in everything we do here at Hollygrove. Even though we are no longer an orphanage as when she lived here, her legacy lives on in the hundreds of children we serve each year who, like her, have suffered abuse, neglect, or mental health struggles. We like to think that Norma Jeane would have enjoyed our unique therapeutic programs that provide help and hope to our community's children, such as art therapy in our therapeutic summer camp or the mini-plays we put on in our after-school program to help build skills and confidence. Or, perhaps she would have really benefitted from our Family Search and Engagement program that helps reunite our children with healthy, positive family members they've lost touch with.

However, Marilyn/Norma Jeane's spirit lives on in other ways: we are so fortunate that those who resonate with Marilyn continue to hold a special place in their hearts for the children of Hollygrove. We receive donations in her honor on a continual basis, especially around her birthday and the anniversary of her death. In August 2017, the Marilyn Remembered fan club held a reception at Hollygrove to commemorate the fifty-fifth anniversary of her passing. But perhaps the most significant indication of the impact Marilyn/Norma Jeane still has on Hollygrove is the fact that our annual fundraiser is called the "Norma Jean [sic] Gala" and has become one of the go-to events in Hollywood each year. In Marilyn's spirit, the gala celebrates our impact as being part of one of the largest, most comprehensive behavioral and mental health agencies in California, Uplift Family Services.

Thanks to money left to psychiatrist Marianne Kris, Marilyn's legacy also helps children in the United Kingdom. "The Anna Freud National Centre for Children and Families benefited greatly from a bequest from a beneficiary of Marilyn Monroe's estate," said Peter

Fonagy, chief executive of the Centre. "It enabled us to expand our work and to build our worldwide reputation as leading researchers and practitioners in child mental health and to improve mental health for children in Britain and beyond today."

IN 1963, LEE AND Paula Strasberg announced that people from all over the world had written to ask if there was some way of honoring Marilyn and her work at the Actors Studio. After much thought, they believed that money should be raised so that the studio could build an extension for her, and help young actors in her name. In documentation to support the cause, it was revealed that Marilyn had two major interests: helping young people to deal with their problems, and theatrical techniques that would help her become a better actress. Happily, two Marilyn Monroe Theatres now exist, in New York and Los Angeles. Both are part of the Lee Strasberg Theater and Film Institute and are a permanent reminder of Marilyn's existence in an industry she felt so proud to be part of.

THANKS TO THE MODERN women's movement during the 1960s, the lives of women gradually began to evolve for the better. New wives were no longer expected to give up work to take care of the household, and many returned to employment after having children. However, even today society still has a long way to go, and sexism and ageism are rife in many quarters. While women now have more of the same rights as men, their salaries and levels of respect are often not on a matching scale at all.

In Hollywood, sexual harassment of young women became a hot topic again with allegations against studio executive Harvey Weinstein coming to light in October 2017. The debate about the lack of serious and fantastic female roles rages on, and the majority of directors and producers are still men. Equality has moved forward to the point where an actress is no longer mocked for starting a film company, but to find a powerful female producer or director is still a fairly rare occurrence. Since the Academy Awards began in 1929, only four women have ever been nominated for Best Director. Of those, only one, Kathryn Bigelow, has won, for her direction of 2008's *The Hurt Locker*. In 2015, Oscar-winning actress Nicole Kidman gave her opinion that female directors were not being given the chance to build their careers and become great in their field. In short, women in Hollywood are still fighting for much the same opportunities that Marilyn did, over sixty years later.

MARILYN MONROE HAS BEEN given many labels, both during her life and after. Probably the two most insulting are that she was a dumb blonde and a victim. She was neither. The characters she played on-screen were often harebrained and made people laugh, but that did not mean that the real-life woman was dumb. She lost some battles and her ending was tragic and devastating, but that does not make her a victim. On the contrary, her determination to fight in such a male-oriented and hostile industry makes her one of the bravest women of her generation.

Mental health is a topic that is still frequently dealt with behind closed doors, and the knowledge that Marilyn felt deep despair at times often makes people uncomfortable. Agreeing with the official verdict of probable suicide is seen as greatly disrespectful by some, though perhaps it is more discourteous to believe the conspiracy theories of murder. It is vital to accept that Marilyn did have issues, and to look at them in a way that can provoke discussion and help spread the word about mental health is of paramount importance. Knowing that Marilyn suffered too may help those struggling with problems of their own, and she would have been terrifically proud of that.

THE TRAVILLA-DESIGNED DRESS THAT Marilyn made famous in *The Seven Year Itch* continues to intrigue people today. Numerous actresses have worn replicas of it, including Anna Nicole Smith and Madonna, and every time a celebrity is caught in a gust of wind, the media automatically dubs it their "Marilyn Monroe moment."

In 2011, the costume was immortalized in a twenty-six-foot statue that toured the world. Photographs showing passersby sheltering under the skirt during a Chicago rainstorm went viral, before the statue then moved on to Palm Springs and even Australia. The original dress caused a media frenzy when it was sold by actress Debbie Reynolds at auction in June 2011. The winning bid was by a private collector, who paid a whopping $5.6 million, including commission. Since then it has been seen only once—in an October 2012 exhibition at the Victoria and Albert Museum in London.

More than sixty years after Marilyn stepped onto a New York City grate, the scene and the costume remain just as iconic. "Clients usually ask for the white dress for functions," explains Monroe tribute artist Suzie Kennedy. "It has become as universally known as the Elvis jumpsuit and it doesn't matter who wears it, everyone knows the dress is supposed to be Marilyn's."

Willem Dafoe proved this to be true in 2016 when he wore a replica during a commercial for Snickers chocolate bars. The advertisement starts with a bored Dafoe shooting the famous skirt-blowing scene. As the electric fan lifts the dress high into the air, Dafoe fights with the material and angrily shouts about the absurdity of the situation. The director complains about the attitude of "Miss Monroe." A member of the crew hands over a Snickers bar, and suddenly Dafoe is transformed into the real Marilyn, with her skirt flying up and a beaming smile on her face.

THE MARILYN MONROE SEEN in manipulated images, fake stories, and false quotes is not the person who really existed. The icon of T-shirts and coffee mugs, key rings and statues, is just that—an icon, a legendary figure who really has no bearing on the human being at all. By allowing ourselves to see only the legend, we reduce Marilyn to merely a character—somebody who has no more bearing on real life than Betty Boop or Mickey Mouse.

The fake quotes that have appeared in recent years read like lines from a bad self-help book, and comparing them to subjects Marilyn actually spoke about shows them to be even more ludicrous. Out goes the human being who loved literature and music, and in comes a character even fluffier than the ones she played on-screen. The real woman is still out there—she can be found in interviews and photographs that have existed for the past seventy years—and yet some still prefer the fake, dumb blonde who gives girls advice on shoes and sparkle. Perhaps the real woman—the woman of poetry, politics, and playwrights—is too much to handle. Maybe she was always too much and the fake version fits a certain mold that people are more accepting of.

By humanizing Marilyn, we are each given a lesson in empathy. Realizing that she was a person made of flesh and bone hopefully forces even the staunchest of detractors to see Marilyn in a more sensitive and caring light. For a woman who fought her entire life to be recognized as an intelligent, functioning human being, the least we can do is understand that while she often played ditzy women on-screen, the opposite was true in real life.

In 1954, after making *The Seven Year Itch* and creating the image that made her an immortal, Marilyn Monroe reached the unprecedented decision to walk away from her Hollywood career. Through taking on the industry and winning the right to work in her own way, she contributed to the ultimate breakdown of the studio system, therefore impacting the course of history. In turn, this helped push forward the women's movement. Her strength, determination, and fight inspired women, men, and businesses the world over, and continue to do so to this day.

Passing the Torch

THEY SAY THAT WHEN a butterfly flaps its wings in New Mexico, it can cause a chain of events that lead to a hurricane in China. This philosophy is true in the case of Marilyn Monroe. Her fights, struggles, and successes have helped thousands of women to find their truth and live their dreams. Here then are just a few whose lives have been changed because of her existence:

Suzie Kennedy, actress and Marilyn Monroe tribute artist: "Marilyn had many sides that women can relate to. She inspires me, as she shows that I can use my femininity as a strength, not a weakness. To be strong and succeed while being who I am is important."

Tara Hanks, author: "Marilyn Monroe inspires me firstly because of her talent. I could watch her movies forever, and she was a genius before the camera. Secondly, despite little formal education, she was intelligent and cultured, always eager to learn. And thirdly, she had great warmth and integrity. I've been a fan for most of my life, and she has been a huge part of my work as a writer. *The Mmm Girl*, my novel about Marilyn's life, was published in 2007, and since 2010 I've been posting Monroe-related news and reviews on the Everlasting Star blog. The constant rumors about her love affairs and her death are less interesting to me, as I believe they're mostly exaggerated, but nonetheless I want to give people a true picture of Marilyn and to respect her humanity, because so many young fans still idolize her. Although her life ended too soon, I'm in awe at the many obstacles Marilyn overcame—from childhood trauma to the pressures of her career and relationships, and of course, her struggles with addiction and depression. Marilyn Monroe was a remarkably brave woman who never lost her humility. Her path wasn't an easy one, but she had true grit. My only regret is that she never knew lasting happiness, because what she gave us is immeasurable."

Daisy Morgan, student and aspiring author: "I am thirteen years old and think that Marilyn Monroe is a good influence for my generation because she fought for the rights of women and spoke out against misogyny. She also supported those who were different or had less power than herself. Her achievements have shown me that there is always a chance to have success in my life."

Andrea Pryke, book reviewer and vlogger: "Ever since I was a little girl, I have been aware of Marilyn. Everything about her was elegant: her face, her clothes, her deportment. She inspired me to embrace my femininity, not reject it. Then I watched her films and was inspired by her talent. . . . Marilyn motivated me to love all films and theater, not just the heavy classics but the fun as well. As I grew older and read more about her I was encouraged by her strength and her determination. She taught me to try things that other people would be afraid of and because of her I went to drama school and studied musical theater, acting, and I wrote and performed a monologue based on Marilyn's last 1962 interview. Most of all, her strength has helped me to realize that life isn't always clear, that we are all human beings, wonderful and imperfect. She has helped me through the darkest times of my life and is a shining example to all of us of how life should be lived: with the determination to be the best that we can be."

Susan Griffiths, actress and Marilyn Monroe tribute artist: "Marilyn changed my life completely. Having no idea of her, then being told I resembled her, set into motion a life-changing experience. She has been the biggest influence in my life and has led to my thirty-five-year career. As far as a role model, she had many problems, challenges, setbacks, and some would say she should not be admired because of them, but I think she should. Marilyn gives women hope that with all she faced, she still rose to the top. Sadly in the end it was too much, but she fought the good fight her whole life. It has been an honor and extreme privilege to portray her."

Emma Watson, actress: "I think [Marilyn] was just trying to find her feet in the midst of this kind of crazy circus that went on around her, and trying to find some sort of balance and some sort of normality in her life, and I can definitely relate to that."

Michelle Williams, actress: "I have always been drawn to Marilyn, but that doesn't make me special in any way. She has that magnetism and that draw for so many people, so I read about her when I was young, devouring biographies. I'm most interested in her life before she became Marilyn. For me, the interest wasn't so much in this larger-than-life personality."

Gloria Steinem, author and feminist icon: "What makes her so riveting for women especially since the advent of the modern women's movement, is that we wonder if we could not have saved her by making a place where she could tell everything. Because that's what we have done for each other."

Linda Kerridge, actress: "I discovered Marilyn as a teenager after reading *Marilyn* by Norman Mailer. I identified with her immediately and wanted to be her! I had no identity at that point, having survived physical, emotional, and sexual abuse as a child and I had completely lost myself. In Marilyn I saw that it was okay to feel sad and vulnerable and still be worthy of love. She embodied such beauty of soul, spirit, and femininity and she became my beacon of light and role model until I walked my own path and learned how to accept who I was. I still loved her but in a more balanced way. I stopped trying to *be* her. That was just the folly of a sad young girl. Besides there will only ever be one Marilyn. She was unique, original, and magical."

A Woman of Culture

FOR THE BENEFIT OF fans who wish to find out more about Marilyn's literary and philosophical tastes, the following is a list of works and people mentioned in this book that she read, studied, performed, admired, or listened to.

Books, Poems, and Plays

A Hatful of Rain by Michael Gazzo

A Streetcar Named Desire by Tennessee Williams

A View from the Bridge by Arthur Miller

Abraham Lincoln by Carl Sandburg

An Actor Prepares by Konstantin Stanislavski

Anna Christie by Eugene O'Neill

The Ballad of Reading Gaol by Oscar Wilde

Bernard Shaw and Mrs. Patrick Campbell: Their Correspondence by Bernard Shaw

The Brothers Karamazov by Fyodor Dostoyevsky

Building a Character by Konstantin Stanislavski

Bus Stop by William Inge

Captain Newman, M.D. by Leo Rosten

The Caucasian Chalk Circle by Bertolt Brecht

The Cherry Orchard by Anton Chekhov

Damn Yankees by George Abbott and Douglass Wallop

Dance to the Piper by Agnes de Mille

Death of a Salesman by Arthur Miller

The Diary of Anne Frank by Frances Goodrich and Albert Hackett
(based on the book by Anne Frank)

Enemy of the People by Henrik Ibsen

Fallen Angels by Noël Coward

Faust by Johann Wolfgang von Goethe

Focus by Arthur Miller

Gertrude Lawrence as Mrs. A. by Richard Stoddard Aldrich

Golden Boy by Clifford Odets

Hamlet by William Shakespeare

House of Flowers by Harold Arlen and Truman Capote

King Lear by William Shakespeare

Lysistrata by Aristophanes

Macbeth by William Shakespeare

Maiden Voyage by Paul Osborn

Middle of the Night by Paddy Chayefsky

"Never Give All the Heart" by William Butler Yeats

Pygmalion by George Bernard Shaw

Rain by Somerset Maugham

Romeo and Juliet by William Shakespeare

The Seagull by Anton Chekhov

The Seven Year Itch by George Axelrod

The Sleeping Prince by Terence Rattigan

The Smiling Rebel by Harnett T. Kane

The Teahouse of the August Moon by John Patrick

The Thinking Body by Mabel Elsworth Todd

Three Sisters by Anton Chekhov

To Kill a Mockingbird by Harper Lee

To the Actor: On the Technique of Acting by Michael Chekhov

Ulysses by James Joyce

Untitled biography of Albert Schweitzer

Will Success Spoil Rock Hunter? by George Axelrod

Actors, Writers, Philosophers, Philanthropists, and Scientists

Albert Einstein

Aldous Huxley

Antoine de Saint-Exupéry

Bertha Spafford Vester

Carl Sandburg

Carson McCullers

Dame Edith Sitwell

Eleonora Duse

Fleur Cowles

Franz Kafka

Greta Garbo

Harold Clurman

Henrik Ibsen

Karen Blixen

Leo Tolstoy

Marie Dressler

Robert Frost

Rudolf Steiner

Seán O'Casey

Sigmund Freud

Somerset Maugham

Thomas Jefferson

Thomas Mann

Thomas Wolfe

Truman Capote

Walt Whitman

Musicians and Composers

Earl Bostic

Ella Fitzgerald

Frank Sinatra

Jelly Roll Morton

Louis Armstrong

Ludwig van Beethoven

Ottorino Respighi

Tomaso Albinoni

Wolfgang Amadeus Mozart

Artists and Sculptors

Auguste Rodin

Edgar Degas

Édouard Manet

Francisco José de Goya

Honoré Daumier

Michelangelo

Pablo Picasso

Paul Cézanne

Selected Bibliography

Arnold, Eve. *Marilyn Monroe: An Appreciation*. London: Hamish Hamilton, 1987.

Axelrod, George. *The Seven Year Itch*. New York: Dramatists Play Service, 1980.

Banner, Lois and Mark Anderson. *MM—Personal: From the Private Archive of Marilyn Monroe*. New York: Abrams, 2011.

Buchthal, Stanley and Bernard Comment. *Fragments: Poems, Intimate Notes, Letters by Marilyn Monroe*. London: HarperCollins, 2010.

Bus Stop: The Story of the Twentieth Century-Fox Film Starring Marilyn Monroe. London: Charles Buchan's, 1956.

Carpozi, George Jr. *Marilyn Monroe: Her Own Story*. New York: Belmont Books, 1961.

Christie's Auction House. *The Personal Property of Marilyn Monroe*. New York: Christie's, 1999.

Cohen, Lola, ed. *The Lee Strasberg Notes*. New York: Routledge, 2010.

Cowles, Fleur. *Friends and Memories*. London: Jonathan Cape, 1975.

De La Hoz, Cindy. *Marilyn Monroe: Platinum Fox*. Philadelphia: Running Press, 2007.

Franse, Astrid and Michelle Morgan. *Before Marilyn: The Blue Book Modeling Years*. Stroud, UK: History Press, 2015.

Greene, Joshua. *Milton's Marilyn*. Munich: Schirmer/Mosel, 1998.

Guiles, Fred Lawrence. *Legend: The Life and Death of Marilyn Monroe*. Lanham, MD: Scarborough House, 1992.

Harris, Radie. *Radie's World*. London: W. H. Allen, 1975.

Haspiel, James. *Marilyn: The Ultimate Look at the Legend*. London: Smith Gryphon, 1991.

Hedren, Tippi. *Tippi: A Memoir*. New York: William Morrow, 2016.

Hethmon, Robert H., ed. *Strasberg at the Actors Studio: Tape-Recorded Sessions*. New York: Theatre Communications Group, 2003.

Julien's. *Marilyn*. Catalogs for November 17–19, 2016, auction, four volumes. Los Angeles: Julien's.

Kazan, Elia. *Elia Kazan: A Life*. New York: Alfred A. Knopf, 1988.

Kobal, John. *People Will Talk*. London: Aurum Press, 1986.

LaBrasca, Bob. *Marilyn: Fifty-Five*. London: Bloomsbury, 1990.

Leaming, Barbara. *Marilyn Monroe*. London: Weidenfeld & Nicolson, 1998.

Logan, Joshua. *Movie Stars, Real People, and Me*. New York: Delacorte, 1978.

Miller, Arthur. *Timebends: A Life*. London: Minerva, 1990.

Monroe, Marilyn with Ben Hecht. *My Story*. New York: Taylor Trade, 2007.

Morgan, Michelle. *Marilyn Monroe: Private and Confidential*. New York: Skyhorse, 2012.

Murray, Christopher. *Sean O'Casey: A Biography*. Dublin: Gill and Macmillan, 2004.

Nicholson, Virginia. *Perfect Wives in Ideal Homes*. London: Penguin Random House, 2016.

Olivier, Laurence. *On Acting*. Kent, UK: Hodder and Stoughton, 1987.

Rattigan, Terence. *The Sleeping Prince: An Occasional Fairy Tale*. London: Samuel French, 1956.

Riese, Randall and Neal Hitchins. *The Unabridged Marilyn: Her Life from A to Z*. London: Corgi, 1988.

Rosten, Norman. *Marilyn: A Very Personal Story*. London: Millington, 1974.

Shaw, Sam. *Marilyn Monroe in the Camera Eye*. London: Hamlyn, 1979.

———. *Marilyn: The New York Years*. Berlin: Lardon Media, 2004.

———. *Marilyn Monroe as The Girl*. New York: Ballantine Books, 1955.

Shaw, Sam and Norman Rosten. *Marilyn Among Friends*. London: Bloomsbury, 1987.

Spoto, Donald. *Marilyn Monroe: The Biography*. London: Chatto and Windus, 1993.

Steinem, Gloria and George Barris. *Marilyn: Norma Jeane*. London: Victor Gollancz, 1987.

Strasberg, Anna and Bernard Comment. *Marilyn Monroe: Girl Waiting*. Paris: Editions du Seuil, 2012.

Strasberg, Susan. *Marilyn and Me: Sisters, Rivals, Friends*. London: Doubleday, 1992.

VeVea, April. *Marilyn Monroe: A Day in the Life*. CreateSpace, 2016.

Victor, Adam. *The Complete Marilyn Monroe*. London: Thames and Hudson, 1999.

Vitacco-Robles, Gary. *Icon: The Life, Times, and Films of Marilyn Monroe: Volume 1, 1926 to 1956*. Albany, GA: BearManor Media, 2014.

———. *Icon: The Life, Times, and Films of Marilyn Monroe: Volume 2, 1956 to 1962 and Beyond*. Albany, GA: BearManor Media, 2014.

Wagenknecht, Edward. *Marilyn Monroe: A Composite View*. Philadelphia: Chilton, 1969.

Wallach, Eli. *The Good, the Bad, and Me: In My Anecdotage*. Orlando, FL: Harcourt Books, 2005.

Zolotow, Maurice. *Marilyn Monroe*. London: W. H. Allen, 1961.

Source Notes

Preface: Rebellious Starlet

"Oh, I don't think so." "Cheesecake Hasn't Hurt Acting Career Says Starlet," *Newport Daily News*, November 19, 1951.

"I was broke and needed the money." "Marilyn Monroe Nude Pose Paid Rent," *Long Beach Independent*, March 14, 1952.

"If anything, the busty, blond bombshell." Gerry Fitz-Gerald, "Will Nude Art Hurt? Marilyn Monroe Asks," *Stars and Stripes*, May 21, 1952.

"No! I'm for her." Earl Wilson, "That High-Collar Girl, She's Hildegarde Neff," *Winona (MN) Republican-Herald*, October 17, 1953.

Phil Max arrest. "Marilyn Monroe Pix Brings Cops," *Times-Bulletin*, February 20, 1953; "Showing Marilyn Monroe Picture Brings Trouble," *Odessa (TX) American*, February 20, 1953; "Nude Calendar Display Results in Fine of $50," *Oil City (PA) Blizzard*, February 26, 1953; "A Postcard from Stan Delaplane," *Reno Evening Gazette*, May 1, 1957.

"I didn't think there was anything wrong." "Marilyn Monroe Gets Publicity, He Gets Fined," *Bakersfield Californian*, February 23, 1953.

"[Marilyn's] going through the same." Erskine Johnson, "Jane Russell Knows Answer to Marilyn Monroe's Problem," *Sunday Tribune*, March 29, 1953.

Information on *Pink Tights*. *Screenland*, May 1954; *Twentieth Century Fox Dynamo*, December 1953; *Film Bulletin*, November 2, 1953; *Film Bulletin*, November 30, 1954.

"I liked his seriousness." Aline Mosby column, *Ames (IA) Daily Tribune*, January 15, 1954.

Wedding to Joe DiMaggio. "Marilyn Monroe Marries," *Yorkshire Post and Leeds Intelligencer*, January 15, 1954; "400 See Marilyn Monroe Married," *Northern Whig*, January 15, 1954.

"Miss Monroe has authorized me." "Marilyn Refuses Script," *Aberdeen Evening Press*, January 26, 1954.

"My only interest is Joe." "I Don't Like the Script, Says Marilyn," *Yorkshire Evening Post*, January 30, 1954.

"Too many kids know." Jack Wade, "The Two Worlds of Marilyn Monroe," *Modern Screen*, November 1954.

"Marilyn was very likeable." Interview with Bob Cornthwaite, March 11, 2006. Published in Michelle Morgan's *Marilyn Monroe: Private and Undisclosed* (London: Constable and Robinson, 2007).

Marilyn's being cast in *The Seven Year Itch* as a reward for returning to the studio has been widely documented in biographies. Her fight with Feldman when it looked as though he would take *Itch* to another studio was told in Barbara Leaming's *Marilyn Monroe*.

"Marilyn Monroe told me." Mike Connolly, "Hollywood—As I See It," *Screenland*, July 1954.

"This was her first triumph." Jack Wade, "The Two Worlds of Marilyn Monroe," *Modern Screen*, November 1954.

Chapter One: The Girl

The Seven Year Itch play. *Theatre World*, September 1953; *New York Times*, November 21, 1952; *Tatler and Bystander*, June 3, 1953; *The Stage*, January 22, 1953.

Making of *The Seven Year Itch*. Hedda Hopper, "Deborah Kerr Held Right for 'Maverick,'" *Los Angeles Times*, August 3, 1954; Herbert Mitgang, "Tom Ewell's Twenty-Year Itch," *New York Times*, September 19, 1954; "Marilyn Monroe Ill After Windy Scene," *Los Angeles Times*, September 19, 1954; *Fergus Falls (MN) Daily Journal*, September 20, 1954; Hedda Hopper, "Tom Ewell Feels Director of 'Itch' Up to Scratch," *Los Angeles Times*, December 12, 1954.

"She should take about fifteen pounds off her fanny." Earl Wilson, "On Again, Off Again," *Motion Picture*, January 1955.

"I never worked with her." Randall Riese and Neal Hitchens, *The Unabridged Marilyn.*

"Everybody worships this gal." Hedda Hopper, "Powell, Heflin, Sought for 'Darling Jenny,'" *Los Angeles Times*, September 24, 1954.

"Marilyn Monroe is here." Walter Winchell column, *Logansport (IN) Pharos-Tribune*, September 10, 1954.

"Howled, whistled and applauded" and "Oh, I love it!" *Long Beach Press-Telegram*, September 18, 1954.

"One of those two is correct." Pete Martin, "Confessions of Marilyn Monroe: Part Three," *Daily Sketch*, June 27, 1956.

"Why should it?" Earl Wilson, "On Again, Off Again," *Motion Picture*, January 1955.

"She would slink off by herself." Richard L. Cox, "The Strange Truth About Marilyn Monroe," *Reynold's News (UK)*, October 30, 1955.

"Alive for the first time in days." "Marilyn, Joe Forget with Work and Golf," *Los Angeles Times*, October 8, 1954.

"There was no suggestion," the comment from Reno Barsocchini, and "A-Bomb. There was no hint." "Marilyn Seeks Divorce from Joe," *Bridgeport (CT) Telegram*, October 5, 1954.

"Often morose baseball-star-with-muscles." Natasha Lytess, "Marilyn Monroe: Her Secret Life: Part 4," *Sunday People*, August 5, 1962.

Tips and expectations of a 1950s housewife. The Doc, "A Little Thought Can Save Your Wife No End of Trouble," *Sunday Post*, February 5, 1950.

Qualities of an ideal wife and mother competition. *Australian Women's Weekly*, March 23–May 4, 1955.

"Christmas morning she'll be happier." "Didn't I Warn You About Serving Me Bad Coffee?" *Daily Mail*, December 30, 2012.

Coronet Instructional Films' *Marriage Is a Partnership,* 1951. "First Year of Marriage—Learning to Live Together—Love & Marriage, Husband & Wife 1950s," YouTube video, 16:16, posted by Historia-Bel99TV, August 20, 2014, https://youtu.be/UdFNUlRqDnU.

Survey of 143 newspaper and magazine editors. Gay Pauley, "Readers Want More Hints on Household," *Los Angeles Times*, November 10, 1954.

DiMaggio relationship and divorce. "The Cerfboard: Marilyn, We Roll Along," *Los Angeles Times*, September 26, 1954; "Marilyn Monroe," *Belfast News-Letter*, October 5, 1954; "Marilyn Monroe Ill," *Belfast News-Letter*, October 9, 1954; "Marilyn Monroe Seeks Divorce," *Yorkshire Post and Leeds Intelligencer*, October 5, 1954; Hedda Hopper, "Marilyn Monroe Will Divorce Joe DiMaggio," *Los Angeles Times*, October 5, 1954; "Marilyn Monroe to Divorce DiMaggio, She Cites 'Conflicting Career Demands,'" *New York Times*, October 5, 1954; "Miss Monroe Files Suit," *New York Times*, October 6, 1954; "Ailing Marilyn Monroe Files Suit for Divorce," *Los Angeles Times*, October 6, 1954; Edwin Schallert column, *Los Angeles Times*, October 7, 1954; "DiMaggio Leaves, Marilyn Unable to Work on Film," *Los Angeles Times*, October 7, 1954; "Marilyn Monroe Given Divorce from DiMaggio," *Los Angeles Times*, October 28, 1954.

Death of Selma Silbert. "Divorce Case Spectator Plunges to Her Death," *Los Angeles Times*, October 28, 1954; e-mail from Sandi Silbert, April 13, 2017.

Divorce of Mr. and Mrs. Parks. "Mate Wanted Another Marilyn," *Los Angeles Times*, July 3, 1957.

Scene with Marilyn and Victor Moore. Hedda Hopper, "Chosen Few Witness Marilyn's Bath Scene," *Los Angeles Times*, November 9, 1954. The scene was eventually shown in *Backstory: The Seven Year Itch*, the August 26, 2000, episode of American Movie Channel's documentary series.

"Working with Marilyn is not." Steve Cronin, "The Storm About Monroe," *Modern Screen*, May 1955.

"I wish to grow as an actress and a person." "Top Stars' 1955 Resolutions," *Oakland Tribune*, January 2, 1955.

"Marilyn has a brassy smile." Elizabeth Toomey, "Glamour Is Rare Outside Hollywood, Photo Man Says," *Vidette (IN) Messenger*, November 16, 1954.

"Although she is personally shy and reserved." Cox, "The Strange Truth About Marilyn Monroe."

Romanoff's party and Gable romance rumors. Hedda Hopper, "Marilyn and Gable Will Be Costarred," *Los Angeles Times*, October 6, 1954; "The Gaze of the Charm," *Los Angeles Times*, November 20, 1954; "No Romance Says Gable," *Sunderland Echo (UK)*, November 22, 1954.

"She was an absolutely perfect." "You Don't Really Know Marilyn Monroe: Clifton Webb in an Interview with Ernie Player," *Picturegoer*, June 11, 1955.

"I looked like the back." Hedda Hopper column, *Los Angeles Times*, November 13, 1954.

Chapter Two: No Dumb Blonde

"People identify me personally." Hal Boyle, "The Symbol of
Success," *Lowell (MA) Sun*, June 10, 1957.

"Marilyn is very sweet." "You Don't Really Know Marilyn Monroe."

"Back when we were close." E-mail from Bill Pursel, December 3,
2016.

Memories of Marilyn's time at the Twentieth Century Fox lessons.
E-mails from David and Cathy Sandrich, March 3 and 5, 2017.

"Marilyn's a great reader." Earl Wilson, "On Again, Off Again,"
Motion Picture, January 1955.

"Himself in the role" and "feared the rehearsals." "Memories of
Stanislavsky [*sic*] by People's Artist of the R.S.F.S.R. Mikhail
Yanshin," *Theatre World*, September 1953.

"First of all, he's a rare human being." "The Men Who Interest Me . . .
by Mrs. Joe DiMaggio," *Pageant*, April 1954.

Chekhov's teachings. Monroe with Hecht, *My Story*; e-mail from Ian
Bevins, administrator, Michael Chekhov Studio London.

"I know (painfully so)." Riese and Hitchens, *The Unabridged Marilyn*.

"Marilyn said she was thinking about shedding." E-mail from Bill
Pursel, December 3, 2016.

"This young fellow" and subsequent comments about Milton
Greene. "The Men Who Interest Me . . ."

Marilyn's letter to Twentieth Century Fox was dated December 11, 1954, and was addressed to Lew Schreiber, Executive Manager. The document was located in the Fox archive, Los Angeles, in 2006.

Publicity campaign for *There's No Business Like Show Business.* "Fox 'Show Business' Tie-In," *Film Bulletin*, December 13, 1954.

"Most assuredly and unreservedly." "*There's No Business Like Show Business*," *Motion Picture Daily*, December 8, 1954.

"Leave Monroe out of this." "What the Picture Did for Me," *Motion Picture Herald*, April 23, 1955.

"The one in *There's No Business Like Show Business.*" Bill Foster, "Marilyn Monroe," *Sunday Graphic*, March 29, 1959.

"'Heat Wave' frankly is dirty." "Ed Sullivan's 'Toast,'" *Exhibitors Forum*, January 24, 1955.

Donald O'Connor's thoughts on working with Marilyn. Hedda Hopper, "Donald's Had Downs in Past but Now It's All Up and Up," *Los Angeles Times*, November 7, 1954.

Marilyn's false name has been reported to be Zelda Zonk for many years. Amy Greene, in conversation with interviewer Scott Feinberg in 2012, remembered it to be Zelda Schnook. "Marilyn Monroe's Best Friend Amy Greene Interviewed by Scott Feinberg," YouTube video, 40:24, posted by "Scott," November 9, 2012, https://youtu.be/Uc_3SYInn9g.

"I would adore to meet Marilyn." "You Don't Really Know Monroe."

Bertha Spafford Vester's memories of Christmas 1954 and Marilyn. Bertha Spafford Vester diary, 1954, Box II: 25, Folder 1, American Colony in Jerusalem Papers, Manuscript Division, Library of Congress, Washington, DC. Reproduced with permission from the Library of Congress. For more information about Vester's children's center, and to support their cause, please visit: http://www.spaffordcenter.org.

Fleur Cowles's memories of Marilyn. Cowles, *Friends and Memories*.

"We'd discuss everything." Helen Bolstad, "Marilyn in the House," *Photoplay*, September 1955.

"I think Marilyn knows exactly where she's going." Earl Wilson, "In Defense of Marilyn Monroe," *Modern Screen*, June 1955.

The "New Marilyn" press conference. "New Role for Marilyn Monroe," *New York Times*, January 8, 1955; "New Marilyn Monroe Has Yen to Produce Her Own Movies," *Galveston (TX) Daily News*, January 8, 1955; "New Marilyn Same as Old and That's Plenty," *Los Angeles Times*, January 8, 1955; "Studio Claims Marilyn Is Still Under Contract," *Los Angeles Times*, January 9, 1955; "Marilyn Forms Her Own Film Company," *Great Bend (KS) Daily Tribune*, January 10, 1955; Hedda Hopper, "Marilyn Stirs Storm with Latest Attitude," *Los Angeles Times*, January 12, 1955; Philip K. Scheuer, "Frenke Receptive to Monroe Wish to Play in *Karamazov*," *Los Angeles Times*, January 16, 1955.

"There has been a change in her public relations." No title, *Independent Film Journal*, January 22, 1955.

"Milton Greene has been a disturbing influence." Jim Henaghan, "My Love Affair with Marilyn," *Motion Picture*, January 1955.

"She is one of the most talented actresses." Aline Mosby, "Marilyn May Lose Her Public by Holding Out," *Great Bend (KS) Daily Tribune*, January 23, 1955.

"I realized that just as I had once fought to get into the movies." Monroe with Hecht, *My Story.*

"I was born under the sign." "Skyrocket a Star Is Born," *Screen Fan*, October 1952.

"You don't seem to get the idea." Elsa Maxwell, "Marilyn Confesses to Elsa Maxwell: I'll Never Be the Same," *Modern Screen*, July 1956.

"It didn't take any courage." Ibid.

"That, brother, was criticism." Thomas M. Pryor, "Hollywood Canvas," *Los Angeles Times,* January 16, 1955.

"The studio will use every legal means." "Monroe Contract Still in Force," *Motion Picture Daily*, January 11, 1955.

Attempts to replace Marilyn with Sheree North. "Dorothy Kilgallen's Exclusive Movie Gossip," *Screenland*, May 1954; *Motion Picture Daily*, March 23, 1955; *Motion Picture Herald*, June 11, 1955; *Motion Picture Daily*, December 7, 1955.

Information about the Oakland *Seven Year Itch* audience appeared in a memo from Zanuck to Skouras sent on January 29, 1955. Found in the Spyros Skouras Collection, Special Collections, Stanford University Library.

Stockholder who claimed he wanted Marilyn fired. Hedda Hopper, "Group Seeks Removal of Marilyn at 20th," *Los Angeles Times*, February 18, 1955.

"I thought the audience would." Hedda Hopper, "Lancaster Seeking Bogart as Costar," *Los Angeles Times*, February 21, 1955.

"There is a small shrewd group that insists." Alice Finletter, "Don't Call Me a Dumb Blonde," *Modern Screen*, April 1955.

"More than anything else." Ibid.

Marilyn was reading a biography on Albert Schweitzer. "New Pin-Up Queen Book Reading Type," *Ironwood (MI) Daily Globe*, January 6, 1951.

Marilyn's favorite authors in 1951. List entitled "Wolfson Notes on Monroe," Maurice Zolotow Collection, Harry Ransom Humanities Research Center, University of Texas at Austin. It would appear from the document that the original list came from *Collier's*, September 8, 1951.

"Please get this straight." Florence Epstein, "Paar for the Course," *Screenland*, January 1958.

"A girl can get along for quite a while." "Marilyn Monroe Has Problem Too," *Cedar Rapids (IA) Gazette*, July 15, 1951.

"I'd like to be smart and chic." Michael Ruddy, "Is This the End of Marilyn?" *Sunday Chronicle*, February 28, 1954.

"I'm beginning to understand Shakespeare." Logan Gourlay, "I've Not Begun to Earn Much Yet," *Sunday Express*, November 8, 1953.

"I've just discovered Tolstoy." Elizabeth Frank, "Fall Girl," *The People*, circa August 17, 1953.

"I'm trying to find myself." Aline Mosby, "Marilyn Monroe Has Her Eye on Movie Oscar," *Lowell (MA) Sun*, November 24, 1952.

Philippe Halsman's thoughts. Ralph Hattersley, "Marilyn Monroe: The Image and Her Photographers" in Edward Wagenknecht's *Marilyn Monroe: A Composite View*. Note: the article was originally published in *Popular Photography*, January 1966.

"I don't know whether." Earl Wilson, "Film Husband Tells All About Marilyn," *Lima (OH) News*, June 24, 1956.

"Marilyn thought of herself." Earl Leaf, "The Marilyn I Used to Know," *Movie Time*, December 1954.

"I was afraid to talk about what I wanted." Tex Parks, "Lessons I've Learned in Hollywood," unidentified magazine, 1951.

"I once thought that this girl" and "I've been on a lot of pictures." Cronin, "The Storm About Monroe."

"I would listen to his advice." Milton Schulman, "Will Mr. M. Rewrite the Monroe Story?" *Aberdeen Evening Express*, July 18, 1956.

"I have no doubt." Ibid.

Chapter Three: Behind the Tinsel

"The day of the 'Casting Couch.'" Irving Wallace, "All This Is Hollywood Too!" *Modern Screen*, February 1941.

"I didn't have much trouble brushing them off." Florabel Muir, "Wolves I Have Known," *Los Angeles Mirror*, September 22, 1952, in Riese and Hitchins's *The Unabridged Marilyn*.

"I beg your pardon?" Earl Wilson, "MM Invited to Pose Nude for Calendar," *Long Beach Independent Press-Telegram*, August 23, 1959.

"I never did sleep with anyone." E-mail interview with anonymous actress, March 23, 2017.

"When I come to look back." E-mail interview with anonymous photographer, May 11, 2017.

"But look at you." Earl Wilson, "MM Invited to Pose Nude for Calendar."

"I think women collectively are much to blame." "This Week's Best Letter," *Australian Women's Weekly*, March 23, 1955.

"[Marilyn] just never wants to get out." Sidney Skolsky, "Sidney Skolsky Gives the Lowdown on Hollywood Women," *Modern Screen*, March 1954.

"Marilyn looked upon New York as a shrine of culture." William Barbour, "The Very Private Life of Marilyn Monroe," *Modern Screen*, October 1955.

"I met Marilyn about a year and a half ago." Alice Finletter, "Don't Call Me a Dumb Blonde," *Modern Screen*, April 1955.

"This book will show the new Marilyn." "'New Monroe' to Come Out of 2-Weeks' Rest," *Chronicle-Telegram*, January 6, 1955.

"Please let me tell you why I formed my own company." Louella Parsons, "Louella Parsons in Hollywood," *Modern Screen*, April 1955.

"Technically, I'm not under contract." Finletter, "Don't Call Me a Dumb Blonde."

"Bunch of bunk." Ibid.

"Absolutely wonderful in the role." "You Don't Really Know Monroe."

"Considering the architecture with which." "Coulter Column," *Film Bulletin*, January 24, 1955.

Richard Avedon on photo shoots. Hattersley, "Marilyn Monroe: The Image and Her Photographers."

"I act when I'm posing." Skolsky, "Sidney Skolsky Gives the Lowdown on Hollywood Women."

Marilyn's notes about directing lectures and *The Misfits*. Stanley Buchthal and Bernard Comment, *Fragments: Poems, Intimate Notes, Letters by Marilyn Monroe*.

Female film directors and producers. "A Tour of Today's Talkies,"
Modern Screen, December 1936; Alma Whitaker, "Woman Film
Director Needs Tact," *Los Angeles Times*, February 21, 1937; "616
Players, 293 Writers, 129 Directors Contracted for 1938–39
Programs," *Motion Picture Herald*, March 26, 1938; "They're
Doing a Man's Job," *Dundee Evening Telegraph*, March 18, 1940;
"We Take Our Hat to Miss Jill Craigie," *The Sketch*, August 7,
1946; Milton Bracker, "Story of a Determined Lady," *New York
Times*, June 7, 1953.

Chapter Four: A Serious Actress

"She was in a shell." Aline Mosby, "Marilyn Monroe Learned to Talk
in 'Bedroom Voice' After Movie Flops," *Coshocton (OH) Tribune*,
November 25, 1952.

"Practically un-coachable." Fess Parker, "Our Kids Are Hero
Happy," *Los Angeles Times*, October 9, 1955.

"Her face was as wooden as a ventriloquist's dummy." Natasha
Lytess, "Marilyn Monroe: Her Secret Life: Part 1," *Sunday People*,
July 15, 1962.

"Not a peep." Hedda Hopper, "Jane Russell Will Star in 'Gibson
Girl,'" *Los Angeles Times*, March 19, 1955.

"One of the few women" and "I have come to the conclusion."
Cronin, "The Storm About Monroe."

"Well just call it a visit." "DiMaggio Denies He and Marilyn Are Reconciled," *Modesto Bee and News-Herald*, January 25, 1955; "Just Call It a Visit," *Aberdeen Evening Express*, January 25, 1955.

"You can bet I'll be there." "Jolter Tops Ballots as Lyons, Vance Hartnett Also Honored," *San Mateo Times*, January 27, 1955. The Hall of Fame is also mentioned in the *Northern Whig and Belfast Post*, January 27, 1955.

Details of Marilyn's studies with Constance Collier. Truman Capote, "A Beautiful Child," from *Music for Chameleons,* reprinted in Schirmer's Visual Library's *Marilyn Monroe: Photographs 1945–1962* (Munich: Schirmer/Mosel, 1994).

Constance Collier. "Stars' Coach Is Dead," *Aberdeen Evening Express*, April 26, 1955; "John Burrell's Appointment," *The Stage*, February 24, 1955.

"No Method-man." Charles Marowitz, "Paganism in the West End," *Theatre World*, April 1958.

"There's really no such thing." Rahna Maughan, "Meet the Goddess," *Screenland*, March 1958.

"We have made history." James Roose-Evans, "The Actors Studio," *Theatre World*, January 1957.

"As Mr. Nelson admits." Eric Johns, "Survival Through T.V.," *Theatre World*, October 1956.

"Instinctively smart, nobody's fool." Susan Strasberg, *Marilyn and Me: Sisters, Rivals, Friends.*

"Marilyn has a God-given talent." Louella Parsons, "I Am Going to Adopt a Baby," *Modern Screen*, July 1960.

"What the heck." Joan Copeland, "They Really Liked Me!" *Modern Screen*, January 1957.

"Actually nobody's being snooty." Gene Houseman, "The Strange New Life of Marilyn Monroe," *Movie Life*, March 1956.

"Therapy is likely to start." E-mail interview with Dr. L. Ruddick, clinical psychologist, August 17, 2017.

Delos Smith Jr.'s observation that Marilyn withheld information during therapy and was fascinated with suicide. Strasberg, *Marilyn and Me: Sisters, Rivals, Friends*.

"I'm not taking a full course." Logan Gourlay, "Marilyn Incorporated," *Sunday Express*, October 30, 1955.

"He's the one I believe in." Logan Gourlay, "Marilyn Monroe on Middle Age," *Sunday Express*, no month, 1960.

"I've read a little of Freud." Pete Martin, "Confessions of Marilyn Monroe: Part Three."

"I decided it wouldn't be fair." Wilson, "In Defense of Marilyn Monroe."

The payment of $175,000 was mentioned in memos from and to Zanuck and Skouras, dated April 13, 1955, and May 3, 1955, Spyros Skouras Collection, Special Collections, Stanford University Library.

"I'm not interested in money." Pete Martin, "Confessions of Marilyn Monroe: Part One," *Daily Sketch*, June 25, 1956.

"I didn't go into movies." Skolsky, "Sidney Skolsky Gives the Lowdown on Hollywood Women."

Feingersh photo shoot. Ed Feingersh and Bob LaBrasca, *Marilyn: Fifty-Five.*

"Dogs never bite me." Capote, "A Beautiful Child."

Darryl F. Zanuck comments about Marilyn. Floyd E. Stone, "Zanuck Tells Press of New Process, Product Plans," *Motion Picture Herald*, April 16, 1955.

Offer of a Las Vegas show. Cronin, "The Storm About Monroe."

Marilyn's interest in Nehru. Edward R. Murrow, "Are Celebrities Human?" *Los Angeles Times*, November 6, 1955.

Murrow's gift of Winston Churchill's speeches. Lot 258, Marilyn Monroe letter from Edward R. Murrow, sold at Julien's on November 7, 1955.

Person to Person program. "Marilyn Monroe Rare Live Television Appearance—"Person to Person" Interview 1955," YouTube video, 14:26, posted by Marilyn Monroe Video Archives, August 16, 2013, https://youtu.be/L05TYBXwU3A.

Marilyn's disappearance from New York. Hedda Hopper, "Curtis Will Introduce Find in New Picture," *Los Angeles Times*, April 12, 1955.

"I'm insane about jazz." Bill Foster, "Marilyn Monroe," *Sunday Graphic*, March 29, 1956.

Songs played on piano. Gourlay, "I've Not Begun to Earn Much Yet," *Sunday Express*, November 8, 1953.

Marilyn's observations of cab drivers and nightmares. Buchthal and Comment, *Fragments: Poems, Intimate Notes , Letters by Marilyn Monroe.*

"Any success I've had." Hedda Hopper, "Niven Wins Big Role in 'Around the World,'" *Los Angeles Times,* April 30, 1955.

Eli Wallach's reaction to theater acting. Looker-on, "Whispers from the Wings," *Theatre World,* June 1954. Wallach also spoke about Marilyn's New York years in his book, *The Good, the Bad, and Me: In My Anecdotage.*

"Marilyn gave me the kind of advice." Helen Dudar and Jim Cook, "The Rebellion of Marilyn Monroe," *New York Post,* September 28, 1955.

"Marilyn had good experience." Joseph Lionetti interview, March 29, 2017.

"Marilyn should have a show written." Wilson, "In Defense of Marilyn Monroe."

Marilyn's denial of seeing *Will Success Spoil Rock Hunter?* Edwin Schallert, "Monroe Vows a New Effort," *Los Angeles Times,* January 1, 1956.

Marilyn accidentally ruining a play's run. Cox, "The Strange Truth About Marilyn Monroe."

"Sit down in front of me and help block the view." Gourlay, "Marilyn Incorporated."

Jay Kanter's opinion that Marilyn had no desire for theater work. Interview with Jay Kanter, April 9, 2017.

"I think my husband has the solution." Parsons, "I Am Going to Adopt a Baby."

Chapter Five: The Unlikely Feminist

Jane Fonda's memories of Marilyn. "Jane Fonda Talks About Marilyn Monroe," YouTube video, 3:43, posted by "Marmar," January 17, 2016, https://youtu.be/9CaMx-wrcsc.

"Informed, acute and enchanting." Vernon Scott, "Marilyn Monroe Says She's Happy, but Has Not Changed," *Middlesborough Daily News*, October 23, 1958.

"Yes, wouldn't she." Radie Harris, *Radie's World*.

Tippi Hedren's memories of Marilyn. Tippi Hedren, *Tippi: A Memoir*.

Jay Julien party. Jim Cook and Helen Dubar, "The Rebellion of Marilyn Monroe: Part Three," *New York Post*, September 30, 1955.

Amy Greene's memories of Marilyn emptying ashtrays. Helen Bolstad, "Marilyn in the House," *Photoplay*, September 1955.

"All the studios brought their top." Erskine Johnson, "Hollywood's Marilyn Monroe: Blond, Saucy, the New Harlow," *Lima (OH) News*, August 5, 1952.

"He had no clue who she was." E-mail from Huston Huddleston, August 17, 2017.

"Marilyn's effect on high-brows." Milton Schulman, "Will Mr. M. Rewrite the Monroe Story?" *Aberdeen Evening Express*, July 18, 1956.

"I have never been so embarrassed." Elsie Lee, "Why Women Love Marilyn Monroe," *Screenland Plus TV-Land*, July 1954.

Joan Crawford's complaints about Marilyn. Bob Thomas, "Crawford Aims Barbs at Monroe," *Syracuse Herald-Journal*, March 3, 1953.

"With all the publicity I've had." Louella Parsons, "Joan and Marilyn Talk," *Modern Screen*, July 1953.

"I'll never quit that!" Earl Wilson, "The Things She Said to Me!" *Photoplay*, May 1956.

"I think we've been held back by all the publicity." Lee, "Why Women Love Marilyn Monroe."

"Gosh, I thought you'd skin her alive." Cox, "The Strange Truth About Marilyn Monroe."

"Nobody can hurt [Marilyn]." Erskine Johnson, "In Hollywood," *Walla Walla (WA) Union-Bulletin*, April 22, 1953.

"I'll tell you a girl." Bob Thomas, "The Face Is Familiar," *Modern Screen*, June 1954.

"No, I'm the Marilyn with clothes on." Bob Thomas, "Two Marilyn's Provide Some Confusion," *San Mateo Times*, January 9, 1953.

"Well, there have been nude models before." "Dame Edith Sitwell—Face-to-Face Interview 1959," YouTube video, 26:27, posted by EckingtonParishTV, November 18, 2014, https://youtu.be/Q5l3UPlO60M; Elspeth Grant, "Miss Monroe Stops the Traffic," *Tatler and Bystander*, October 31, 1956.

"Of course I'd be delighted to play." William Barbour, "The Very Private Life of MM," *Modern Screen*, October 1955.

"I've taken plenty of criticism." Parsons, "Joan and Marilyn Talk."

"Here was a girl." Jon Bruce, "The Inside Story of the Marilyn-Jane Feud," *Screenland Plus TV-Land*, April 1953.

"I'd like to be known as a real actress and human being." Foster, "Marilyn Monroe."

"An ardent feminist is." "Finger in the Pie," *The Scotsman*, March 4, 1950.

"I am not a feminist." "Mr. Nehru to Stay with Sir Anthony," *Yorkshire Post and Leeds Mercury*, July 8, 1956.

"I cannot understand how any woman." "A Suffragette Retires," *Belfast News-Letter*, June 26, 1951.

"Feminism is something that cannot be put into words." "Feminist Eartha," *Northern Daily Mail*, June 27, 1956.

"A woman only hurts herself." Pete Martin, "Confessions of Marilyn Monroe: Part Two," *Daily Sketch*, June 26, 1956.

"Marilyn's one of the most." Wilson, "Film Husband Tells All About Marilyn."

"Selfish career women." "Equal Pay Will Force Wives to Go to Work," *Sunderland (UK) Echo*, April 23, 1954.

"Throughout her short life." E-mail interview with Gabriella Apicella, April 1, 2017.

Joe and Marilyn attend a Sammy Davis Jr. concert. Interview with Jay Kanter, April 9, 2017.

Marilyn's insistence that she would never marry DiMaggio again. Maurice Zolotow, "The Mystery of Marilyn Monroe (VI)," Maurice Zolotow Collection, Harry Ransom Humanities Research Center, University of Texas at Austin.

"A brilliantly produced version." Review of *The Seven Year Itch*, *Film Bulletin*, June 13, 1955.

"The big achievements in humor." Review of *The Seven Year Itch*, *Motion Picture Daily*, June 3, 1955.

"A top-notch sophisticated comedy." Review of *The Seven Year Itch*, *Harrison's Reports*, June 11, 1955.

Skirt-blowing scene cutout. "Change of Scenery," *New York Times*, May 24, 1955.

Unveiling by Roxanne. "What the Showmen Are Doing," *Film Bulletin*, May 30, 1955.

The Seven Year Itch publicity. "The National Spotlight," *Motion Picture Herald*, June 18, 1955; "Showmen in Action," *Motion Picture Herald*, June 25, 1955; "Showmen in Action," *Motion Picture Herald*, July 9, 1955; "It's the Windy City," *Motion Picture Herald*, July 16, 1955; "What the Showmen Are Doing," *Film Bulletin*, July 25, 1955; "Exhibition Highlights of the Week," *Independent Film Journal*, September 3, 1955; "Pills Unnecessary for 'Itch,'" *Film Bulletin*, September 5, 1955; "A Bell-Ring Shatters the 'Great Lovers' Fantasy," *Aberdeen Evening Express*, November 15, 1955.

Weekend business of *The Seven Year Itch*. "Itch Pulls $50,000 for Weekend Mark," *Motion Picture Daily*, June 7, 1955.

"Dear Marilyn: We need you." Wilson, "In Defense of Marilyn Monroe."

John Steinbeck's autograph request. Lot 259, Marilyn Monroe letter from John Steinbeck, dated April 28, 1955, property from the Estate of Lee Strasberg, sold at Julien's in November 2016.

Marilyn on the Monroe Six. Hedda Hopper, "Marilyn Studying, Enjoys Anonymity," *Los Angeles Times*, April 28, 1955.

"I thought she was extremely brave." Michelle Morgan, *Marilyn Monroe: Private and Confidential.*

"For the first time I felt accepted." "The Scared Little Girl in a Woman's Body Grows Up at Last," *Daily Herald*, May 23, 1956.

"You get such wonderful thoughts." "Home Life of a Hollywood Bachelor Girl," *Television and Screen Guide*, August 1951.

"My poems are kind of sad." "Marilyn Is Two Girls," unidentified newspaper, June 10, 1951.

Poetry reading and trip to see Emil Giles. Norman Rosten, *Marilyn: A Very Personal Story.*

"Never Give All the Heart" by William Butler Yeats was published in 1906.

Marilyn's poetry. Buchthal and Comment, *Fragments: Poems, Intimate Notes, Letters by Marilyn Monroe.*

"I know just the monsters he paints." Tim Connelly, "Marilyn's New Pitch," unidentified newspaper, circa October 1957.

Marilyn's portraits. Anna Strasberg and Bernard Comment, *Marilyn Monroe: Girl Waiting.*

Lover Watching His Love Sleep. Lot 521, sold by Julien's in November 2016.

Nude portrait for Boris Aronson. Lot 986, sold by Julien's on June 26, 2015.

Norman Rosten's memories of Marilyn and *The Hand of God.* Rosten, *Marilyn: A Very Personal Story.*

Chapter Six: Inspirational Woman

"There are two schools of thought about her." Martin, "Confessions of Marilyn Monroe: Part Two."

"I first became aware of Marilyn after seeing her in cinema newsreels." E-mail from Maureen Brown, May 16, 2017.

"Like everybody else." E-mail from Virginia Nicholson, March 17 and 18, 2017.

Gloria Steinem's early feelings about Marilyn are well known. One interview: "Gloria Steinem on Marilyn Monroe | American Masters: In Their Own Words," YouTube video, 2:39, posted by American Masters PBS, June 23, 2016, https://youtu.be/fvDz-WCUv20.

Steinem also wrote about the actress in *Marilyn Monroe: Norma Jeane.*

"Quite simply, I do not believe." E-mail from Gabriella Apicella, April 1, 2017.

"He is one of the few contemporary playwrights." "The Men Who Interest Me . . ."

"I was with her morning, noon and night." Terrence Feely, "What Marriage Is Doing to Marilyn," *Sunday Graphic,* July 1956.

"I am in love with the man, not the mind." Parsons, "I Am Going to Adopt a Baby."

Hedda Hopper's amused reaction to the Greenes' European trip. Hedda Hopper, "John Forsyth Will Co-Star with Olivia," *Los Angeles Times,* July 14, 1955.

Marilyn's invitation to Washington. "Marilyn Declines," *Aberdeen Evening Express,* August 19, 1955.

"It seems to me she's not there." "Russians See Marilyn Film," *Aberdeen Evening Express,* July 28, 1955.

Marilyn's trip to Fire Island. Cox, "The Strange Truth About Marilyn Monroe"; Susan Strasberg, *Marilyn and Me: Sisters, Rivals, Friends.*

"At least I haven't made any appointments." "Divorce of Marilyn and Joe Now Final," *Lowell (MA) Sun,* October 27, 1955.

Divorce. "Marilyn Gets Final Decree from DiMaggio," *Los Angeles Times,* November 1, 1955; "Marilyn Monroe Just a Step from Freedom," *Los Angeles Times,* October 28, 1955.

"The public deserves its money's worth." Edwin Schallert, "Marilyn Monroe Seeks Best Direction," *Los Angeles Times,* November 17, 1955.

Marilyn's feelings on the character of Pola. Edwin Schallert, "Monroe Vows a New Effort," *Los Angeles Times*, January 1, 1956.

Marilyn's appearance on an unnamed radio show during *The Rose Tattoo* premiere. "Marilyn Monroe RARE Radio Interview—The Rose Tattoo Premiere 1955," YouTube video, 14:00, posted by Marilyn Monroe Video Archives, April 3, 2013, https://youtu.be/Klr4hamwroQ.

"On the stage there is a feeling of integration." "Marlon Brando: Unaccustomed as I Am," *Modern Screen*, October 1955.

"My fight with the studio is not about money." Maurice Zolotow, *Marilyn Monroe*.

"They were pretty tough on Marilyn." John Gold, "The Man Behind Marilyn," *Aberdeen Evening News*, February 8, 1956.

"What I have settled for is a compromise." Wilson, "The Things She Said to Me!"

Frank Delaney's memories of the new Fox contract appear in a letter he wrote to Inez Melson, dated June 22, 1965. She responded on June 24, 1965.

Frank Delaney's thoughts on Marilyn's debt appear in Maurice Zolotow's notes on Frank Delaney, Maurice Zolotow Collection, Harry Ransom Humanities Research Center, University of Texas at Austin.

John Huston to direct *The Sleeping Prince*. "Miss Monroe, Olivier to Star," *New York Times*, January 2, 1956.

"Gave Vivien Leigh." Looker-on, "Whispers from the Wings," *Theatre World*, December 1953.

"One wonders if there might be." Ibid.

Meeting between Marilyn and Olivier. Interview with Jay Kanter, April 9, 2017.

Marilyn and Olivier see *Anne Frank*. April VeVea, *Marilyn Monroe: A Day in the Life*; Strasberg, *Marilyn and Me: Sisters, Rivals, Friends*.

Olivier's experience of an Actors Studio class. Laurence Olivier, *On Acting*.

"I wish you would use some of that." Roose-Evans, "The Actors Studio."

"Marilyn is an expert" and "Olivier has always." "Marilyn Monroe to Star in British Film," *Hartlepool (UK) Northern Daily Mail*, February 10, 1956.

"She is very sweet." "Marilyn 'Sweet and Charming,'" *Hartlepool (UK) Northern Daily Mail*, February 11, 1956.

"I cannot think of anyone better than Miss Monroe." "Marilyn Monroe to Team with Sir Laurence Olivier," *Belfast News-Letter*, February 10, 1956.

Alan Brien on Marilyn winning the battle. Alan Brien, "Marilyn Leads the Revolt," *Aberdeen Evening Express*, February 15, 1956.

"You can hardly expect Marilyn Monroe." Thomas Wiseman, "Uncle Edgar Comes Before Cousin Marilyn," *Aberdeen Evening Express*, May 1, 1956.

"Perhaps only a husband and wife." Looker-on, "Whispers from the Wings," *Theatre World*, December 1953.

"If you pay that driver." Robert J. Levin, "Marilyn Monroe's Marriage," *Redbook*, February 1958.

"Believe me when I say" and "She displayed—you know." Copeland, "They Really Liked Me!"

Kim Stanley's recollection of *Anna Christie*. John Kobal, *People Will Talk*.

"Like an over-excited child asked downstairs after tea." "Marilyn Monroe's Beauty Biography," *Los Angeles Times*, December 11, 1960. Note: the newspaper credits as the original source for the quote Cecil Beaton's *The Face of the World* (New York: John Day, 1957).

Chapter Seven: Performance of a Lifetime

"Nobody believes it now." Mawby Green, "Echoes from Broadway," *Theatre World*, April 1955.

"A unique work of art." "Marilyn Monroe, the Unique Work of Art," *Radio Times*, October 8, 1970.

"I don't really believe in ignoring traffic citations." "Footage of Marilyn Monroe at Court 1956—'I Don't Really Believe in Ignoring Traffic Citations,'" YouTube video, 1:17, posted by Marilyn Monroe Video Archives, May 6, 2016, https://youtu.be/WOqiQ3DpTHk.

Meetings between Jane Wilkie and Natasha Lytess and the unpublished manuscript. Maurice Zolotow Collection, Harry Ransom
Humanities Research Center, University of Texas at Austin.

France-Dimanche buying Lytess's story. Memo to Pat Newcomb
and Arthur P. Jacobs, dated May 11, 1962, Charles Von der Ahe
Library, Loyola Marymount University.

"Marilyn Monroe: Her Secret Life" by Natasha Lytess was serialized
in the *Sunday People* on July 15, 22, and 29, 1962, and August 5
and 12, 1962.

Natasha Lytess's death was reported in a document entitled "Report
of the Death of an American Citizen," dated June 5, 1963, and
found on Ancestry.com. Her name is given as Natasha Frank
(aka N. Lytess and N. Lewis), and her place of death Switzerland.
Prior to her death, the teacher was living in Italy with her
daughter, Barbara.

"If I keep it there much longer," "though that doesn't mean," and
"That would make a good photograph." Thomas Wiseman, "I've
Nothing Against Women—But I Prefer Men Says Marilyn,"
Evening Standard, March 3, 1956.

"I like Arthur very much." Maxwell, "Marilyn Confesses to Elsa
Maxwell: I'll Never Be the Same."

Joshua Logan spoke many times about his way of directing Marilyn in letters between Laurence Olivier and Logan. Letter from Olivier to Logan, June 9, 1956, and letter from Logan to Olivier, June 20, 1956, both Logan Box 31, Folder 13, Joshua Logan Papers, Manuscript Division, Library of Congress, Washington, DC. Also of interest, "Director of Bus Stop, Joshua Logan, Interview About Marilyn Monroe," YouTube video, 2:29, posted by Marilyn Monroe Video Archive, August 22, 2013, https://youtu.be/YC-rwQLWnZ0.

Marilyn's illness and details of scenes filmed in her absence. Letter from Joshua Logan to George Axelrod, April 16, 1956, Logan Box 99, Bus Stop Production, Joshua Logan Papers, Manuscript Division, Library of Congress, Washington, DC.

Logan on Don Murray's future. Letter from Joshua Logan to William Inge, April 16, 1956, Logan Box 99, Bus Stop Production, Joshua Logan Papers, Manuscript Division, Library of Congress, Washington, DC.

Logan swearing on set. "Marilyn Monroe—The Making of *Bus Stop* 1956 [*Backstory:* Bus Stop, AMC Productions, 2001]," YouTube video, 23:06, posted by Marilyn Monroe History, February 10, 2015, https://youtu.be/LOxCP5RXMSI.

Marilyn swiping Murray across the face. Ibid.

Concern that certain scenes may be too risqué. Memo from Frank McCarthy to Buddy Adler, May 16, 1956, Logan Box 99, Bus Stop Production, Joshua Logan Papers, Manuscript Division, Library of Congress, Washington, DC.

Don Murray on trying to keep Marilyn covered up. Earl Wilson, "Memories of Marilyn," *Times Recorder*, April 15, 1973.

Marilyn playing her role charmingly and Logan's concern film was too long. Letter from Joshua Logan to George Axelrod, April 16, 1956, Logan Box 99, Bus Stop Production, Joshua Logan Papers, Manuscript Division, Library of Congress, Washington, DC.

Photographs of Marilyn posing for Joshua Logan can be seen in Strasberg and Comment's *Marilyn Monroe: Girl Waiting.* The book also includes a letter from Logan documenting how the photo shoot took place.

Nedda Logan's favorite scene. Telegram from Buddy Adler to Joshua Logan, July 5, 1956, Logan Box 99, Bus Stop Production, Joshua Logan Papers, Manuscript Division, Library of Congress, Washington, DC.

Logan on working with Marilyn. Letter from Joshua Logan to Lee and Paula Strasberg, April 9, 1963, Logan Box 35, Folder 15, Joshua Logan Papers, Manuscript Division, Library of Congress, Washington, DC.

Alan Dent review of *Bus Stop*. "The World of Cinema: That Girl," *Illustrated London News*, November 3, 1956.

New York Times on *Bus Stop* and "fools the skeptics." "Marilyn Rings the Bell," *Aberdeen Evening Express*, September 10, 1956.

"If that part about my being a symbol of sex is true." Martin, "Confessions of Marilyn Monroe: Part One."

"[She is] the only phenomenon." "Movies Are Declining," *Aberdeen Evening Express*, September 26, 1956.

"I didn't avoid the film." Rahna Maughan, "Meet the Goddess," *Screenland*, March 1958.

William Inge reaction to final film. Undated, Logan Box 99, Bus Stop Production, Joshua Logan Papers, Manuscript Division, Library of Congress, Washington, DC.

Chapter Eight: The Woman Who Impacted the World

"I don't know exactly." "Marilyn Protests as Picture Jumps from Calendar to Glassware," *Lima (OH) News*, December 18, 1952.

Meeting with Dr. Robert Williams. "Doctors Study Picture of Marilyn Monroe," *Belfast News-Letter*, May 3, 1955.

Grantham and District Young Farmer's Club meeting. "Cross Between African Farmer's Wife and Marilyn Monroe!" *Grantham Journal*, December 23, 1955.

"The thing that always takes the trick." "Marilyn Would Take a Trick," *Aberdeen Evening Express*, October 11, 1956.

Plans for the Marilyn Monroe aircraft. "Jet Design Secret Aired by Magazine," *Los Angeles Times*, September 8, 1955; "The Marilyn Shape Makes Planes Faster," *Courier and Advertiser*, September 12, 1955.

Nautilus atomic submarine. Riese and Hitchins, *The Unabridged Marilyn*.

"Figures are dreary." "Miss Monroe Teams Up with Mr. Therm," *Yorkshire Post and Leeds Mercury*, March 5, 1954.

Boy who sold Marilyn's phone number. Gene Sherman, "Cityside," *Los Angeles Times*, January 21, 1954.

"With Jane Russell and Marilyn." "Candid Quotes of the Week," *Luton News and Bedfordshire Chronicle*, December 2, 1954.

"I don't know whether." "Hard on Marilyn," *Portsmouth Evening News*, October 14, 1954.

"Marilyn Monroe is a good walker" and "Which is news if only." Ed Weisman, "You, Too, Can Walk Like Marilyn," *Aberdeen Evening Express*, June 30, 1956.

Dior uplift panty girdle. Olga Curtis, "Fashion Reporter Tests Dior's Latest Style Garment," *Tipton (IN) Daily Tribune*, July 10, 1957.

Penny Wilson winning a Marilyn look-alike competition. "MM on Ice," *The Stage*, July 26, 1956.

Cheryl Ooms impersonation of Marilyn. "List Winners of Events at Steger Fete," *Chicago Heights Star*, August 14, 1956.

Joan Ferchaud wins Marilyn look-alike competition. *Anniston (AL) Star*, August 27, 1957.

Pauline Spanos wins trip to New York. "Ready for the Show," *Lowell (MA) Sun*, April 5, 1959.

Marilyn Monroe hen. "Mary Jane Beats Marilyn Monroe in Egg Contest," *Lovington (NM) Leader*, October 24, 1954.

"The ultimate triumph of alliteration." "The Literific: Fun in Debate at 'Queens,'" *Belfast News-Letter*, October 21, 1954.

"Ill-mannered and boorish behavior." "University Notes: The 'Literific,'" *Belfast News-Letter*, October 29, 1954.

"Then there are other phenomena." "Peer Backs Films Against TV," *Courier and Advertiser*, January 22, 1954.

"They're indecent." "Marilyn Monroe Pictures Burned by Malta Censors," *Los Angeles Times*, August 28, 1954.

Censorship in New Delhi. "Marilyn's Movie Cut by Censors in India," *Los Angeles Times*, November 9, 1954.

"Arousing temptation to lasciviousness." "No Temptation," *Northern Whig and Belfast Post*, December 22, 1954.

Star of Fire Gem Company problems. Riese and Hitchins, *The Unabridged Marilyn*.

Trinidad film censors. "Marilyn Posters Are Banned," *Aberdeen Evening Express*, January 16, 1956.

Japanese ladies copying Marilyn. "Copying Marilyn Monroe," *Belfast News-Letter*, February 5, 1954.

"And what did he put?" "Moonrakings," *Wiltshire Times*, February 20, 1954.

Olivier/Logan correspondence. Letter written by Laurence Olivier to Joshua Logan, June 9, 1956, and Logan's reply, June 20, 1956, Logan Box 31, Folder 13, Joshua Logan Papers, Manuscript Division, Library of Congress, Washington, DC.

"When Arthur's parents told me." Maxine Block, "The Two Faces of Marilyn Monroe," *Screenland*, January 1959.

"A political whing-ding." "Will Mr. M. Rewrite the Monroe Story?"

Miller's contempt-of-Congress charge. "Marilyn's Fiancé May Face Contempt Charge," *Aberdeen Evening Express*, June 22, 1956; "Marilyn Monroe to Marry Before London Visit," *Belfast News-Letter*, June 22, 1956.

"The happiest day" and "I'm sure everything will work out." Stan Mays, "Marilyn Hugs in Street," *Daily Mirror*, June 23, 1956.

Death of Mara Scherbatoff. "Coroner Exonerates Marilyn," *Aberdeen Evening Express*, August 22, 1956.

"There's been a terrible accident!" Christopher Dobson, "Marilyn," *Daily Express*, June 30, 1956.

"Somebody should question you" and "Well, we just had a terrible accident on this road." "Marilyn and Arthur Miller at a Press Conference," YouTube video, 3:47, posted by Iconic, November 17, 2010, https://youtu.be/b_P2FFIVV8A; "Marilyn Monroe at Press Conference in Support of Her Husband Arthur Miller—'Contempt of Congress,'" YouTube video, 1:32, posted by Marilyn Monroe Video Archives, January 10, 2016, https://youtu.be/pY7DHZ4oDzI; Christopher Dobson, "Marilyn."

"It's as much a surprise." "Marilyn," *Daily Sketch*, June 30, 1956.

"There was no question of controlling onlookers." Dobson, "Marilyn."

"I guess they suddenly decided to go through with it." John Gold, "Marilyn Monroe Weds in Pink Sweater," *Evening News*, June 30, 1956.

Cecil Beaton portrait from Joshua and Nedda Logan. Letter from Nedda Logan to Lee Strasberg, March 5, 1969, and letter from Lee Strasberg to Nedda Logan, March 11, 1969, Logan Box 35, Folder 15, Joshua Logan Papers, Manuscript Division, Library of Congress, Washington, DC.

"Awakened intellectually." Scott, "Marilyn Monroe Says She's Happy, but Has Not Changed," *Middlesborough Daily News*, October 23, 1958.

Chapter Nine: The Power Struggle

"I would like to do *Pygmalion*." "Miss Monroe Wants to Do 'Pygmalion,'" *Daily Telegraph*, July 16, 1956.

"To espouse the Method." Marowitz, "Paganism in the West End."

"She is quite enchanting." "Express from London," *Aberdeen Evening Express*, September 29, 1956.

Sybil Thorndike's methods for happiness. David Lewin, "Marilyn Monroe Talks as She Seldom Has," *Daily Express*, May 6, 1959.

"Apart from closing theatres." Eric Johns, "Sybil Thorndike Looks Back," *Theatre World*, June 1954.

"She has obviously come to England." "Marilyn Monroe, the Minister and the Sage," *Belfast News-Letter*, July 17, 1956.

"I tried to walk like her down the corridor." "Express from London," *Aberdeen Evening Express*, October 20, 1956.

"A bit stuck-up, but nevertheless" and "It was dull working for them." Alan Arnold, "Marilyn: A Bit Stuck-Up but Charming," *Sunday Dispatch*, November 18, 1956.

"I'm telling you, they couldn't." Thomas Wiseman, "Marilyn, Weeping Thinks of Frank and Coca-Cola," *Aberdeen Evening Express*, December 5, 1956.

"Marilyn Monroe! I am not kidding." Nigel Nicholson, "Alma Would Like to Be Marilyn," *Aberdeen Evening Express*, July 27, 1956.

"I would love to see her." "O'Casey to Meet Marilyn?" *The Stage*, July 26, 1956.

O'Casey turning down Olivier's invitation. Christopher Murray, *Sean O'Casey: A Biography*.

In 1959, Dame Edith Sitwell told the BBC's *Face to Face* program about meeting Marilyn and Miller during the London trip.

"The truth is she was very interested." Thomas Wiseman, "The Two Worlds of Arthur Miller," *Aberdeen Evening Express*, October 9, 1956.

"I am familiar with *Lysistrata*." "Marilyn Too Busy for Radio Part," *Belfast News-Letter*, August 11, 1956; "Marilyn Sorry, but Too Busy," *Northern Daily Mail*, August 11, 1956.

Vivian Blaine's Vegas invitation. Edwin Schallert, "Drama," *Los Angeles Times*, October 12, 1955.

Offer of *Maiden Voyage*. Letter from Arthur Miller to Kermit Bloomgarden, September 20, 1956, and letter from Bloomgarden to Miller, October 1, 1956, Kermit Bloomgarden Papers, Box 52, Folder 25, Wisconsin Historical Society.

"[Marilyn] had the courage to challenge the big movie moguls." Maxwell, "Marilyn Confesses to Elsa Maxwell: I'll Never Be the Same."

"It was remarkable." Arnold, "Marilyn: A Bit Stuck-Up but Charming."

"Definitely not." Ibid.

"What a terrible picture!" Alan Arnold, "Tension Between Marilyn and Olivier," *Sunday Dispatch*, November 11, 1956.

"When a director says, 'Marilyn.'" Gourlay, "Marilyn Incorporated."

"The most interesting event." "Over the Footlights," *Theatre World*, October 1956.

"A very warm person" and "We shan't live in Hollywood." Wiseman, "The Two Worlds of Arthur Miller."

"You!" Arnold, "Tension Between Marilyn and Olivier."

"An Italian marble sphinx." Strasberg, *Marilyn and Me: Sisters, Rivals, Friends*.

"[Olivier] is the greatest actor" and "I have nothing lined up."
"Marilyn Monroe Says Goodbye to Britain," *Belfast News-Letter*,
November 21, 1956.

"She will be president." "Marilyn Monroe Forms British Film
Company," *Belfast News-Letter*, November 17, 1956.

Firing of Milton Greene. "Star Scores Associate," *New York Times*,
April 12, 1957; "Miss Monroe Ousts Business Associate," *New
York Times*, April 17, 1957; "Marilyn Monroe Sued," *New York
Times*, July 12, 1957; "Stock to Miss Monroe," *New York Times*,
February 27, 1958.

"He knows perfectly well." "Marilyn Monroe Feuds with Milton
H. Greene," *Los Angeles Times*, April 12, 1957. A similar quote
appeared in the *Daily Express*, April 12, 1957.

Laurence Olivier made aware of Milton's producing ambitions.
June 9, 1956 Logan Box 31, Folder 13, Joshua Logan Papers,
Manuscript Division, Library of Congress, Washington, DC.

Chapter Ten: The Human Being

"Sounded like an ad for a woman's magazine." Strasberg, *Marilyn
and Me: Sisters, Rivals, Friends*.

"Miss Sellars wonders." Looker-on, "Whispers from the Wings,"
Theatre World, August 1957.

"Does Marilyn Monroe." Readers' questions column, *Modern Screen*,
October 1958.

"It is getting used to it—happiness and belonging." Lewin, "Marilyn Monroe Talks as She Seldom Has."

"What people don't realize about Marilyn." David Lewin, "Marilyn and Miller . . . Bound to Come Unstuck!" *Daily Express*, November 12, 1960.

"It really didn't start out that way." Erskine Johnson, "It's Like Reading Marilyn's Mail," *Rhinelander Daily News*, September 3, 1960.

"No one ever knows how." Erskine Johnson, "Hollywood Today," *Uniontown (PA) Evening Standard*, September 2, 1960.

"You know what I think about Marilyn?" Erskine Johnson, "Marilyn Monroe Views Clift in a Unique Light," *Reno Evening Gazette*, September 3, 1960.

Henry Hathaway on seeing Marilyn on the set of *The Misfits*. Kobal, *People Will Talk*.

"Arthur taught me a lot." David Lewin, "The Girl Who Took On Too Much," possibly *Daily Express*, August 1962.

Miller's letter of resignation is dated November 23, 1960.

"She was absolutely wonderful." Lionetti interview, March 29, 2017.

Anna Sten on Marilyn. Kobal, *People Will Talk*.

Notes from *Golden Boy*. Lot 260, Marilyn Monroe handwritten lines from a scene, property from the Estate of Lee Strasberg, sold at Julien's in November 2016.

Notes from *Streetcar*. Lot 255, Marilyn Monroe notebook with notes from acting class, property from the Estate of Lee Strasberg, sold at Julien's in November 2016. The scene is mentioned in Strasberg's *Marilyn and Me: Sisters, Rivals, Friends*.

"At the Actors Studio." Lewin, "Marilyn Monroe Talks as She Seldom Has."

"I've still a lot to learn." Gourlay, "Marilyn Monroe on Middle Age."

"I want to lead a drive to do something." Louella Parsons, "Louella Parson's Good News," *Modern Screen*, October 1952.

Marilyn's support for the Fox coffee vendor. Gary Vitacco-Robles, *Icon: The Life, Times, and Films of Marilyn Monroe: Volume 2, 1956 to 1962 and Beyond*.

Isidore Miller's comments about Marilyn's charity come from "Remembrance of Marilyn" by Flora Rheta Schreiber. Published in Wagenknecht's *Marilyn Monroe: A Composite View*. Note: the article was originally published in *Good Housekeeping*, January 1963.

"She was shy." Lionetti interview, March 29, 2017.

"All I know is that I'll be back in New York soon." Jonah Ruddy, "Now That I Am 35," *Daily Mail*, June 5, 1961.

Marilyn's statement and telegrams on the firing from *Something's Got to Give*. Arthur P. Jacobs Collection, June 1962, Charles Von der Abe Library, Loyola Marymount University.

"Maybe she was tough," "I was deeply, deeply fond," and "She was difficult to work with." *The Progress*, August 6, 1962.

"It was a tremendous shock to me." Arthur Miller to Robin Stafford, "Why I Say Marilyn Did Not Kill Herself," *Daily Express*, August 7, 1962.

Miller's thoughts on Marilyn's death were also mentioned in a letter from Miller to Joshua Logan, August 14, 1962, Logan Box 29, Folder 17, Joshua Logan Papers, Manuscript Division, Library of Congress, Washington, DC.

"If she was simple." John Gold, "Luck . . . That Is What Marilyn Needed," *Aberdeen Evening News*, August 7, 1962.

"The spirit of Marilyn/Norma Jeane." E-mail from Kathleen Felesina, director of fund development, Uplift Family Services, April 11, 2017. For more information, please visit: http://upliftfs.org/about/hollygrove.

"The Anna Freud National Centre." Quote from Professor Peter Fonagy, chief executive of the Anna Freud National Centre for Children and Families, provided by Tim Linehan, head of communications, on March 2, 2017. For more information, please visit: http://www.annafreud.org.

Marilyn helping young people deal with their problems. Description of the Marilyn Monroe Memorial Fund, circa March 1963, Logan Box 35, Folder 15, Joshua Logan Papers, Manuscript Division, Library of Congress, Washington, DC.

Nicole Kidman on female directors. "Risk Taker: Nicole Kidman," YouTube video, 22:43, posted by Women in the World, October 10, 2015, https://youtu.be/jO-soyHpgW0.

Epilogue: Passing the Torch

All quotes were taken from interviews by the author, except the following:

"I think [Marilyn] was just trying." "Emma Watson: My Life Is Like Marilyn Monroe's," *Daily Mirror*, November 20, 2011.

"I have always been drawn to Marilyn." Will Lawrence, "Michelle Williams: I Was Born to Play Marilyn," *Telegraph*, November 10, 2011.

"What makes her so riveting." "Gloria Steinem on Marilyn Monroe | American Masters: In Their Own Words," YouTube video, 2:39, posted by American Masters PBS, June 23, 2016, https://youtu.be/fvDz-WCUv20.

Acknowledgments

I COULD NOT HAVE written this book without the support of some truly wonderful people:

Bill Pursel, Christina Rice, Virginia Nicholson, Gabriella Apicella, Maureen Brown, Naomi Pieris, Huston Huddleston, Dr. L. Ruddick, Suzanne Sumner Ferry, Yessenia Santos, Sandi Silbert, Kathleen Felesina, Ian Bevans, Jay Kanter, Joseph Lionetti, Emily Wittenberg, the late John Hazell, Lucy Vance Seligson, David Sandrich, Cathy Sandrich Gelfond, Tim Linehan, Peter Fonagy, and Chido Muchemwa have all been extremely gracious in providing support, information, or both. Barbara Bair from the Library of Congress went above and beyond to help me with my research, and I am eternally grateful.

To Suzie Kennedy, Susan Griffiths, Andrea Pryke, Tara Hanks, Linda Kerridge, and those people who contributed memories anonymously, I'm so very grateful for your candor, honesty, bravery, and, of course, your stories. Thanks also to my friends and readers for the constant encouragement shown toward me and my books, and to Marilyn's fans for keeping her unique light burning.

A HUGE thank you must go to my editor, Cindy De La Hoz, for bringing this project to me and for helping it to grow. Cindy, I sincerely hope that we work on many more projects together! I'd also like to thank Amber Morris, Susan VanHecke, and everyone at Running Press for supporting this book, as well as my agent, Robert Smith, and his personal assistant, Gemma Quinn.

A big hug and thank you must go to Mum, Dad, Paul, Wendy, and Angelina, who have supported my writing career since day one. I love you all very much! And to my husband, Richard, and daughter, Daisy: Thank you for the laughs, hugs, and support. I love you to the moon and back. I'd like to add that I'm especially proud and grateful to Daisy for supplying me with her thoughts on how Marilyn is inspiring her generation.

To anyone I may have mistakenly missed, I'm so sorry for the oversight, but thank you too. x